Is there earthly
conne

Am I an Ari[...]
and relax for [...]
at and where [...]

Am I a Taurus woman who secretly craves to throw caution and the budget to the winds and do something wild and extravagant?

Am I a Gemini woman who would love people to know I'm not all fizz and bubble, and I suffer from doubts and fears like everyone else?

Am I a Cancer woman who is sick of being taken for granted, and would love to be lavishly pampered and looked after?

Am I a Leo woman who'd like to prove I'm more intelligent and nicer than the bossy, loud person I'm often taken for?

Am I a Virgo woman so busy solving other people's problems there's no time to solve my own so I can be more self-contented?

Am I a Libra woman who longs to be respected for her deep understanding and perception, and not just her romantic outlook on life?

Am I a Scorpio woman who knows she is not the domineering type others see her as, but loyal, loving and compassionate?

Am I a Sagittarius woman who needs to change her scene, her outlook and her image, and be taken more seriously as a thinking individual?

Am I a Capricorn woman tired of climbing the same mountain, bashing her head on the glass ceiling and not being appreciated for what she is?

Am I an Aquarius woman who knows her head is not always in the clouds, and is more warm and generous than given credit for?

Am I a Pisces woman tired of being dismissed as a dreamer incapable of making decisions, when I could easily outwit the lot of them?

If your answer is 'yes', *The Perfume Zodiac* will uncover your hidden assets.

If your answer is 'no', *The Perfume Zodiac* will reveal even more of your hidden assets.

THE
PERFUME ZODIAC

JOHN OAKES

PRION

Published in 2000 by
Prion Books Limited
Imperial Works
Perren Street
NW5 3ED
www.prionbooks.com

First published in Australia in 1998
by HarperCollins*Publishers* Pty Limited
25 Ryde Road, Pymble
NSW, Australia 2973
This revised edition published by arrangement with
HarperCollins.

ISBN 1 85375 405 6

British Library Cataloguing in Publication Data
A catalogue record for this book is available from the British
Library.

Jacket design: Bob Eames
Printed in China by the Everbest Printing Company

This book is dedicated with
gratitude to
Mylène Boulting and Denise Barnes
who inspired its idea;
and to a trinity of earthly guardian
angels:
my kind critic Rosemary Penman,
my indefatigable agent Fitzroy
Boulting,
and my lifelong mentor Magda
Wollner.

CONTENTS

The cosmic connection:

PERFUME AND STAR SIGNS

You know yourself pretty well — the nice and not-so-nice things, as well as other traits that don't seem quite so obvious about you, because you are either too reticent about showing them or you simply don't know how. But whatever you do show the world, naturally you want it to be your best. You cultivate the nice things and put them on display as your public image. The more private and secret things you usually don't let others see. So this is, more or less, the way you want people to see and appreciate you.

Of course you don't deliberately show the negative traits — or at least you try not to. They're for you to privately deal with and hopefully improve. Who knows? They might even turn into positive things to add to your general impressiveness as you get to know yourself even better. And what about those private little things you don't seem to display — what do you do about them?

Well, let's see. Even a cursory knowledge of your particular astrological star sign will tell you what you're basically like — the good and the not-so-good, the positive and the negative, and all the possibilities. Of course it can only be a general outline, but it's usually amazingly accurate.

I'm not talking here about those daily or monthly predictions in newspapers and magazines — that's way out of my line. I'm simply talking about your basic characteristics, your personal makeup. I realise that a lot of other factors, such as heredity and environment, come into the picture to shape the finer, intensely individual parts of your complex character — and these influences may make you deviate in one way or another from your astrological basics — but again, those basics are still there underlining you as a guide to your beliefs, attitudes and aspirations.

Now, if you accept all this so far, then there's absolutely no reason why you can't apply your characteristics to other important parts of your life, such as the material things — your possessions and how and why you choose them. They speak volumes about your personal taste, your likes and dislikes. You choose them for their suitability to yourself — colours, clothes, accessories, flowers, furniture and furnishings, makeup and — of course — perfume!

*They **express** you.*
*They **represent** you.*
*They **define** you.*
*They are your **impact** on others.*

Therefore they must be chosen and selected carefully. And quite often when faced with a bewildering number of choices, we tend to go off the rails and make misjudgments. Or we allow ourselves to be influenced by others whose tastes may be quite different from ours. Then disaster strikes!

This is particularly true when it comes to choosing perfume for yourself. Too often too many outside influences get in the way. Or, because you may not know what you want, or what it is that's being suggested to you, you get lost. And getting lost when it comes to perfume is a very expensive and frustrating exercise.

Okay, you might have an idea of what you want to try. But where did the idea come from? A magazine or TV ad? A perfume promotion in a store? You smelt it on someone else and liked it? Your best friend told you about it? Don't trust any of them! It's *you* who's the prime consideration. *You're* the one who has to wear it, or pretend you never bought it. Therefore, the perfume or perfumes you ultimately choose must be *compatible* with your nature, your lifestyle and your aspirations.

So, do you trust blind instinct or female intuition while you're standing there and the salesperson looks as if she's about to pressure you into a perfume she *thinks* might suit you? You can, but it's better if you retrack and start thinking it all through before you get yourself in a pickle. And that's where this book comes in.

The Perfume Zodiac lets you sort yourself out by relating your astrological characteristics — the outer and the inner qualities — to suggested

The Cosmic Connection

choices of perfumes that I think are best suited to those personal, basic features. It's as simple as that.

The way you smell isn't primarily for the benefit of those around you. It's for you. Your perfume, scent or fragrance has to be, first and foremost, an extension of not just your personality and your taste, but also an extension of how you feel. If you don't feel good wearing a particular perfume, then there's something wrong. It could be it just doesn't suit you — it may be too overpowering, too assertive, too seductive or too flowery and sweet. Or maybe the season's wrong for it — there are perfumes that definitely smell their best in certain weather conditions. Maybe it's what you're wearing that's the problem — jeans and a blouse just don't go with sophisticated perfumes, just as heavy oriental-type perfumes smell decidedly over the top if you're in a pretty little party dress. Change it for a slinky off-the-shoulder number, and you're in business!

Change is a key word. Perfume does not change for you. It is itself — its own thing. It's *you* who has to change, to measure up to its message. And if you've chosen the right perfume to wear with the right clothes (or at least the right colours) at the right time, and you're in the right mood, then you've got it all going for you. Who knows, this fabulous (and very easy to achieve) combination — this perfumed powerhouse — may come as something of a shock to those around you! They may have to rethink everything they've ever thought about you. Wouldn't that be nice?

Now, this may be all well and good for your usual public persona — your upfront image — but what about those hidden feelings and potential attributes you may not have exploited or not known how to make the most of? We all have them but might be a little wary of exposing them. Why? They could open up a whole new dimension! And, best of all, the magic of perfume caters for them as well as it does your basics. In other words, perfume can bring out the *hidden* you as well as the obvious you.

Let's say, for instance, you're a nice reliable Cancerian wife and mother, devoted to home and family but feel sometimes you're a bit put-upon or taken for granted by your nearest and dearest. Yet you don't want to make waves. Cancerians are not supposed to. Rubbish! You not only have a partly-hidden temperament that can be quite fiery, you also do not consider yourself a well-oiled, uncomplaining machine either. So let them know. And the quickest way to do that is to reveal another image, another aspect of yourself — one they least expect. Go out and have a pampering facial, get a new hair style, get into a daring dress they've never seen before, and choose a perfume you might not normally wear but have always suspected might be just the thing to get your point across loudly and clearly! Then see them sit up and take notice. Don't be surprised if you're suddenly whisked off to dinner in a swish restaurant and you find yourself ordering beluga caviar and the best champagne, and not giving a damn about the family budget! I can promise you it won't be the first time you'll kick up your heels. Of course you may have to make lamingtons for the school fête, and do the ironing the next day, but you know you've got that ammunition at the ready if they try burying you up to your neck in household chores again.

Another example? You're a Libra who's quite used to flattery. You lap it up, you flirt! But you may have become so used to it, you start to wonder if there's something more to your life than fun and games. What about that fine brain, that incisive sense of evaluation you know you have? Why aren't you using it? Why do they think you're superficial and not deep and meaningful when you know you are? Well, show them! Get out of those sexy numbers, put your hair up (wear glasses if you must!), and appear all smart and *chic* in a totally different outfit, complete with that vital change of perfume. Instead of always being enveloped in pretty, romantic fragrances, go for something smooth, dry, calculated and super-sophisticated. They'll show you a new sense of respect!

To put it in a nutshell, what you're doing by choosing perfumes that suit your astrological personality is heightening your potential with a wardrobe (or 'arsenal' as I call it later on) of perfumes that intrinsically attract and become part of you, as well as widening your options with other perfumes you keep for those times when you want to make people really see you in a new and different perspective.

At this point, I'd better talk about those of you who were born on the cusp. In case you don't know, when

The Perfume Zodiac

you're born either at the very end of one star sign or at the very beginning of another, you are born on what is known in astrology as the cusp. So you can, if you like, assume the best characteristics of both! But, if you're being truthful and constructive with yourself you'll be honest and know which of the influences of both signs you have in your makeup — the good and the not-so-good. Although it might look as though you can easily choose what you like from either sign's perfume suggestions, I'm sorry to say that's not the way it works. Just as if you were born in the middle of a star sign, if you are born on the cusp you will have to assess what you're really like and align the findings to the perfumes that complement those personal characteristics and leanings. But I've made it a bit easier by suggesting some perfumes especially for cusp people, which you'll find towards the end of each star sign chapter. These, I hope, will take the confusion out of what can otherwise be a difficult choice.

Remember, *The Perfume Zodiac* is all about pleasing yourself as well as those you want to please! It's a simple, down-to-earth guide that leads your nature and your nose in the right direction. Hopefully it will cut out a lot of expensive and frustrating trials and errors when you make your perfume choices. But remember, it is not written in cement and it can't cope with all the extraneous factors in your basic star sign's characteristics. Treat it as your guiding star in the wonderfully complex and endlessly fascinating world of perfume. It should be quite an adventure!

The earth connection:

COMPATIBILITIES, CATEGORIES
AND CROSSOVERS

L et me explain briefly and simply how I've come to outline my observations of each star sign's basic characteristics and choose the perfumes I think are most compatible with them.

I am not a professional astrologer but an avidly amateur one. Through my intense interest in the subject I've gleaned lots of information and formed personal ideas and observations. I've asked hundreds of people first-hand what they think they're all about astrologically, and to this I've added quite a bit of good old intuition to allow me to feel confident in my evaluations and summations of each sign. I've exhaustively gone through my list of perfumes (some readily available, some a little off the beaten track) and again, through knowledge and instinct, aligned each one with a star sign. It's this alignment that I feel reveals the compatibility or incompatibility of perfumes with a particular star sign and therefore, ultimately, with you.

It's quite obvious to me there's a solid compatibility, a complementary *simpatico* between certain types of women and certain types of perfume. Again, this is generalising, but I think you'll find it pretty accurate anyway. But there's a compatibility that goes even deeper — that peculiar but fairly obvious sympathetic relationship that exists between certain colours, clothes, seasons, occasions, moods and perfume — how they can tie in together as if made for each other. That's where *you* come in.

Take colour, for instance, in the case of people born under the sign of Pisces. In my experience, they're invariably more attracted or at home with sea colours, so their clothes and furnishings, the flowers they like best and so on are more likely to be the greens, blues and purples in all their shades, rather than the reds, oranges and fiery yellows beloved by Scorpions, even though both are water-signs and attracted to each other. And since colour plays such a dominating role in our lives, when it comes to perfume it's fascinating to realise that each perfume, apart from its own distinctive smell or personality, also favours some colours over others — for instance a pretty and feminine perfume like Estée Lauder's **Pleasures** conjures up a picture of pinks and mauves quite unlike those of one of its sister perfumes like **SpellBound**, which exudes the drama of black, gold and scarlet. It follows that you wouldn't smell quite right spraying yourself in **Pleasures** after zipping up in black leather or dousing yourself in **SpellBound** and twirling off in lilac organza frills!

Categories

Just as the zodiac wheel divides into its twelve houses or signs, perfumes are usually divided into certain categories. The number can range from four to twenty, depending on how pernickety one wants to be, but I think five is plenty as far as the basic, easily-recognised categories go.

Florals

These perfumes are principally floral bouquets — meaning they are made up of a number (any number) of flower smells as their dominant theme. A few claim to have just one single flower as their theme, but that single floral 'note' always has to be backed up by other ingredients, even if they're only the base notes or fixatives which hold the perfume in place so it won't evaporate on exposure. The most common bouquet is what is known as an 'accord' of rose and jasmine. The majority of perfumes, grand or otherwise, have this accord as their basis, but to differentiate themselves their creators add various combinations of other flowers and other ingredients like fruit, spice, moss, musk and so on, to make the perfume uniquely distinctive. The most famous and classic examples of this beautiful accord or duet are probably Jean Patou's Joy, Lanvin's **Arpège** and Chanel's **No. 5**, but the reason they smell totally different from one another is that the rose–jasmine accord is transformed into its own unique scent by the complex addition of other ingredients to create the unique formula or recipe. There are other florals whose bouquets don't have this combination at all — intensely floral perfumes such as Cacharel's **Anaïs Anaïs**, which is based on lilies, tuberose and orange blossom, and Guerlain's **Champs-Elysées**, which combines rose, mimosa and buddleia (the lilac-smelling butterfly bush), for a totally different floral effect. But the one thing these florals do have in common is their intense femininity and romantic charm — in varying degrees of sweetness or freshness.

Fruity

These rather salivating perfumes have as their dominant note a combination of different fruits which can come from as far afield as a Mediterranean or French country orchard or an exotic oriental jungle. Of course, if they were composed of nothing else you'd probably end up smelling like a fruit salad, which is not the desired effect. So they are always wedded to certain flowers (usually blossoms) and spiked with spices, herbs and green notes to give them that outdoor freshness and delicious, just-plucked bloom. They can be either extremely sophisticated and alluring like Rochas' peachy-rosy **Femme**, or fresh and exuberant like Nina Ricci's **Deci Dela** bursting with raspberry, peach and freesia, or Dior's young and spirited combination of lemon, orange, melon, basil and carnation in **Diorella**. Or they can be as vivacious and vivid as in **V de Valentino**, which is dominated by sun-ripened Tuscan melon infused with tangerine, orange bergamot, pepperberry and jasmine. But the one thing these fruity types have in common is, as you'd expect, a glowing, sunny and vibrant warmth that's hard not to lick your lips at.

Woody

This can mean either perfumes with a distinctly wood or timber/bark smell of such things as sandalwood, cedarwood, pine, rosewood, or things that you'd find in a forest or wood, such as moss, fern, leaves or lichen. There are barely any perfumes available today that are dominated by the scent of wood or forest, but still quite a formidable few that are distinguished by those characteristics. Most are heavily garlanded with greenery and spices, some with the smell of burnished leather (which is a rare, but haunting, ingredient in perfume), some with forest, woodland or even jungle flowers, and almost all of them with the soft warmth of amber. What they have in common is a rich, smouldering smokiness that gives them an immense sense of mysterious power and individuality. If you can find it, **Montana Parfum de Peau** (in the cobalt blue box) is the modern quintessence of this category with its sweep of rare woods, amber, cassia, pepper, vetiver and ylang ylang. **Vanderbilt** also has very pungent and warm woody undertones of cypress with musk and spicy flowers, and Shiseido's haunting **Feminité du Bois** is almost entirely based on the hypnotic and calming effects of Moroccan cedarwood from the Atlas Mountains. I also find Chanel's **No. 19** a perfume very reminiscent of an enchanted forest with its lilting *mélange* of leaves, moss, sandalwood and white flowers, and even the very majestic **Bal à Versailles** by Jean

Desprez, although laden with richly opulent flowers, has a very woody and smoky glow from its extravagant use of Mysore sandalwood and spicy vanilla. This category can certainly boast its unique influence in some of the most audacious and classic perfumes.

Greens

This category is almost self-explanatory but it's actually much more complex than the others. Basically, a green perfume is one that immediately reminds you of, or even transports your imagination to, the outdoors — all fresh and breezy and sunny. Suddenly you can smell new-mown grass, sap-laden green leaves, ferns and mosses, even crushed citrus leaves and almost certainly herbs and meadow flowers. Some of them use as their base a very classic formula called *chypre*, which is pronounced 'sheep-ruh'. This is a strong and quite intoxicating mixture of (usually) the orange-type oil called bergamot, galbanum (a very rare and expensive oil from Persian ferula plants), tree resins, ferns and mosses. It is very beautiful and unmistakably green. Coty first used it after the First World War in his ground-breaking **Chypre**, as did Guerlain in the incredibly haunting **Mitsouko**, which added peach to *chypre*. Much later on, after the Second World War, Pierre Balmain revolutionised perfume with his greener-than-green dazzling masterpiece **Vent Vert**. Continuing the green revolution is **Paloma Picasso**, which adds lots of Spanish spiciness to its seductive, dark green base, and Jean Couturier's even spicier **Coriandre**, which not only uses coriander and geranium leaf but also oakmoss and angelica to give its green theme an emerald sparkle. Greens have come in and out of fashion but never disappear, simply because of their heady, breathtaking freshness and clean crispness. They also have the advantage of making you feel very, very young all over again.

Orientals

These are the seductresses of the perfume galaxy. They can be very heavy and dark, or lighter but still highly sensual, and are almost always best worn in the evening and preferably in autumn and winter. They are exotic and intense and are not known for their subtlety, so it follows that younger women should avoid their sultry smoulder and leave the field to their elders. Orientals are composed of opulent and heady flowers such as jasmine, carnation, tuberose, gardenia and more exotic eastern charmers such as ylang ylang, orchid, osmanthus, plus lashings of spices like cinnamon, clove, coriander, pepper and vanilla, rich resins like balsam and amber, plus fruits, woods and grasses as well as mango, coconut, patchouli, vetiver and sandalwood. They can be sweet and sensual like Guerlain's great classic **Shalimar**, or lighter (but no less seductive), like their beautiful **Samsara**. Yves Saint Laurent's **Opium** is another great success with its jasmine, incense and vanilla sophistication, as is Estée Lauder's enduring and very pervasive intoxication, **Youth Dew**, a dark enchantress you have to be careful with. If you are emotionally equipped to wear an oriental (and there are plenty of women who feel too shy to go near them) you know you're in for an exotic and sometimes thrilling adventure. Only you will know if you can handle it!

Crossovers

Although you'll get to recognise the five basic categories, it's not all that easy when it comes to 'crossovers'. These are sub-categories which combine one or more of the five basics. You might come across such things as the so-called 'florientals', which are basically florals with a touch of oriental influence (or the other way around). Then there are fruity florals, fruity greens, woody greens and so on. You get the picture. They're not really the categoric hybrids or new breeds they pretend to be — they simply heavy up on their basic category by adding a fair whack of another one, or even more than one. But your nose will soon tell you what the main plot really is, and, after all, it's your nose that makes the final decision, and it's only interested in what it likes — regardless of anything else.

The counter

connection:

CHOICES, AND HOW TO MAKE THEM

E ven if you've had plenty of experience when it comes to making that crucial perfume choice, it's a good idea to remind yourself of a few things — such as where to find what you want, in what formulation, how to handle the salesperson (rather than have her handle you) and the basic rules of getting to know a perfume that is new to you. These are things that, no matter how dab a hand you might be, should always be taken into consideration when you front that glamorous and glittering perfume counter. If you haven't had much experience in these enjoyable but tricky matters, then this section is invaluable reading.

First off, where do you find what you want? This is trickier than you think and often a source of disappointment so I might as well be blunt about it from the start. Big department stores and, to a lesser extent, big pharmacies carry a large range of top-flight, expensive perfumes as well as a smaller, but comprehensive, range of less expensive and less-known perfumes. I must point out here, though, that they do not stock perfumes that do not sell in large quantities. In other words, if a perfume does not sell, and continue to sell, in budgeted quantity they will drop it. So, if you're looking for an unusual perfume, or one that's gone past its 'new' attraction, or one that's ignored by the big local distributors as being unprofitable to import, then look elsewhere (unless the store or pharmacy is prepared to order it in for you — they're usually quite obliging about doing so).

But look where? Again, it's not cut and dried, nor easy. Capital cities and larger cities or towns are bound to have specialist perfume shops or boutiques. These are your best bet for the perfumes you can't find in the big stores. They carry exclusively imported names, or perfumes that have a special but not large appeal, and are usually extremely helpful in obtaining one that you like that they may not have in stock at the time. They usually have mailing lists and facilities to cater to those of you who don't live in very populated areas. In any case, your phone book is your best source to finding these specialist stockists. Personally, I think that they're also more exciting because of their rare and sometimes surprising variety of unusual or hard-to-find perfumes. Also, if they don't have exactly what you want, they're more likely to suggest a suitable alternative.

Duty-free shops are also very good if you're eligible to buy their product. They will always have the leading brands, as well as some very famous ones not handled by department stores and pharmacies. Unfortunately you won't find much in the way of the 'older' perfumes — again here it's the new and popular that rule the roost. And, of course, the prices are considerably lower than normal retail outlets.

Speaking of prices, I'd like to digress slightly and point out a few salient truths about what might seem like the exorbitant cost of perfume. Aside from the very considerable government tax put on these so-called luxury items (which is no fault of the perfume makers, distributors or retailers), I don't believe good — repeat, good — perfume is outrageously expensive. Perfumes which have been created with extraordinary creative imagination contain only the very highest quality ingredients, whether they be synthetic or natural, or both. (By the way, perfumers don't consider 'synthetic' to be a dirty word. Without synthetic or chemically-constructed ingredients we would still be inhumanely killing animals for fixatives such as musk, ambergris and so on, and would not have half the perfumes available to us if we relied on prohibitively natural ingredients and processes.) And because such perfumes are of such high quality and high concentration, they do not require great lashings of application to make their message clear. In fact, in almost all cases, you need very very little of a perfume for it to give its all and keep giving it for some hours — four or five quick squirts will do the trick (have a look at the bottle after you've done that and you'll see there has not been a great drop in the level of the precious stuff at all!). In fact, I think that although the initial outlay may be hefty, perfume is not extravagantly exorbitant at all. And that does not include the immeasurable degree of personal pleasure it gives you. Always remember this — cheap perfumes are cheap because they contain cheap (meaning inferior) ingredients, which is exactly why they *smell* cheap (and so might *you* wearing them).

Back to the perfume counter. Don't make up your mind about exactly what you think is best for you and go charging up to the salesperson and buy it without trying, or at least asking a few questions about what you think is *the* one for you. No matter how persuasive a description of a perfume is, it is after all just that — a description which can't take into account all the nuances and subtleties that your mind or your nose or even your skin might have. *Always try it first — and always on your skin.* Don't ever be fobbed off with those paper strips sprayed with the perfume — you are not made of paper, and every skin is different. Some skins take to particular types of perfumes more agreeably and lastingly than others. It depends on your personal degree of acidity or alkalinity as to how a perfume reacts and sits on you. That's why you must try the perfume first. Have it sprayed quite generously (and closely) on your inner wrist and let it settle at least a minute (even longer if you can). Don't be embarrassed about waving it around in the air a bit so it dries quicker. Never, never rub it into your skin, especially on your other wrist! All you'll do is bruise the all-important gradation of the perfume. The gradation of a perfume is a very vital element in knowing whether you like it as it begins its journey of revelation. This is done usually in three stages*:

The top or head notes form the first impression — the volatile onset of the perfume's initial character. Think of it as a leading lady making her entrance onstage. These notes say quite emphatically what they have to say, but last no longer than a few nose-dazzling minutes. *Never judge a perfume on these top notes* — they act as the enticement to lead you further and deeper into the perfume's personality or character.

The middle or heart notes reveal the heart and soul, the true message or voice of the perfume in all its complex and compelling splendour. This is the leading lady's big scene, with all stops out where she wants to woo and win you completely. Take a good, deep breath to get its message (just as you would with the first sip of a good wine), and judge whether the perfume speaks your language. This is the crucial stage.

The base or soul notes are not as assertive as the head or heart notes, but are just as complex and interesting. They are there to give the perfume its true depth and staying power, as well as to smooth and fix the whole composition with a warm fullness. Without the soul notes, all the former brilliance would evaporate or just go unpleasantly stale. They also have a complex

There are some new perfumes that claim to have all their ingredients bonded and combined into one consistent and persistent note right from beginning to end, and therefore do not go through the three usual stages. In other words, what you smell when you first apply them is what you get all the way through.

character of their own, and lead inevitably to the graceful and lingering fadeout. It's as if the leading lady has taken her final bow and, loaded with floral tributes, disappears enigmatically behind the curtain.

Salespersons at perfume counters usually have a fair amount of product knowledge at their disposal. But do be careful they don't bamboozle you with too much of it. Too often it's been force-fed into them and they're now doing the same to you. Be brave and *ask questions* — such as what season is it best in, or what colours or clothes to wear with it, how much is it and does it have staying power or fade away quickly? This will bring her to its formulations, which usually fall into the following categories.

Extrait or **concentrate** is the real unadulterated thing. This is strong, pure perfume you use very little of, which is why it lasts longer, and also why it's so expensive. If you can afford it, I think it is the best buy of all.

Eau de parfum is the next best thing to the *extrait*. It is quite powerful and lasting (depending always on the formula of the particular perfume — some are naturally or intentionally stronger than others), with a 10–20% concentration of the perfume essence diluted in 80–90% proof alcohol. It's a very wise economical option and will give you a truly faithful idea of the concentrate.

Eau de toilette is the most popular form which gives a very distinct impression of the perfume concentrate without being too assertive or long-lasting. It contains less than 10% concentrate diluted in 90%

proof alcohol and, being less expensive than *eau de parfum*, can be used more lavishly, which makes it ideal for layering on the skin if you've used some of the bath or body product lines of the perfume. These bath and body products are not only a wonderfully pampering way to envelop yourself in the perfume's scent, they are also a good and practical way to get to know what the perfume is like on your skin before you make a bigger outlay.

Eau de cologne is entirely different from the above formulations in that cologne is, strictly speaking, a formula of its own, having originated in the German city that bears its name. It is made from a fairly strict (and once secret) recipe of citrus oils, herbs, spices and flowers. It is often erroneously confused with *eau de toilette*.

The personal connection:

THE QUEST, THE QUALITY,

THE QUANTITY

I'm always surprised that a lot of women use only the insides of their wrists or little dabs behind the ears and then expect the perfume to blaze forth in all its glory to carry the message loud and clear! Of course they're great places to wear it, but so are the insides of elbows, the 'v' and the nape of the neck, the cleavage of the bust, along the hairline, behind the knees, at the ankles and even between the fingers — all done with discretion of course. At least the perfume has various vantage points from which to infiltrate its presence and purpose. Or, if you like the sheer blissful extravagance of it, spray the perfume in front of you and simply walk through it (twice!) — it feels wonderful as well as achieving a veil-like effect.

If you are unfortunate enough to be slightly allergic to some perfumes, you don't have to touch your body with a beautiful fragrance at all — simply apply the perfume to little balls of cotton wool and secrete these where they won't actually touch the skin (in a handkerchief, pinned to the inside of a scarf, in a purse or between your stockings and shoes).

And here's a personal tip: if you're having trouble getting to sleep, a judicious spray of one of your more soothing perfumes (nothing too dramatic) on your pillow or in the 'v' of your collarbone, should have you wafting off in no time.

Take care

Now you have the precious commodity you've been looking for, make sure you take tender, loving care of it. Being so complexly constructed and so costly, perfume is to be treated with the proper respect it deserves.

Once you have it safely at home, please don't display it unless you feel you *have* to show it off. Perfume is extremely sensitive to light, and will discolour and decompose — if not rapidly then at least doggedly over repeated exposure. **Never** leave it out of its outer packaging no matter how spectacular the bottle might be. **Always** leave it in the dark protection of its carton, **always** leave the carton in a dark or darkish place — and **always** upright if it is not the spray variety. Leakage (which will almost always be your fault for not putting the stopper back firmly) can occur while you're not aware of it, with disastrous results. It's best to have a special little place for your perfumes — preferably behind a closed door, such as in a deep-sided box or carton inside a cupboard or drawer which you can keep closed.

Try not to take a large size with you on your travels, whether it be to work or on holiday. Buy a smaller, more portable purse- or travel-size or a refill bottle if you can. If this isn't possible, keep the bottle upright in its carton surrounded by soft materials which will help protect it. If your perfume is not a spray but has a glass or metal stopper, always make sure you replace it firmly after use without using brute strength or you may find it will jam in the neck and be almost impossible and dangerous to pull out again.

The collection

It never ceases to amaze me that there are still some women who are so faithful to one perfume they will not use, or even try, anything else. It amazes me not because it appears to be a blinkered approach but because it ignores the endless pleasures of variety. To be synonymous with a single perfume is not wrong in itself, except that it can become too much of a trademark and can turn you into a perfumed *cliché*! Aside from which you don't know what you're missing out on by sticking stubbornly to it.

After all, you change your clothes and their colours, your hair, makeup and accessories to suit the mood and the occasion. Surely it follows that your choice of a perfume should complement your whole presentation. There is no such thing as an all-weather, all-purpose perfume, and featuring the same one time and time again, no matter what, is asking too much of it (and your friends!). This is why I think it's absolutely essential, and much more interesting, to have at your fingertips a wardrobe or arsenal of perfumes to choose from. Of course, I know it's an expensive proposition, but you can do it gradually.

Start off by adding one or two to your faithful favourite, and you're on your way. And remember, the more you have to choose from, and use, the more you spread out their rate of consumption.

Assuming you've found your absolute favourite, think about adding one that's quite different from it (but still within the range of your astrological temperament), then perhaps one that's in-between. It's a good idea to have a perfume that's great for warmer weather (something light and breezy), one for cooler times (perhaps an oriental) and your standby. But don't stop there — keep collecting. I firmly believe every woman who loves and is sensitive to the power and persuasion of perfume should have at least six at her disposal at all times. Frankly, I don't think any woman can have too many, as long as you don't over-favour some at the expense of others. If you find yourself not using one or two, try giving them to someone who will appreciate having them — perhaps someone just starting off a perfume collection. Don't be mean and let them languish and go sour and stale in their beautiful bottles, will you?

The creative connection:

A GLOSSARY OF INGREDIENTS

In the fascinatingly complex creation and composition of a perfume, hundreds of ingredients are either considered or tried until the right recipe is achieved and the new perfume is born. Most of them will be familiar to you because most of them are well-known exotic or home-grown flowers. But there are many, many others that may be a mystery to you, and since they all play important, supporting or sometimes even starring roles in the final product, I thought you might like to know what they are and what they contribute to the particular perfumes which would be the less without their contribution. I've narrowed them down to these, and added simple pronunciations where necessary.

Aldehyde (AL–duh–hyde): organic compounds from natural or synthetic sources are created in the laboratory and chemically manipulated to smell sharp, powdery, glowing, vivid, intense, green or woody, or to create a scent not found in nature. They add originality and versatility. For example, Chanel's **No. 5** uses aldehydes in conjunction with floral and fruit essences to achieve a complexity and synthesis that is indefinable to this day.

Amber: a processed amber-coloured resin from fir trees with a warm, autumnal, smoky smell. It can be used to 'fix' or cement a formula, or can be used as a starring ingredient (as in Calvin Klein's **Obsession**).

Balsam: a tree resin with a sweet and warm fragrance that can be used as a supporting star or a fixative in the base notes of a perfume. It is used mostly in oriental perfumes for a lightly sensuous note.

Bergamot (BERGA-mot or BERGA-mo): a bitter, inedible citrus fruit whose peel is used to extract a highly aromatic lemon/orange oil. It gives a citrus note to genuine *eau de cologne* and combines with heady floral scents in perfumes.

Benzoin (ben-ZWARN): a resin from the styrax-benzoin tree of South-East Asia, with a sweet chocolate/vanilla fragrance. Benzoin is usually used as a fixative and to impart a rich, confectionery finish.

Bulgarian rose: the world's finest rose attar (or oil) is extracted from flowers grown in Bulgaria's Valley of Roses. It takes about 2,500 roses to yield one gram of precious attar, so it is only used in high quality perfumes.

Cassia: cinnamon-smelling bark and leaves of the Chinese cassia tree.

Cassis (kass-EECE): aromatic oil from the buds of blackcurrants.

Castoreum (karst-or-EE-um): originally a leathery-smelling secretion gathered from the lymph glands of the Canadian beaver, but now synthetically made in the laboratory, and used as a very powerful fixative.

Chypre (SHEEP-ruh): French for 'Cyprus', this is a combination of various leaves, grasses, ferns, mosses, resins and green buds, mixed with bergamot to resemble the green smell of cypress oil, and used as the basis of tangy 'green' perfumes.

Civet (SIVV-itt): a glandular secretion taken from the farmed Abyssinian civet cat with an extremely repugnant smell, and used in minute quantities to add an earthy note, as well as being a powerful fixative.

Clary sage: a meadow-sage herb with a sweetish mint/citrus smell.

Coumarin: a mostly synthetic sweet vanilla and hay-like smell resembling the natural fragrance of the tonka bean.

Galbanum (GAL-ban-um or gal-BAIN-um): intensely green-smelling oil from the sap of Iranian ferula plants, it is vital in giving the leafy freshness and piquancy to all 'green' perfumes.

Grasse (GRARSE): not the smell of freshly-cut grass found in many green perfumes, but the perfume capital of France in southern Provence, where hillsides of flowers are grown and distilled into the essences used in hundreds and hundreds of fine perfumes. Very popular with tourists.

Heliotrope (HEEL-ee-o-trope): a bright purple

flower with a cherry and woody fragrance (most notably used in Guerlain's **L'Heure Bleue**).

Iris: found in up-market perfumes and called Florentine iris, or sometimes called orris. It comes from the iris roots (not the flowers), which are peeled, dried and stored, then distilled to exude a sweet violet-woody scent. It is very, very expensive.

Labdanum (LAB–den–um): a dark, leather-smelling resin from the rock–rose herb (which is sometimes called cistus).

Leather: usually obtained from rawhide treated with birch tar and then boiled down to a rich, smoky essence with a burnished leathery smell. It is used in highly sophisticated perfumes, such as **Fendi**.

Living Flower: a modern technique whereby the intensely fresh smell of a newly-opened flower is captured and sealed in a bell jar, then broken down chemically and re-created with astonishing fidelity in the laboratory. The result is highly intense and radiant.

Mimosa (mim–O–suh): European name for the blossoms of the acacia or wattle tree.

Musk: nowadays, musk is usually chemically created to resemble the glandular secretion of the rare male musk deer. It has an erotic image because of its use in oriental perfumes. The smell is rich, sensuous and pervasive.

Myrrh (MERR): a liquorice-sweet smelling gum from a Middle Eastern shrub. Myrrh is used sparingly, mostly in oriental perfumes.

Oakmoss: a velvety green, earth-smelling resin

from the lichen growing on or under oak trees from Central Europe. Oakmoss is a vital component of many classic perfumes, especially the 'greens'.

Opoponax (o-POP-o-nax): the warm, woody, animalic odour from the gum resin of the Horn of Africa tree.

Osmanthus: a small flower grown on trees in the Far East with a mysterious perfume reminiscent of jasmine, plums and raisins.

Patchouli (paht-CHOO-lee): the oil from the leaves of the patchouli plant grown in South-East Asia. It achieved legendary status in the '60s for its intensely earthy, musky, sexy and sweet pervasiveness. Patchouli is an essential in straight oriental or floral–oriental perfumes. Strong stuff!

Petitgrain (PETTY-grain): delicate citrus oil from the leaves and stems of the bitter orange tree. It is used extensively in *eau de cologne*.

Rose de mai (rose duh MAY): a small *centifolia* Moroccan rose now grown extensively in the Grasse district of Southern France whose highly fragrant oil is used in many classic floral perfumes.

Rosewood: the fragrantly woody, spicy oil from the Brazilian rosewood tree.

Sandalwood: a soft, sensuous, creamy oil from the matured Indian sandalwood tree grown extensively around Mysore. Sandalwood is used as a starring, supporting or fixative role in the very best perfumes.

Tonka bean: sweet and penetrating caramel/vanilla/marzipan-smelling beans from the pods of

The Creative Connection
31

South American tonka trees.

Tuberose (TUBA-roze): not a rose at all, but a tall-stemmed type of many-flowered lily with an intensely heady, pervasive sweet smell some people find cloying. Tuberoses are used extensively in sensuous, exotic perfumes.

Vanilla: the seeds from the pod of a South-East Asian climbing orchid. Its scented extract is very tenacious and sweet, and makes an excellent fixative.

Vetiver (VETTY-vair): an earthy, woody, pungent scent from the roots of a tall grass grown in Haiti, Reunion Island, Brazil and Sumatra. Vetiver is used as a green element in both men's and women's fragrances.

Violet leaves: the oil from the leaves and the stems is used to add a subtle violet/cucumber note, and as a booster to iris/orris violet-like essences.

Ylang ylang (il-LANG-il-LANG): the legendary tropical 'flower of flowers' from Madagascar, the Philippines, Indonesia and the Comores Islands, has an intensely lush, exotically earthy, almost hypnotic scent.

Words of
caution

F inally, before we launch on our perfumed
astrological journey, three things must be
clarified.

The first is that the principal ingredients described
by me in the following sections of *The Perfume Zodiac*
are as accurate as I've been able to confirm. They may,
however, differ here and there from those of the actual
formulation, which is known only to the manufacturers
and is, quite understandably, not available for outside
perusal.

Secondly, the generalised opinions in the star sign
sections are based only on my personal observations and
assessments, and therefore cannot hope to be entirely
accurate about personal and private characteristics of
any individual. I'd also like to point out that personal
taste, likes and dislikes, might find you discovering a
perfume not suggested for your star sign, but which may

suit you perfectly. If that's the case, go for it!

Thirdly, remember that nothing — least of all an inexact science such as astrology — is infallible, and a certain amount of elasticity and, above all, levity is necessary to enjoy both the adventure of discovering yourself through astrology, and the pleasure of discovering perfume as linked in *The Perfume Zodiac*. It's meant to be fun as well as being helpful — and I hope you'll enjoy it on that level.

Aries

The ram
March 21—April 19

You and the Yellow Brick Road

It's very hard to resist children, no matter how demanding they can be, and the same can be said about you. The Aries woman, no matter how old she is, still has a marvellous childlike quality about her, and that's what makes her all at once seem innocent, appealing, energetic, sometimes a little too persistent, but most of all, irresistible.

No other star sign is as indefatigable, as questing and questioning, as straightforward (sometimes to the point of embarrassment!) or as uninhibited.

Everything is interesting to you and you'll have a go at anything, usually at breakneck speed. And if you make a mistake, you're not in the least deterred. You'll either try again and again until you've cracked it, or do a quick reverse and find something else that looks promising. You like to win — in fact, you have to win — second-best is not in your nature, and that goes not only for your life but your life-style.

But sometimes the Yellow Brick Road has too many turns, detours and dead-ends, and like an impatient and frustrated child you wear yourself out. This can lead to tears of frustration, sulkiness, sudden outbursts of temper and foot-stamping. But you get over it. You have to, because people will either ignore or steer clear of you until the storm passes. However, you bear no grudges, and soon you're back on your Yellow Brick Road of discovery and achievement. And you enjoy every bit of it!

Life is all a marvellous wonder to you — new things are not only fascinating but absolutely necessary. You have to find out how things tick, but sometimes you forget to include people in this as well, which gets you the reputation for being uncaring. Nothing could be further from the truth. You are a very caring, kind, and extremely generous person, but you don't show it with a great deal of false modesty. You don't even care all that much for compliments, and can be quite shy about receiving them (secretly you knew you were going to get them, anyway!).

You don't particularly like having to face the

negative parts of your characteristics. You can be very intolerant of inefficiency (although you know you can be a bit slapdash yourself), and patience is not one of your virtues. Criticism, especially if it's personal, is particularly resented and you've been known to lash out at anyone who dares to question you. And even if you do listen to well-meaning advice it will be rather painful, but you'll try your hardest to be polite (briefly and tersely) and pretend to take notice of it. It's a fear of failure that you're really terrified of. That makes you nervous, frustrated, unhappy — and unhappiness is just not in your book! Nor is disillusionment. The thought of not being liked can be a crushing blow. But the good thing about you is your childlike optimism in the face of disaster. Somehow you put on a brave face, rev up those engines, and *meep-meep! vroom!* — you're off like the Roadrunner in those cartoons you split your sides laughing at!

But, of course, everyone runs out of energy — even you. This you find hard to cope with. It's as if the wind's suddenly gone out of your sails and you're becalmed. This confuses you. Still waters are too deep and scary for you and you get into a panic. You shouldn't because this is where the secret part of Aries lies. You may not know it, but you are not only a softie, you can be incredibly wise. *Wise?* I hear you say. *Me?* Yes, you are, in a beautifully disarming and simple way. You can see straight to the heart of matters and find out what's gone wrong — just like your natural ability to know what part of a machine or gadget has malfunctioned and needs fixing. This is your hidden strength and the positive characteristic you should cultivate, nurture and put to good use. Suddenly you're not the blustering, impetuous, impatient steamroller you're often taken for but a helper, an adviser and, if necessary, a defender — in fact you'll defend a friend with your life! It's your innate optimism that gives you this ability to see the problem and help, and this is the rare quality you should always keep as your guiding light — as well as your fearless honesty and directness. That's what people love you for — especially when it's accompanied by one of your widest, most winning big-kid smiles.

Aries style

Your canvas is a broad and sweeping one — like a cinematic wide-screen complete with blazing colour and full-on sound. Subtlety is not one of your strong points, and neither should it be with your demonstrative and big-hearted personality, so you can forget any attempts at minimalism or cool, calculated austerity. It just isn't you.

Your tastes are clear-cut. There's a naive, no-nonsense approach to the things you like and those that express, even underline, your sense of style. For instance, red might have been invented just for you —

any red, although you usually go for the fire-engine end of the spectrum! This is because red expresses speed, efficiency and passion. You're usually attracted to its secondary colours — yellow, orange, and especially gold. You dote on anything with a touch of gilt to set it off. Cobalt blue and emerald green come into your life a lot too, and anything metallic. Like the grown-up child you are, you like to make an immediate and unmistakable impression — bright, breezy, even a touch blatant. It's not that you don't admire understatement. It's just that it might be fine for others, but leaves too much unsaid — it's too cold and boring in your eyes.

Even the way you dress is testament to your unerring sense of the overall impact. Details are not usually important as long as the 'big impression' is clearly made. Flamboyance is second nature to you, yet you try never to overstep the mark into vulgarity. In fact, you think appearance should not only be colourful but fun! Good on you — you'd look awful in grey with touches of pink — you'd feel a bit of a galah really, when you'd rather be a beautiful, dazzling lorikeet! And when it comes to perfumes, the same rule of thumb applies. You wouldn't fool anyone in a sweet, young, romantic fragrance, least of all yourself. You'll never be a shy retiring violet, so stick to your guns and express yourself the way you want to — big, bold and unabashed. That's what people love about you. In fact, you always come undone when you try to deny your own judgment of what suits you.

What suits you best is *you!*

Your outer expression is *excitement*. Your inner core is *kindness*.

Here's how you translate all of that into the best perfumes for you.

I have divided your perfumes into two sections:

1. *The big guns* — the all-important basic perfumes that should suit you best. They form the core of your perfume arsenal.

2. *Your secret weapons* — these augment the basics and are more daring and unusual, but still should suit you.

There is also a choice of perfumes for those of you born on the cusp of Aries/Taurus, as well as a selection of men's fragrances suitable to give the Aries male. (If you were born on the cusp of Pisces/Aries see pages 454–458 for your further perfume choices.) I have given each perfume a category, and a simple and easy guide to its correct pronunciation. At the end of the chapter I have summated all of the perfumes into a table that tells you whether they're best on young or mature women, in warm or cool weather, day or evening, for fair or dark complexions.

The big guns:
the indispensable basics

To me, the Aries personality and her behaviour is

summed up in the ball scene of a 1938 American movie called *Jezebel*, where the very headstrong and rebellious character played by Bette Davis flatly refuses to appear in a virginal, white crinoline like all the other Southern belles and shocks the pants off society by turning up in a scarlet one! It's not so much that she's kicked over the traces, but more that she wants to be noticed for what she is — a fearless individual. And I think it's the fearlessly individual perfumes that are truly compatible with you. But I must stress this doesn't mean your perfumes should be overtly seductive and sexy — you are not a natural vamp. So, generally speaking, the orientals are not really for you. And it follows that sweetly romantic trifles won't stand a chance when you hit your top speed. Nor does too much elegant sophistication sit easily on your shoulders — subtlety makes you suspicious. But perfumes that are outspoken and assertive, those that underline your cheerful, no-nonsense attitude will do wonders to complement your expectations and your aspirations. One word of warning though — don't overdo the dosage. They are all powerhouse perfumes and must be treated with a little caution, even though you might be tempted to go slightly over the top in your well-meaning efforts to impress. This is one race you will only win by sticking to the rules of good taste and not succumbing to that typical Aries overkill. Here they are:

- **Le Feu d'Issey** by Issey Miyake
  Pronunciation: ler fer DISS-ee/
  ISS-ee me-YAR-kee
  Type: oriental
- **Calandre** by Paco Rabanne
  Pronunciation: kal-ARND-ruh/PAR-ko rar-BARN
  Type: floral/green
- **Ma Griffe** by Carven
  Pronunciation: mah-GREEF/kar-VAN
  Type: floral/green
- **Escape** by Calvin Klein
  Pronunciation: KAL-vin KLINE
  Type: floral/fruity
- **Ferre** by Gianfranco Ferre
  Pronunciation: fair-AIR/jarn-FRANKO fair-AIR
  Type: floral
- **Rive Gauche** by Yves Saint Laurent
  Pronunciation: reeve GOASH/eve-sarn-lor-ON
  Type: floral/fruity

LE FEU D'ISSEY — because it's fiery

What do you follow a roaring success with — in Issey Miyake's case the phenomenal **L'Eau d'Issey**, a perfume so revolutionary it caught everyone by surprise? Well, he had no intention of repeating himself and that's why **Le Feu d'Issey** probably disappointed a lot of women who expected more of the same, and not this topsy-turvy little devil!

Mind you, many Aries find **L'Eau d'Issey** a bit too wet and wimpy for their assertive natures and tastes, but **Le Feu d'Issey** (or Issey's Fire, if you like) is more of a flamethrower that ignites the right sparks in you and sends you rocketing off in all directions. It's so individualistic it takes the bravery and fearlessness of Aries to handle it without getting burnt.

Just one look at the cute but vaguely sinister round red bottle tells you it contains something incendiary — it looks a bit like a time bomb ticking away, ready to explode. It's not really dangerous, but it means business with its initial blaze of rich Bulgarian roses to get you off on the right foot before the oriental heavies take over. You and the roses are plunged into a cauldron of spicy Sichuan pepper and guaic wood, which has an unusually haunting smell of violets and Chinese tea, plus a generous handful of pungent coriander leaves to really stir things up. The result is not as fearsome as you might think, but a fascinating and compelling bit of alchemy that sends shivers of sensuality up and down your spine.

Le Feu d'Issey has a smouldering sexiness without resorting to the corny tricks of too many oriental perfumes that smell cheap by comparison. It's a true trail-blazer, not a cheong-sammed assembly-line seductress. Like anything with the Miyake label, it's a genuine one-off, just like you! You might find **Le Feu d'Issey** is just the cheeky little firecracker you need to light your fire and keep it burning bright right through to the sizzling climax and beyond!

CALANDRE — because it's still radical

Calandre gives the impression of being a brilliant and rather reckless perfume, but actually has a surprisingly soft heart. This perfectly complements the two strong forces of the Aries astrological character — the high-energy outer shell and the soft inner core.

As you might know, **Calandre** is no longer the spring chicken it was. It was first released in 1969, but has endured so easily it could just about lay claim to being a modern classic! It has an extraordinarily faithful following and doesn't deserve to be passed over in favour of newer, flashier perfumes (although I can't think of one that is too similar to it). It's a radical perfume full of surprises. If you don't know it, give it a try.

Calandre hits you like an accident — and no wonder! The word is French for the front grille of a car. **Calandre**'s up-front notes are so strong you'll probably reel from the onslaught of green leaves enhanced with some high-pitched aldehydes for an even more acerbic zing. But almost immediately you find yourself plunged into a whirlpool of flowers bolstered by aldehydes to smell sharper and more focused than they usually are — lily of the valley, jasmine and rose. It's rose that lies deep at the heart of **Calandre**, rose in a concentration so emphatic it becomes quite intoxicating. This is the soft centre of the perfume, edged with the dry and pungent punch of geranium leaf, oakmoss and bergamot. The sheer success of **Calandre**'s effect is its ability to balance a very high-powered, almost metallically-sharp theme with a throbbing heart of romantic flowers. While there's nothing pretty about **Calandre**, it exudes a persistent magnetism. But it's the pulsating roses in its depths that keep things purring. It's like having your motor running — at the ready!

MA GRIFFE — *because it's defining*

In French, *griffe* can mean anything from claw to designer label to signature. In this exquisite perfume, they all apply, but I think 'my signature' is probably the most persuasive because **Ma Griffe** is a perfume that can become indelibly and uniquely yours. Like **Calandre, Ma Griffe** is always in danger of being passed by for something newer, which is not always necessarily a wise thing. Certain perfumes endure over many decades because they had something important to say in the first place — something that set them apart from the also-rans. That thing is, simply, originality. And **Ma Griffe** is a true original.

In 1946, it ushered in an entirely new breed of perfume — green aldehydes fused with floral aldehydes. This simply means both green and floral ingredients were used but synthetically bolstered — almost re-invented — rather than based on purely natural essences (which would have still been in pretty scarce supply after the ravages of the war). This doesn't mean for a second that the word 'synthetic' should be sneered at — since Chanel's heyday in the '20s, hundreds and hundreds of successful perfumes veered off the 'natural' track and added synthetic elements to their formulas to create brand new scents without the familiar pure smells of 'rose' or 'jasmine' or 'violet' or whatever. In other words, they invented their own mysterious gardens and bouquets of flowers, fruits and so on. **Ma Griffe** simply took the process one exciting step further.

It's a perfume full of white flower scents — gardenia, jasmine, rose — almost swamped by the sharp green of galbanum, clary sage and vetiver. Also present to add an exotic touch are ylang ylang and sandalwood, along with styrax, which is a resin with a heady narcissus/hyacinth note. Sharpened and glossed with its aldehydes, **Ma Griffe** creates a compelling, sophisticated character all its own — an individuality that is at once both elegant and vivacious. It is assertive but never stridently so, gregarious but not boisterous, and has such an informal and cheerful approach I think it will appeal to the Aries woman who wants to be admired for her good taste and self-confidence without shouting about it.

I think you'll find **Ma Griffe** such a reliable friend that likes to make friends, you'll wonder why you hadn't thought of wearing it before. And, I'm glad to add, it still comes in its straight, no-nonsense bottle packed in the unmistakable vivid green and white diagonal striped presentation.

You could very well make **Ma Griffe** your own unique signature perfume.

ESCAPE — because it's a great traveller

You never run away from situations. You'd rather face them fair and square. So, in the case of this perfume, don't confuse escape from responsibility with escape from convention. **Escape** is firmly on the side of the latter. It's your passport to freedom (as if you needed it) — a travelling companion you'll find not only compatible but able to keep up with your hectic schedule. But it also has a surprising asset. **Escape** can actually relax you, if you slow down enough to breathe in its outdoor freshness and ozonic drifts — truly! So you've got it both ways with this one!

Escape is versatile and unpretentious enough to stick by you in just about any situation. It's unconventional enough to appeal to the nonconformist in you, and sociable enough to cover for you when you're feeling jaded or bored. It's a cheerful mix of delicious fruits and lush flowers, spiked with spices. The top notes read a bit like a recipe for fruit salad (mandarin, apple, apricot, peach, melon, plum) but their salivating piquancy is pulled slightly into line by some marvellously calming ozonic notes, plus the headiness of jasmine, rose and carnation, which usher in spicy dashes of clove, coriander, chamomile and blackcurrant bud. Sensuously soft hints of musk, sandalwood, cedar and amber help to settle things down, so **Escape** doesn't go reeling off the tracks into over-the-top frivolity.

Aries women like to be unencumbered and **Escape's** lightness is never excess baggage. With its air of casual *joie de vivre*, **Escape** not only gets you to wherever you're going but makes sure you have a good time while you're there. And when you want to go, it's ready!

FERRE — because it's dynamite!

The shiny gold box ought to lure you immediately, and when you extract what looks like a round black bomb covered in silky black mesh with its gold top suspiciously resembling the pin of a hand grenade, you have a fair idea this is something you can't wait to detonate! One squirt of **Ferre** ought to satisfy the incendiary in you — and we all know what a potential pyromaniac Aries (even ladylike ones) can be! This perfume is nothing short of an explosive bombshell.

First of all, **Ferre** might take a bit of tracking down (perfume boutiques are your best bet). Secondly, don't get it confused with its sweet and lovely sister, which is called **Gianfranco Ferre** and comes in virginal white packaging. There is absolutely nothing virginal about **Ferre** by Ferre — it's a very worldly, been-there and done-that cocktail, and only grown-up Aries need apply!

It begins with a bang of volatile orange blossom, bergamot, Bulgarian rose, ylang ylang and (not surprisingly) passionfruit. While these are creating havoc, the heart notes thunder in — mimosa, violet, blackcurrant bud, lily of the valley and peach. So there's not much let up from the fusillade — not even from the base notes of musk, spices, vanilla and amber, which are used not so much as counterpoint but as another line of fire. Of course, it's all Italian bravado and not to be taken as deadly serious. **Ferre** is actually not quite as ferocious as it sounds — its melange of high-powered flowers is unashamedly sensual and dazzling and it's more a game than a battle of seduction. Ferre starts and finishes in a blaze of triumph — which should please a red-blooded, relentless Aries woman no end!

RIVE GAUCHE
— because it couldn't care less

Rive Gauche was introduced in a blaze of prêt-à-porter glory as long ago as 1971, but like the genius of its creator it has taken on an enviable agelessness that springs eternal just as much as Saint Laurent's couture does. What's more, I firmly believe it's one of those very rare beauties that can be worn by any woman from teenager to dowager. **Rive Gauche** has such affable and insouciant charm it brings out the blithe spirit that Aries automatically possess but also adds its own dimension of easy-going *panache*. It radiates such friendly vibrations it could easily convince you that you're quite sophisticated — an aspiration that sometimes you feel is a bit beyond your uncomplicated unpretentiousness.

Its name simply means 'left bank' — in this case

referring to the left bank of the River Seine, so straight away **Rive Gauche** firmly announces its bohemian inspiration. With its entrancing bouquet of honeysuckle, magnolia, gardenia, lily of the valley and jasmine you might think it's heading for an all-white floral arrangement, but strong fruit notes of bergamot, peach, vetiver and tonka bean swerve it into another direction altogether. So by the time dashes of vanilla, sandalwood and geranium leaf are added, **Rive Gauche** has definitely turned the corner into racier, more raucous hot-spots. And just to make sure it's not just a city slicker, the entire creation is doused with a bunch of sharp, breezy greens, giving it a pastoral *chypre* flourish. The exhilaration and gregarious charm of Rive Gauche gives the all-action Aries woman a feeling as exciting as a reckless dash on a high-speed Harley, with herself at the controls!

Your secret weapons: the surprises

Now to your love of the unexpected, the unusual, the unpredictable. For those times when you're cooling off (or feel you should before collapse sets in), when you don't feel like being your usual dynamo, these gentler, more relaxed perfumes can give you another kind of lift altogether. They help bring out your lighter, less energetic characteristics to surround you with an impression of friendly approachability. You may not be overly sentimental (or want to show it if you are) and nor are they. They are all strongly individualistic but not quite as assertive as your Big Guns. If you're in the mood, or want to be, they can radiate your simple honesty and niceness without being cloying. They might also help you in the romance department — often a source of frustration to your impatience. They might even be able to relax you enough to let someone take over for a change. Who knows? You might even like the change! Anyway, they'll add that extra pleasure to your love of life. They are:

- **Poême** by Lancôme
  Pronunciation: po-AIRM/LARN-kom
  Type: floral
- **Cheap and Chic** by Moschino
  Pronunciation: cheep and SHEEK/moss-KEEN-o
  Type: floral/fruity
- **Estée** by Estée Lauder
  Pronunciation: ESS-tay/ESS-tay LOR-duh
  Type: floral
- **Fidji** by Guy Laroche
  Pronunciation: FEED-jee/ghee la-ROASH
  Type: fruity/floral
- **Fleur d'interdit** by Givenchy
  Pronunciation: fler darn-tuh-DEE/zjhiv-ON-she
  Type: fruity/floral
- **Splendor** by Elizabeth Arden
  Type: floral

POÊME — *because it's peaceful*

The sculpted grace of its bottle will be an instant attraction to the Aries sense of clean-lined beauty. The perfume it contains will either carry you away or disturb you with feelings of vague restlessness. **Poême** is so original, so individual it seems to polarise opinions, but to a battle-fatigued or brain-fagged Aries it may well offer the peace and tranquillity to fix things in the most soothing and sensuous manner. It is quite sweet but not cloying, romantic but not mushy, memorable without being pushy. It is, I think, a perfume that is both peaceful and poignant.

Lancôme has constructed it along highly unusual lines. It is made entirely of flower scents — no fruits, spices, greens or oriental accents to give contrast — the flowers say it all. But they're not your usual flowers.

The principal alliance is between a highly-seductive desert flower called *datura candida*, and the legendary and extremely rare Himalayan blue poppy. This has a sweet, singing, ecstatic perfume that disappears when picked. So Lancôme use the Living Flower technique to extract the essence, seal it from evaporation and then duplicate the scent in the laboratory. The result is obviously successful because in combination the two principal flowers in **Poême** smell like nothing you'd find in a garden! A sunny theme of freesias, yellow roses, mimosa and vanilla flowers completes the unique and perfectly-poised harmony.

Poême is not designed to cater to all tastes. It is one of those rarities that will attach itself to the right person and then radiate a singular beauty that is both sensual and compelling. It is not an epic poem in the grand manner, but more like a lyrical ode that infiltrates and calms the senses. It's for when you want to shine with an inner, secret glow rather than stop a room in its tracks with one of your big entrances.

CHEAP AND CHIC
— because it's crazy like a fox

I doubt if any good-humoured Aries could resist the bottle alone — a cheeky and funny representation of Olive Oyl from *Popeye* — madcap and adorable! What's inside though is another matter altogether. This was Franco Moschino's last perfume, and he obviously wanted it to be even more quirky than his signature **Moschino** perfume (which is almost a parody of **Shalimar**!). **Cheap and Chic** is not cheap in the vulgar sense of the word, and it's not particularly *chic* either — in fact he may as well just have called it Cheeky and Cheerful, because that's what it smells like.

There's nothing world-shattering about its composition. In fact, part of its charm is in its ingenuous and mock-innocent bouquet of flowers —

peony, cyclamen, jasmine, wild rose and water flowers up against bergamot with its citrus twist, petitgrain and rosewood, and other accompaniments of white orchid, tonka bean, vetiver and a dash of bourbon — if you please!

It all comes out in a rush of impish naughtiness but an underlying prettiness. But you get the idea the whole thing's a bit of a satire, although a good-natured and nose-tingling one. Moschino's creed was 'I remove impositions' and he's certainly torn down the barricades here.

But don't take it too seriously. **Cheap and Chic** is meant for fun — it laughs at itself as it laughs at the world. It has that wonderfully refreshing 'who cares?' attitude to life, which makes it just fine for Aries who like to live theirs slightly off the beaten track. Splash it around enough, and who knows? Your Popeye could pop up to strut his stuff just for you.

ESTÉE — *because it's theatrical*

Now to sterner, more serious stuff. This is a perfume whose almost infallible effect comes only from the confident but refined way you feature it. **Estée** is not to be trifled with and treated casually, nor does it like to be prettied up. Its world is one of impressive presence and theatrical effect without ever hamming it up. The very fact that Estée Lauder named it after her august self should give you an idea of the elegant clout she insisted it should convey in no uncertain terms.

For the Aries woman who has a secret desire to be onstage and the centre of attention, but may be a bit scared of such exposure to limelight, **Estée** can be a godsend with its flashing brilliance, its dazzling sophistication. I wouldn't exactly call it elegant, but it certainly has heaps of self-confidence and magnetism. But do be careful of it — it's a very potent concoction and too much will turn a star-turn into a turn-off.

It begins with a blast of raspberry backed with citrus oils and peach, plus a strong whiff of acerbic coriander. Then a huge procession of flowers takes over — rose, lily of the valley, jasmine, carnation, ylang ylang laced with seductive musk and styrax. There's even some rich honey present to emblazon it with a sweet glow. Obviously, **Estée** is no slouch — it means to be noticed, and hopefully applauded.

While it may not appeal to sports-crazed Aries, or even those who have curbed their penchant for showing-off, it will become quite a favourite of those who want to bask in more social and refined circles. It will even help to boost your social self-confidence while keeping it within the boundaries of feminine attraction. And that's precisely what **Estée** is all about — winning hearts with its well-bred seduction while maintaining its brilliant and provocative poise. You'll know you've succeeded if you hear people wondering just what it is that you're wearing that makes you so obviously magnetic! Take my advice — don't tell them a thing.

FIDJI — because it's luscious

Whether you imagine yourself cutting a swathe through an exotic jungle path or languishing in a hammock with a wicked hibiscus behind your available (or even unavailable) ear, **Fidji** is the tropical cocktail Aries can't resist when they want to be anywhere else but where they are. It's extravagant, lavishly over-the-top, and totally irresistible. What's more, **Fidji** has been wowing women who wear it, and men lured into its seductive sultriness, since it first arrived like a perfumed cyclone in 1966! It may have cooled off a little since then in popularity, but I don't know anyone who still can't be swept away in a tidal wave of nostalgia when they have another whiff of its siren call.

What's amazing about it is that for all its tropical evocation, **Fidji** is actually created from rather genteel flowers such as rose, carnation, jasmine, hyacinth and violet — although they are given an explosive boost of ylang ylang and tuberose. But it all seems too floral for a perfume that is resoundingly redolent of ripe mangoes, coconut and frangipani! That's the magical art of the perfumer at work — creating a scent that gives a definite impression of something that isn't actually in its composition. But who cares, when **Fidji** is such a glorious and gorgeous knockout!

It's the sort of perfume men love to give women for reasons that might be a bit obvious. But you can play innocent and be more tantalising than submissive. **Fidji** might make you feel passionate, but that doesn't mean you're a pushover! Play the game your way — **Fidji** is on your side. Don't forget to take it with you on your next tropical holiday — preferably alone. You won't be for long.

FLEUR D'INTERDIT — because it's adorable
This charmer is for when you're breezing, not rushing, down your Yellow Brick Road. It's for coasting, for stopping long enough to release all that nice simplicity in you. You won't even mind if the world passes you by. You know you'll catch up with it later on, anyway.

Fleur d'interdit was the last parting tribute to Givenchy's muse Audrey Hepburn before he handed over the reins of his fashion empire to younger and more aggressively modern interests. Its gentleness and poise belie an inner strength of great beauty, but a beauty without any pretensions. It arrives in a lovely apple green and bright pink box which opens to reveal a beautiful frosted bottle containing the rose-pink perfume. Even before you smell it, you're half in love with it. **Fleur d'interdit** is composed of raspberry, peach, melon and a touch of cucumber which are then infused with roses, lilac, lily of the valley, violet leaves and the merest hint of gardenia. Then a hazy veil of vanilla is floated over, along with some serene sandalwood. It's like smelling the first fragrant breeze after the sun's up on a dewy spring morning — perfectly fresh, perfectly beautiful.

The message of **Fleur d'interdit** is tranquillity that suddenly explodes into light-heartedness. Its cheerful exuberance and youthful charm are not made for standing still for too long — it wants to set out and explore the day, but in a purposeful stroll, not in a hurry. It smells like it's ready to let go with an infectious laugh — and Aries like a good laugh, don't they?

SPLENDOR
— because it'shimmers

This is another softie, but one with a cunning strategy. It's a bit like Grace Kelly — all cool, almost icy beauty on the outside but seething with inner passion the right person will unleash in a barrage of fireworks! That's why **Splendor** is such a terrific secret weapon to have in your Aries arsenal — it's the old story of what others might see in you is only the tip of the iceberg! But you'll be glad to know you don't have to look like Grace Kelly did to fall in love with the sweet charms of **Splendor** — just have a picture of her (and maybe Cary Grant) firmly in your mind when you wear it.

It's an unpretentious but imaginative perfume with all the Elizabeth Arden trademarks of prettiness, elegance and romantic inclinations with a little sophistication thrown in to bolster your sometimes fragile ego. It begins its little web of intrigue with the springtime pleasures of sweet pea, hyacinth, white peony and luscious, honeyed drifts of wisteria, then makes gentle waves with jasmine, magnolia and waterlily before the warm depths of satinwood, ebony wood and white musk settle it all down in a tranquil and serene pool of moonlight. It doesn't rock the boat or cause a tsunami of unbridled sensuality, but knows exactly where it's going and gets there calmly and quietly with deliciously sweet persuasion.

Splendor has an ability to keep developing on you, so that it doesn't fade away just when you're getting to the crunch. Instead it persists ever so gently in its own shimmering orbit while you weave you own gossamer web. It's a very comforting perfume, light and lilting but not the least saccharine or slushy. It has enough sparkle to keep you smiling, and it's a great antidote to those times when you feel jaded by romance or just plain disillusioned with your lot in life. A little dash of **Splendor** will get your belief in yourself going again — just keep thinking of Grace, the Ice Princess who melted all too willingly in some very accommodating and handsome arms and pretended it was all a big surprise!

The advantage of the cusp: taking your pick

It's not all confusion — being neither one star sign nor the other, or feeling you're partly both — if you're born towards the very beginning of Taurus*.

You can of course pick and choose from the perfumes suggested from Aries and Taurus, but be careful. Depending on your characteristics, they may not all sit easily on you. That's why I've come up with a selection of extras that might solve any perfume problem or indecision you might have. Anyway, the choice is yours, so have fun finding out!

They are:

- **Tuscany per Donna** by Aramis
  Pronunciation: TUSK-anny per DONN-uh
  Type: floral/fruity
- **Byzance** by Rochas
  Pronunciation: biz–ANSE/ro–SHAR
  Type: floral/oriental
- **Narcisse** by Chloé
  Pronunciation: nar–SEASE/KLO-ee
  Type: floral
- **Ocean Dream** by Giorgio Beverly Hills
  Type: floral

If you were born towards the very beginning of Aries, you might like to check out the choices for those born on the cusp of Pisces/Aries on pages 454–458.

TUSCANY PER DONNA
— because it's vivacious

This is not exactly an adventurous perfume, but I think it will appeal to Aries who have the Taurean trait of the need for order and comfort in their lives. **Tuscany per Donna** is relaxed, friendly and flirtatious. It loves company and fits easily into almost any situation without wanting to steal the show. It's composed of jasmine and orange blossom placed over a bed of lily of the valley, rose, honeysuckle and hyacinth. Citrusy smells of mandarin, bergamot and grapefruit infiltrate but never dominate the all-white floral bouquet, and it's only when the creamy-rich presence of sandalwood (lots of it!) is suffused through the fruit and flower harmony that **Tuscany per Donna** really makes its point. And the point is peaceful and pastoral. If it carries you away to the hazy hills and poppy-strewn fields of sunny Tuscany, the smell of fresh-picked herbs and fresh-baked bread, you're not far off the track — **Tuscany per Donna** was created to do just that. Perfect for putting the brakes on Aries, and for the Taurean love of nature in all its impressionistic imagery.

BYZANCE — *because it's enigmatic*

Don't you sometimes just yearn to be called mysterious, unfathomable, fascinating? They're not traits found in too many Aries, but with a little Taurean influence coming your way, it's not impossible at all. Your frame of mind will help you — being purposeful but not impatient, definite but willing to acquiesce — and wearing something as equivocal and lovely as **Byzance**. This is the perfume where East meets West, without a border war. Named after the ancient city of Byzantium, it is all at once dazzlingly exotic, sophisticated and haunting. Once you get over the fabulous brilliance of its Mediterranean-blue orbed bottle, gilded seal and cyclamen ribbon, **Byzance** opens its heart to you with magnificent Turkish delights of rose, jasmine, tuberose and white stocks, then tantalises your nose and head with the spicy exotica of cardamom, musk, vanilla and basil. There's a piquant whiff of mandarin, a dash of ylang ylang, a whisper of sandalwood to consolidate the oriental opulence, and the entire accord is heightened with a glamorous gloss of aldehydes to make **Byzance** an almost impenetrable but very flattering mystery. I think it's a marvellous bridge between the impressionability of Aries and the sensuality of Taurus. In any case, leaving a trail of its loveliness in your floaty wake (no rushing, please!) will make you enticing and fascinating — even enigmatic!

NARCISSE — *because it's emphatic*

Although it could be named after the beautiful white narcissus, **Narcisse** is not a straight-out, single-scented tribute. It has the heady delights of narcissus in its composition, but a lot of other surprises as well, which leads me to think it might have been secretly named after the Greek youth Narcissus who fell in love with the reflection of his own beauty. But whatever inspired it, **Narcisse** is a perfume that will appeal to Aries for its frankness, and to Taureans for its passion. Along with narcissus, the flower that makes a big impact in its overall effect is plumeria (which we call frangipani). This is the red West Indian variety so you know it's going to pack something of a powerful tropical punch. Together these flowers are olfactory dynamite, especially when apricot, marigold and orange blossom are added to the cocktail. **Narcisse** is not subtle. It's potent and tenacious (so do be discreet with its application). It's vivacious and gregarious. It makes no pretence about being noticed — it is unashamedly seductive, and self-assured of its success. You'll certainly make your presence felt wearing it — even long after the battle's over!

OCEAN DREAM
— because it's a breath of fresh air

Ocean Dream is like an underwater floral ballet. It's said to be composed of flowers not grown on land, but in the ocean or at least in water. The choreography does a grand jeté into white water freesia, lotus and water clover, delicate mermaid flower (grown in the Pacific shallows) and vanilla-scented sea heliotrope before surfacing to float among Californian orange blossom and blue musk — a new synthetic variety noted for its soft sensuality. The effect is, as you'd guess, rather like watching Esther Williams up to her old MGM mermaid tricks — dazzling, fascinating, fantastic. Despite its name, **Ocean Dream** does not take a dive into mysterious depths. It far prefers lounging gracefully and not getting wet. Aries will find it surprisingly soothing when they run out of puff, and Taureans will be thankful for the tranquil smell of the sea, rather than the unglamorous paddock.

The Aries male: gifts for his personal best

He may not always win the race, but you must always treat him as if he's the champ. The Aries male is so competitive, so aggressive and enthusiastic he thrives on success and craves recognition — just don't ever tell him he's failed. You'll lose a good friend if you do. He loves challenge, he loves to show off, so consequently he takes immense pride and care of his appearance at all times. He loves the bathroom, and gets dressed with meticulous attention to detail. When he's finally ready for inspection he'll look so proud of himself you'll want to pat his head like the very good little boy he really is. He may not be the most sophisticated man in the world, but he thinks he is, so be a sport and go along with it. Like all children, he goes bananas over gifts, and anything that helps him achieve success will be appreciated with a genuine display of thanks. The best fragrances to adorn him are ones that smell to him of adventure and top honours — he'll wear them like laurel wreaths! So, nothing too complicated or super-smooth. Nor anything subtle, because he'll miss the point! Light but intense and bright are your best bets — and nothing that smells of sweetness either (he abhors anything that might detract from his macho image). These have proven track records:

- **Polo** by Ralph Lauren
  Pronunciation: PO–lo/ralf lor-ENN
  Type: green/herbal
- **Allure Homme** by Chanel
  Pronunciation: al-YURE om/shar-NEL
  Type: spicy
- **Escape for Men** by Calvin Klein
  Type: woody/fruity
- **Boss Sport** by Hugo Boss
  Type: fruity/spicy

Polo

Not to be associated with rich men's games, but with Lauren's signature Polo range of clothes and toiletries, which are smartly stylish but approachable and affordable. **Polo**, the fragrance, has become something of a classic — a guarantee of masculine good taste assertive enough to be recognisable but never strident enough to be intrusive or obvious. I think the original version is the yardstick which the others in the range (**Polo Sport**, **Polo Crest**) live up to, and is the pick of the bunch for Aries.

It has a sharp, clean scent of greenness (like new-mown grass) combined with freshly aromatic herbs, a touch of light pine for woodiness, a dash of tobacco leaf and oakmoss for depth, and an underpinning of leather — a rich, burnished smell that is used here to give the fragrance warmth and staying power. **Polo** is clean-cut and bracing — and certainly not snooty.

Allure Homme

Everyone, even including himself, seems to expect the Aries man to be something of a non-stop macho man, all aggression and raw animal magentism. Well, nobody can keep that up without wishing there was something a bit more sophisticated around the corner. Give the poor bloke a break and give him a bottle of this terrific new bracer from Chanel. He deserves it, doesn't he? Happily, the only thing it shares with its stunning female counterpart is the classic bottle shape and the clout of Chanel. But **Allure Homme** gives him the chance to consider himself a bit alluring in a butch sort of way with its blast of sexy tonka bean trumpeting over the cooling earthiness of vetiver, cedar and labdanum, which is the herbal-type resin from the rock rose, all sprinkled liberally with hot pepper!

Escape for Men

If he doesn't feel well-dressed without some evidence

of Calvin Klein, then give him this. It's a very Aries concoction — almost an assault — of tangy citrus oils mixed with fresh herbs, green leaves and the dryness of cypress pine with vetiver and a dash of velvety oakmoss to give it a nice soft bed. **Escape for Men** is one of those masculine fragrances that appeals to men who love to get out and do things and show off their prowess — physical or otherwise. It's assertive, immensely self-confident, bursting with energy and enthusiasm. Sound like an Aries male to you? He'll be in his element in this as long as he's not the sophisticated type. It's not quite refined enough to satisfy finicky tastes, but if he wants to be noticed (muscles and all) **Escape for Men** is his passport to male liberation.

Boss Sport

If he finds the generic **Boss** too complex and businesslike, then try **Boss Sport** if only to give him something to display in his bathroom cabinet that testifies to his domestic or professional superiority. (It doesn't matter if you know otherwise.) **Boss Sport** is simplicity itself with its bracing display of citrus oils spiked with pungent lavender (no longer exclusively in the female fragrance domain), a generous gathering of fresh green herbs, geranium leaf and vetiver to give it a darker green undertone. **Boss Sport** has a breezy outdoors vivacity that will get that famous Aries adrenalin pumping. It's a good bet for men who don't like to be overly associated with the use of male fragrance, but want to smell as if they'd just conquered the perils of some super-tricky white water, even if they've never set foot in a raft.

Who suits what, and when: getting the best out of your perfumes

Because perfumes become not only extensions of your personality but also give emphasis to the way you look and the mood you're in, naturally, to bring out their best, they should be treated with due understanding with regard to their own characteristics and qualities. They too have limitations and strengths, just as we all have. So, the following table outlines when best to wear them (Day, Night), the age-group most suited to them (Young, Mature), the general complexion of the wearer (Fair, Dark), and the seasons they bloom best in (Spring/Summer – S/S, or Autumn/Winter – A/W). This table is meant only to be used as an approximate guide or reference point — it is not a hard and fast set of rules by any means.

rfume	Day	Night	Young	Mature	Fair	Dark	S/S	A/W
Feu d'Issey		•		•	•	•		•
landre	•	•	•	•	•	•	•	•
a Griffe	•	•	•	•	•	•	•	•
cape	•		•		•		•	
rre		•		•		•		•
ve Gauche	•	•	•	•	•	•	•	•

YOUR SECRET WEAPONS

rfume	Day	Night	Young	Mature	Fair	Dark	S/S	A/W
ème	•	•	•	•	•	•	•	•
eap and Chic	•		•		•		•	
tée		•		•		•		•
lji	•		•		•			•
eur d'interdit	•		•		•			•
lendor	•	•	•	•	•		•	

ARIES/TAURUS CUSPS

rfume	Day	Night	Young	Mature	Fair	Dark	S/S	A/W
scany per Donna	•	•		•	•	•	•	
zance	•	•	•	•	•	•	•	
rcisse	•	•	•		•	•		•
ean Dream	•							

PISCES/ARIES CUSPS

rfume	Day	Night	Young	Mature	Fair	Dark	S/S	A/W
ontana								
arfum de Peau		•		•		•		•
acas	•	•	•		•	•		•
ue Grass	•		•	•	•		•	
nia Rykiel		•		•	•			•

MEN'S FRAGRANCES

rfume	Day	Night	Young	Mature	Fair	Dark	S/S	A/W
lo	•	•	•	•	•	•	•	•
ure Homme	•			•	•			•
cape for Men	•			•	•		•	
ss Sport	•		•		•			•

Taurus

The bull

April 20—May 20

Chanel.

You and the china shop

I suppose you get sick and tired of being the butt of that tired old cliché about the poor lost bull blundering around somewhere he's not supposed to be and didn't want to be in the first place. The analogy doesn't really apply to Taureans anyway, except perhaps that when they are put in a difficult spot they tend to get frustrated and are inclined to paw the ground and try to charge their way out of things. But that's not really their style at all, and Taureans, especially Taurean women, have quite a lot of personal style (and delicacy) they're sometimes not credited with.

You are not usually clumsy and wouldn't dream of destroying anything beautiful, especially if it's valuable (you have an eagle eye for value!). In fact you're one of the least destructive signs of all. You're a great lover of beauty — in appearances, ideas and thoughts. You see not only what is obviously lovely but what lies beneath, the inner beauty and harmony, because you possess inner beauty and harmony yourself.

You like to choose things with a careful eye, although your selections may be a little on the conservative and classical side rather than the wilder, more outrageous and unconventional choices of those more impulsive and capricious. You don't care for flashiness or surface glitter because it somehow offends your sense of good taste. You subtract rather than add to achieve simple elegance and refinement.

The trouble with all of this is that you are too often inclined to camouflage your best (and often hidden) asset. And that asset is passion. Didn't you realise you are a very passionate creature? Or don't you know how to express it without fear of embarrassment (and you're terrified of embarrassment!)? Every Taurean woman I've ever known has revealed herself to be passionate and highly romantic under her ladylike and composed exterior. This makes you vulnerable and susceptible to flattery and seduction, so you try to be stoic and almost shy. An outward show of feelings is not very Taurean, unless your sensual interest is aroused, which could lead to throwing your usual caution to the winds with abandoned gusto! But too often your down-to-earth commonsense tells you it's not the sensible thing to do, and you are a stickler for commonsense, aren't you?

This leads everyone to expect you to be always practical, comfortable, reliable, unchangeable (also stubborn), so they don't suspect your other side. They know about your unpredictability, which comes out as sudden outbursts of ferocious temper. But they also know it's all over in a flash and you forget it as quickly as it overtook you (unfortunately *they* don't).

Taureans are legendary for these terrible tempers and have been known to clear a room when they start snorting fire and charging at red rags! This happens when their plans get upset. You have everything already mapped out and see that as the way it has to be done. If anyone questions it or dares to try to change it — whammo! Your sense of rightness and harmony has been assaulted. But there's no use trying to change that fiery temperament. After all, you don't actually make a habit of losing it if you can help it.

You are noted for your courage in the face of almost anything (short of uprooting your entire life and moving house to Tierra del Fuego), so why not let go and surprise yourself by doing something totally unexpected and daring? This can be anything from embarking on a new love affair to splashing out and buying something extravagant for yourself — like a new perfume or two! You have scads of good taste and a terrific capacity for romanticism, yet too often your commonsense stops you from doing something that might shock your friends but pleases you no end.

I can just hear you saying 'But that costs good hard-earned money!', and so it might. We all know Taureans might not be exactly tight with their purse-strings but can account for every cent they spend or might spend. We all know you work hard to get the money you deserve and don't want to fritter it away unless you can see something solid for it, but come on — you can actually bury yourself in solid possessions that are more like boring investments than acquisitions of love, and you already have a sneaking suspicion some people regard you as too possessive and cautious — so to hell with it! Start being actually opulent! You'll unleash that subterranean, throbbing, smouldering passion you've been squashing. And you'll love it, I'll bet!

Taurus style

As far as you're concerned, the grass is never greener in someone else's paddock. *Your* paddock is exactly the right shade of green because you've chosen it! This is invariably true of the Taurean woman. You are utterly sure of your innate good taste and how to express it. In fact, you never look at other people's efforts without silently thinking you could have done it just that little bit better! This is because you know what goes with what and what doesn't. It's your uncanny eye for beauty and harmony.

You are never attracted to the merely pretty, the frilly or the tizzy. You are attracted to simplicity of line and form, unity, solidity and to rich, warm colours. Your house and its garden may not always be immaculately tidy (let's face it — you like the 'lived-in' look and hate trendy minimalism, whose message escapes you entirely) and you're not much for stiff formality either. Comfort is your key word — presentable comfort. Your personal surroundings are your anchor and you'd be utterly lost without them, no matter how old or even tatty they've become. You take great pride in them, just as you do with yourself. Your possessions are more than mere objects — they are treasures that have been lovingly chosen to be your companions of comfort. They represent security, which is a commodity you think you cannot live without. Creatively, you are constantly striving for honesty, integrity, simplicity but with a certain emotionalism others (but not you) would unashamedly call sentimentality. You are so secretly sentimental it almost makes you cringe, but it shouldn't. There's nothing wrong with showing your softer side — it makes you more endearing and approachable. Just don't let the love of your precious possessions get in the way of your actual longings.

You usually love all the warm, earthy colours — reds, browns, oranges, and your love of the sun and nature explains your fanatical devotion to yellows and greens. You also have a penchant for metallic colours and objects such as copper, bronze, and of course, gold. Rubies, emeralds, sapphires, mysterious topazes and tourmalines warm your heart more than diamonds, which to you are only attractive because of their financial worth and status. You also look stunningly elegant in black — it suits your idea of simplicity — but you will almost always add a bright stroke of colour or a flash of jewellery to relieve its severity. Severity reminds you of poverty, which is the one thing you absolutely fear and dread!

So, the expression of your style comes down to this: a warm-hearted, well-chosen harmony of classical beauty that is approachable and easy to live with, and reflects your elegantly conservative good taste. Just lighten it a little now and then — you don't want to be thought of as dull, do you?

Your outer expression is *comfort*. Your inner core is *passion*.

Here's how you translate all of that into the best perfumes for you.

I have divided your perfumes into two sections:

1. *The big guns* — the all-important basic perfumes that should suit you best. They form the core of your perfume arsenal.

2. *Your secret weapons* — these augment the basics and are more daring and unusual, but still should suit you.

There is also a choice of perfumes for those of you born on the cusp of Taurus/Gemini, as well as a selection of men's fragrances that are suitable to give a Taurean man. (If you were born on the cusp of Aries/Taurus see pages 60–64 for your further perfume choices.) I have given each perfume a category, and a simple and easy pronunciation guide. At the end of the chapter I have summated all of the perfumes into a table that tells you whether they're best on young or mature women, in warm or cool weather, day or evening, for fair or dark complexions.

The big guns: your indispensable basics

Good taste has two meanings when it comes to wearing perfumes that Taureans are immediately attracted to; firstly, in the cultured sense and secondly, in the delicious sense. Delicious? Most certainly. The perfumes I think ideal for your personality and temperament as well as your style have either a predominantly fruity or complex floral/fruit theme that will practically have your mouth watering and your head reeling with intoxication. In other words, they are earthy, woody, aromatic, but intensely romantic in a sophisticated way. They are neither dry nor acerbic, nor sweet and pretty — which are not smells which basically appeal to your discerning and discreet nose. Most of these are indeed big guns. I don't think Taureans are attracted to too much subtlety. You are what you are, and that is self-assertive, straightforward, earthy, and — let's face it — lusty without being the slightest bit vulgar or over-the-top. Just don't ignore the romantic and sentimental side of you. I haven't in these choices:

- **Femme** by Rochas
  Pronunciation: FAMM/ro-SHAR
  Type: fruity/floral
- **Fendi** by Fendi
  Pronunciation: FEN-dee
  Type: floral/oriental
- **Casmir** by Chopard
  Pronunciation: KAZ-meer/SHO-par
  Type: oriental
- **No. 5** by Chanel
  Pronunciation: numba FIVE/shar-NEL
  Type: floral
- **No. 19** by Chanel
  Pronunciation: numba nine-TEEN/shar-NEL
  Type: woody/green
- **Roma** by Laura Biagiotti
  Pronunciation: ROH-muh/LOW (as in WOW)-ruh bee-adj-ee-OTTIE
  Type: oriental

FEMME — because it glows

You have a highly-developed appreciation and admiration for the finer things of life, and **Femme** is one of perfume's supreme achievements in expressing sheer artistry in the most refined manner possible. Yet it is anything but formal or aloof. It positively glows with radiance and a discreet passion. You may not at first think that it lives up to its name by being the quintessence of the female psyche, but deeper acquaintance will have you under its mesmerising, sensuous, ambery, peachy spell. It is a perfume so unassailably feminine not even the most rabid of feminists could object to its celebration of nature and woman's place at its centre.

Marcel Rochas was one of the leading couturiers in Paris during the late '20s and all through the '30s and even managed to survive the ravages of the Second World War. He proudly introduced his new, limited edition perfume in 1944. **Femme** turned out to be his supreme creation, and has far eclipsed the memories of his famously daring dresses. He had always been an innovator — he invented the two-thirds length coat, was the first designer to put deep pockets into skirts, and the first to cinch the waist with the infamous *guêpiere* corset. He was not afraid of slashing cut or riotous colour, but all of this Parisian panache and showmanship was always underlined with a strict sense of classicism of line. One could well say the same of **Femme**. It was daring for its time, and there is still nothing to match its warm collection of sun-ripened fruits and full-blown flowers bedded down with a superbly extravagant gathering of musk, woods and spices. But the overwhelming impression is of richly delicious peach, plum and orange suffused with jasmine, *rose de mai*, Bulgarian roses and ylang ylang. The final note is a suffusion of amber, which gives the whole glorious mélange its golden glow and heady allure. It's intriguing, mysterious, passionate and sensual but totally friendly and approachable from its warm heart to its tantalising fadeout. I've been told it's been slightly 're-orchestrated' but, having smelt it recently, it doesn't seem to have been radically altered at all. **Femme** is a supremely comforting and quietly seductive perfume. Best of all, it's a perfume you can wear anywhere, anytime once it becomes synonymous with your warm-hearted, nostalgic nature.

FENDI — because it has flair

The Fendi sisters became famous initially for their collectively creative genius and good but daring taste in fine leathergoods and high fashion furs and only decided in 1987 to enter the rather frenetic and over-crowded arena of designer perfumes. They did it with characteristic style and considerable extravagance, and the whole shebang went off like Roman fireworks. Fortunately, the perfume was good enough to match the promotional hype, and although it hasn't really maintained its original position in the mainstream of top-sellers and is consequently not stocked as readily as it used to be, it is still available — much to the relief of its considerable number of ardent devotees. It is not a warm weather perfume and wilts under pressure, so don't take it on holidays unless you're going skiing. **Fendi** was made for the luxury of furs, but even though they're not politically fashionable at the moment, it revels in autumn and winter, and positively glows in big occasions. **Fendi** adores company — it's not Roman for nothing! — and is one of the most gregarious perfumes I know, so if you're a party-going Taurean, take it with you. However, it loves nothing better than adding a slightly mischievous touch to dinner parties with its rather witty sparkle.

Underneath all that, though, **Fendi** is a big, sentimental softie. It has armloads of rich jasmine in its generous bouquet of rose, ylang ylang, carnation and geranium, which it spikes with some fizzy citrus top notes plus plenty of fruit and spice before succumbing to the soft woodiness of rosewood, sandalwood and a dash of oriental patchouli. In fact, despite its Italian pedigree, the Far East is lurking just below the surface to give the proceedings a little sexy nudge. **Fendi** also features (appropriately) a tantalising whiff of leather to give it a rich, ambered burnishment. So, you can see it's not a simple concoction but a highly complex creation. It's one of those breed-apart perfumes with a slightly snooty, patrician ambience that can't quite conceal a sociable and fun-loving nature — but is always well-mannered and elegant, of course! Just like you.

CASMIR — *because it smoulders*

This relatively new perfume (first released in Europe in 1991, much later in Australia) is half a world away from the civilised orchards of France and the elegant energy of Rome. Its inspiration springs from the northern Indian area of Kashmir (after which it is named) with its image (now sadly shattered) of exotic allure, its serene but disturbing beauty. **Casmir** is not an immediately likeable perfume, but it stands its ground (which should appeal to you) until you get its throbbing, relentless message. Pretty or romantic it's not. Nor is it urbane or sophisticated. It gives the impression of a haughty, wilful beauty that has been somewhat tamed but might break out with a vengeance at any time. You might even call it tempestuous!

Casmir is an Indian bazaar loaded with luscious fruit and festooned with garlands of jasmine and lily of the valley. Take a deep breath with your eyes closed and your mind focused on things oriental, and you'll slowly be immersed in its huge whiffs of coconut, mango and peach among wafts of vanilla, cinnamon, musk and patchouli. But the effect is concentrated — you certainly won't smell one scent predominating.

It's as if all these exotic ingredients had been flung into a copper cauldron then stirred and simmered until an indescribably rich and resonant essence emerged to infiltrate and seduce the senses. It's distinctly Indian but not heady. It smoulders with depth and mystery. It broods and slowly unleashes its considerable seductive powers like a magic love potion. Above all, it's earthy and warm. You'll either be irresistibly drawn into its depths or be rather wary of its powers, but it does suit the Taurean penchant for hidden passions if you're feeling a bit reckless or out to seduce. In any case, **Casmir**'s beautiful Taj Mahal-inspired bottle and its graceful lotus flower stopper will probably get you so fascinated you'll at least want to try it.

No. 5 — because it's the classic of classics

You can count yourself among the fortunate if this marvellously enduring perfume comes to have pride of place in your perfume arsenal. It may or may not be the greatest perfume ever created (I don't think it is, but millions of women do) but it's without doubt one of the great treasures as well as being the perfume that has become synonymous with perfume itself! **No. 5** has that indefinable air of being head and shoulders above anything that dares to imitate or compete with its august but always approachable presence. It is haughty but warm without being sentimental, challenging without being presumptuous, charming without being cloying. It is absolutely irresistible and instantly recognisable. So is the woman who wears it. She seems to automatically assume a sophistication that is not calculated but sits easily on her, adding to her own attraction, complementing her own self-assurance.

No. 5 is an extraordinarily original fusion of what were once (in 1921 when it was created by the great perfumer Ernest Beaux) very daring synthetic ingredients called aldehydes, allied with a profusion of rich floral and amber scents. The aldehydes proved to give an edge and polish that brought out the hidden depths of masses of *rose de mai*, jasmine and ylang ylang, and seemed to give even more smoothness to the vetiver, sandalwood and patchouli that gave the formula its soft pulsation. **No. 5**, in one fell swoop, changed not only the way perfumes were formulated, but changed the attitudes of women who wore it with a new self-confidence and elegance that seemed to emanate naturally from the uniqueness of its character. **No. 5** is an eternal pleasure — intriguing, supremely feminine and civilised. It is also a fabulously unique security blanket. No wonder Taureans dote on it!

No. 19 — because it's so sweetly earthy

Aren't you the lucky one having two Chanels to choose from, depending on your age, mood and where you're going? Age is an important consideration with this beguiling but strikingly individual perfume. It really smells much more naturally beautiful on the young and the young-mature rather than anyone over thirty-five. Mood is another vital factor in the successful wearing of **No. 19**. It dislikes seriousness because of its sunny personality and prefers not to be forced into important social occasions — it's much happier in less formal surroundings, especially the outdoors.

No. 19 has always been something of a problem to pin down. It's often classified as a green/floral but I think it's much more earthy, woody and glowing than that. It's a wonderfully original gathering of foresty notes reminding you of moist earth, fallen leaves trodden underfoot, smoky wisps trailing up through tall green trees to a shimmering blue sky. In actual fact it's loaded with white hyacinth, iris, *rose de mai*, ylang ylang over orange blossom, sandalwood, green galbanum, violet leaves, sycamore and sandalwood and a hush of golden amber and oakmoss. It's mysterious and enveloping but never heavy or demanding.

No. 19 has a romantically inclined shimmer and dazzle that give it a unique feeling of happiness that's not too far away from haunting nostalgia. It will appeal to Taureans who love the earth, understand nature and can't live without the tang and zing of fresh air. It might also lead you to thoughts of a quiet stroll through an enchanted forest, either with a loved one, or by yourself in the hope that some magical being might suddenly appear and whisk you off your feet to unknown pleasures. Wouldn't that be nice for a change?

ROMA — *because it's brave*

The Eternal City — irrepressible Rome — calls you again, and it's a pretty demanding invitation at that. This is a perfume to be reckoned with and only the most individually minded and courageous of Taureans will have the confidence to wear it. Those that do will pin it proudly to them like a medal! **Roma** does not hide its light under a bushel, as they say. It is one of the most outgoing and extroverted perfumes I know of, but it's also so persistently beautiful you could call it downright ravishing!

This is *Roma alla tempestosa* — wild, exciting, uninhibited. Is that you? You bet! It's the perfect perfume for Taureans who love to let their hair down and get in amongst the action — as down-to-earth and passionate as possible. So if you're the more stay-at-home, security-conscious type, best give **Roma** the go-by on your perfume itinerary. Then again, you'll never know if you don't at least try it once!

It's a great way of drawing attention to yourself with its full-on spectacle of explosive herbs and spices (cardamom, mint and myrrh) mixed with the smoulder of carnation, patchouli and blackcurrant bud, cooled down a bit with jasmine, lily of the valley and oakmoss. There is nothing subtle about it, and it's so powerful you have to be very discreet with its application (it's a great stayer, I warn you). But it has a brash, almost opulent beauty all its own, and a certain vulgar enticement you might find impossible to resist. **Roma** is so warmly embracing and suggestive, you could find the conservative, sensible part of you suddenly flung into an unbridled celebration of *la dolce vita* — Fellini-style!

Your secret weapons: the surprises

You might be reeling from the high-powered line-up of the preceding perfumes, but here are your second-string choices — the back-ups, if you like. They're no less important in that they're the ones that are more than capable of showing you in something of a new light. Of course you can't expect miracles from them — that has to come from you, but I'll bet at least one or two of them will not only add a new and fascinating loveliness to your perfume arsenal, but also bring out those not-so-public assets you otherwise might consider a bit too unconventional to suit your precious image. In other words, go for them — they're passionate and beautiful revelations! Here they are:

• **Ivoire** by Pierre Balmain
  Pronunciation: ee-VWAH/pee-AIR bal-MARN
  Type: floral

- **Tocade** by Rochas
  Pronunciation: tock-ARD/ro-SHAR
  Type: fruity/floral
- **Kenzo** by Kenzo
  Pronunciation: KEN-zo
  Type: floral/oriental
- **Ysatis** by Givenchy
  Pronunciation: ee-SAR-teece/zjhiv-ON-she
  Type: floral/oriental
- **Givenchy** III by Givenchy
  Pronunciation: zjhiv-ON-she THREE (or, if you're
  in France: TWAR)
  Type: woody
- **L'Aimant** by Coty
  Pronunciation: lay-MON/CO-tee
  Type: floral

IVOIRE

— because it melts your heart

Ivoire is a magical perfume that's so rapturously beautiful it makes your heart ache for those fleetingly memorable moments of sheer heaven on earth that can sometimes obliterate everything awful in your world. That's the good news. The not-so-good news is that it is not easy to find, but far from impossible — boutiques and duty-free outlets usually stock it. When you do find it, it's like discovering something rare and beautiful you've been longing for all your life. Now if that doesn't satisfy a romantic and secretly sentimental

Taurean, then there's something amiss!

Not long before he died, Pierre Balmain (who in his palmier days was one of the *couturier* greats) saw a fabulously beautiful woman dressed in ivory silk elegantly descending the grand staircase of the Paris Opera before vanishing into the night. The apparition haunted him so much he had this perfume created as an anonymous tribute to her fleeting beauty. It is a truly heavenly perfume so full of softness and roundness, sensuousness and radiance, it transports the wearer and anyone in her orbit into another, vanished world of charm and grace.

Ivoire is composed of a complex harmony of jasmine, lily of the valley, violet, Turkish rose, carnation and ylang ylang over a suspended hush of gentle, powdery spices and soft green leaves. It always reminds me of a tangled flower garden giving up its intertwined perfumes after a shower of summer rain. It possesses the cool tranquillity of ivory as well as its subtle lustre. And it settles so beautifully and so immediately it manages to wrap you in an aura of pure pleasure and repose that can't fail to reach those that come into your enchanted circle. If you think I'm waxing too lyrical, then you obviously haven't yet fallen under **Ivoire**'s mesmerising spell.

TOCADE
— *because it's luscious*

If you adore the creamy and sensuous smell of vanilla,

you will more than likely find your nose titillated and your tastebuds salivating when you breathe in the heady delights of this recent arrival from the revered House of Rochas. **Tocade** can mean either 'infatuation' or 'love at first sight' so you get the message that this is intended to be a romantic and feminine perfume, and so it is. But, like all perfumes with a great Parisian pedigree, **Tocade** springs a few surprises on what can be a fairly conventional theme of roses and bergamot. First of all there's gardenia — rich and creamy and sumptuous — then iris root, which gives a beautiful violet-like radiance, and finally a more than generous dousing in pure vanilla. The effect is vivacious and disarming.

   Tocade is one of those seemingly sophisticated perfumes you might at first think is entirely devoted to being cool and elegant, but it isn't at all. It is a bit of a minx — subtle and complex enough to take seriously, but full of capricious good fun when it gets to the heart of the matter. Its heart is not meant to be captured — it is meant to be dallied with first before any other more meaningful business might arise. **Tocade** takes it all in its self-assured step. It can be as whimsical and impetuous or as subtly seductive as you like. It's entirely up to you. But chances are it will be love at first sight when you see the smooth, sleek bottle topped with a jewel-like stopper. It might not be a blockbuster, but it has masses of class under its flirtatious and good-natured exuberance. I think

Tocade is perfect for Taureans who are not quite ready to commit themselves to anything too serious, but want to at least have a good time before they take a deeper plunge. Either way it smells and looks just delicious!

KENZO
— because it's unforgettable

Kenzo is an extraordinary designer genius whose heart has been totally seduced by Paris but remains true to Japan. One look at his fabulous clothes tells you that. They may be oriental in inspiration but they are occidental in technique. The same can be said of this ravishing tuberose-laden perfume. (I must say here that if you don't care for the enveloping richness of tuberose, then **Kenzo** might upset your delicate senses too much.) He has composed his ravishingly lovely perfume on the principles of ikebana with its three stages of intensely simple and sensuous composition designed to emanate a serenity and balance that passes through to the observer (or in this case, the wearer). The principal flowers are tuberose, magnolia, gardenia, jasmine and ylang ylang — all distinctly oriental in their roots. Interwoven through these are the scents of plum and peach, orange and vanilla, cardamom and coriander. All very hypnotic and seductive in the subtlest possible way. The tuberose is persistent though. It seems to throb warmly and suggestively underneath this masterpiece of harmony and contrast. An oriental poet was once moved to describe the mighty tuberose as the 'mistress of the night in the magical gardens of Malay', and its voluptuousness is the key to **Kenzo** — and more than likely the key to the Taurean heart that longs to be transported to a secret region where it can find a new haven and a new outpouring of its desire to exist among all things beautiful. **Kenzo** lifts the veil and allows you to enter, your heart on your sleeve.

YSATIS — *because it's incomparable*

There are certain rare things in life that are so beautifully designed, harmonised and synthesised you really want to call them perfect. If there is such a thing as a perfect perfume, then this classic from Givenchy (before its recent takeover by less classic iconoclasts of design) is near enough to qualify.

Ysatis is so elegant, so poised, so sophisticated it is almost on a pedestal. And I doubt if it has feet of clay, either. It reminds me of a statuesque sculpture from its tall fluted bottle and oriental cap to its immaculately chosen classic components. But to rescue it from being too aloof and cool, it is also anointed with more overtly seductive Eastern treasures that give its alabaster smoothness a living, breathing sensuality.

Ysatis is one of that rare breed of perfumes

constructed as a single entity. Its massive array of ingredients does not go through the normal head, heart and soul stages, but is cleverly harmonised and bonded to form a synthesis that smells exactly the same all through from the first application to the perfume's gracious fade-out. But what a smell it is! If you can imagine a choir singing one pure chord made up of rose, jasmine, ylang ylang, carnation, jonquil, orange blossom, mandarin, coconut, rosewood, patchouli, oakmoss, sandalwood, musk, vanilla and clove, all coming out in a single sustained breath, then you have some idea of the quiet sensation of this extraordinary perfume. Small wonder its devotees simply sigh when its name is mentioned. And when Ysatis, all calm self-assurance and sensual awareness, enters a room, you will probably hear a collective hush of sheer awe. And to think you could be the cause of it!

GIVENCHY III — *because it's rich and rare*
This perfume is from the glory days of the House of Givenchy. It has practically disappeared (certainly from the big outlets) but thankfully is still usually available in boutiques. I don't think it's been totally scrapped yet, but a number of its faithful devotees I know have bought up stockpiles just in case of such a catastrophe! Why? Because it's not only rare in an availability sense, it's also one of those rare woody, smoky, smouldering perfumes so original in formulation it practically invites extinction because of its

uncompromising individuality.

Givenchy III (or simply 'Three' as it is known) is one of those magnificent rebels that is neither blatantly perverse nor flag-waving. It is simply a perfume of great majesty and grace. It is reflective yet surprisingly sensual. It is warm and rich and fascinating, but makes no great waves. Its purpose is romantic serenity and intelligent attachment. It is one of those perfumes that, like a pedigreed cat, may be aloof at first but will eventually take you over in the most subtle way possible.

Givenchy III is composed of beautifully glowing things like mandarin, amber, oakmoss, peach, patchouli, carnation, myrrh and vetiver over which is laid a mantle of rose, jasmine and jonquil petals, then a sensual bouquet of gardenia and lily of the valley. This is all brought to a gentle simmer and left to infuse over rosewood until a soft and smoky murmur arises and infiltrates the very air around it. Wearing it is like suddenly hearing a distant fanfare from burnished trumpets in an autumnal forest that calls for you to follow. I can think of no sensible Taurean who wouldn't heed the plaintive but romantic call of **Givenchy III** — except young, impetuous ones for whom this elegantly mature beauty is obviously not meant. But if you've mellowed a little, this is it!

L'AIMANT — *because it's unpretentious*
One of the great perfumers of the '20s and '30s,

François Coty created this eternally young and exhilarating explosion of roses and jasmine in 1927 and, as was then the new fad, enhanced its rich bouquet with the fashionable, fabulously successful aldehydes that were no longer mistrusted after the huge hit of Chanel's **No. 5**. Suddenly it became a new young classic with its romantic head in the clouds and its feet not quite on the ground. Amazingly **L'Aimant** still survives in the face of relentless opposition. It has repositioned itself somewhat at the less expensive end of the perfume market, and wisely so, because it is affordable to the very people who love it — the young and the young–mature of this fickle day and age.

The reason it has survived is its classic formula — the familiar roses-and-jasmine accord — but tempered with a dash of energetic vetiver, the sensuousness of vanilla and musk, the deliciousness of peach, and (most important of all) a healthy whack of sexy civet, it has a peculiarly magnetic animalic scent that gives out an earthy, erotic invitation to follow. It's worth noting here that **L'Aimant** is translated as 'the Magnet' — get it? Well, it certainly works, and does so with a good deal of self-confidence and sauciness as well. **L'Aimant**'s message of light-hearted flirtatiousness is quite openly stated. There's absolutely nothing complicated or serious about it, and young or young-at-heart Taureans will probably love it for its candour, its uncloying sweetness, and its straightforwardness. It's also the perfect 'first perfume' for young players.

The advantage of the cusp: taking your pick

It's not all confusion — being neither one star sign nor the other, or feeling you're partly both — if you're born towards the very beginning of Gemini*. You can of course pick and choose from the perfumes suggested from Taurus and Gemini, but be careful. Depending on your characteristics, they may not all sit easily on you. That's why I've come up with a selection of extras that might solve any perfume problem or indecision you might have. Anyway, the choice is yours, so have fun finding out!

They are:

- **Romance** by Ralph Lauren
  Type: floral
- **Envy** by Gucci
  Pronunciation: EN-vee/goo-CHEE
  Type: floral
- **Cristalle** by Chanel
  Pronunciation: cris-TARL/shar-NEL
  Type: floral/fruity
- **Calèche** by Hermès

*If you were born towards the very beginning of Taurus, you might like to check out the choices for those born on the cusp of Aries/Taurus on pages 60–64.

Pronunciation: kal-ESH/air-MAZE
Type: floral/green

ROMANCE — because you always need it
Ralph Lauren makes it quite clear he considers himself, his clothes, his perfumes, his style to be a sophisticated notch above his main competitor, Calvin Klein, with a style that's slightly more elitist and definitely more romantic rather than severely pared-down. He appeals to the feminine, not just the female, instincts in a woman. But his kind of woman is not a sit-at-home — he sent her on wild adventures in **Safari** and onto the sporting field in **Polo Woman** for instance. Now he thinks it's time she had some more time in her life for love — so in sashays **Romance**.

Working on the well-founded premise that women are pushovers for roses in all their scented glory, he searched for one that would dominate his new perfume, and found it in the gorgeous and highly-fragrant Sun Goddess rose. This is the heart and soul of **Romance**, so much so that, by and large, he's left it to speak for itself without cluttering it up with too many other scented attendants. But he adds a beautiful harmony of lightly-orchestrated white lilies and wisps of seductive patchouli to underscore the dazzlingly lovely central aria, and not much else, except the necessary base back-up woods and resins to ensure the whole rosy soufflé doesn't collapse under its own airy loveliness.

Romance, in its classically simple bottle (he even had a legal battle with Calvin Klein over its shape that was considered too close to **Eternity**'s and won!) will appeal to the no-nonsense side of Taurus as well as the lovely earthiness of its roses, while Gemini will automatically go into rosy raptures over its romantic possibilities.

ENVY — because it makes others envious
It's quite true! Although **Envy** has been on the market for only a short time, it's been phenomenally successful — and the reason is, I'm quite sure, that those lucky women who can wear it do so with terrific panache, which causes quite a bit of envy from those who for some reason can't quite get to grips with it, or know it's totally wrong for them. Anyway, whatever the reason, it's perfect for you cusp people because it is so sparkling and intoxicating. It has the incredible ability to turn heads — especially male ones, and we all know how vital that is to the Gemini side of you. Taureans will like it for its floral beauty. **Envy** begins with a fantastic rush of high green notes to set up the 'envy' theme (even the perfume itself is a lovely bright lime green), but these are all but overpowered by lush white flowers — magnolia, jasmine, hyacinth and, most importantly, lily of the valley. Lily of the valley is a deceptive little flower, all trembling innocent beauty that has a sweet and utterly captivating perfume. But beware! It's more than

captivating — it can grab you by the throat! Maybe that's the reason for **Envy**'s envied success.

CRISTALLE — *because it sparkles*

This often-neglected and largely unsung beauty is a little charmer that sparkles happily in a world of its own. It's nowhere near as formidable as its Chanel sisters, but doesn't pretend to be anything but a beautifully composed and scintillating fragrance. It's available only in concentrated *eau de toilette* and *eau de parfum* strengths, which means you can use it almost as you would an extrait or concentrate perfume, but with slightly less impact and staying-power. But **Cristalle** has plenty of tenacity without ever being pushy about it. It's a lively mix of spring flowers and sun-drenched fruit — rose, jasmine, lily of the valley, honeysuckle and hyacinth, blushed with citrus oils, peach and mandarin, accompanied by rosewood, vetiver and a daring dash of lavender to give it a Provençal piquancy. **Cristalle** is very bright, sunny and breezy, although it's more than capable of a sly wink or two in the right direction. But basically it doesn't like to be in serious situations, preferring to keep things light and bright and definitely uncomplicated — which makes it fine for both Taureans and Geminis. Its appeal is in its fresh versatility — it doesn't mind where it goes or when. **Cristalle** can be as happy as you are, or simply contented with the way things are. And it's unfailingly reliable.

CALÈCHE — because it has true chic!

And has done since it was first created in 1961! It has
long since entered the revered and respected ranks of
the classics and for a very good reason — **Calèche** is a
masterpiece that manages to be both dazzlingly light
while harbouring serious intentions of seduction. It's a
completely successful interpretation of a floral with
green undertones and aldehydic overtones. This gives it
its incomparable vibrancy and sheen. Thus it appeals to
Taureans for its classic beauty and to Gemini cusps for
its air of excitement and anticipation. **Calèche** is
named after those elegant horse-drawn carriages of the
nineteenth century that were the fashionable way for
sophisticated and worldly women to travel to and from
appointments — clandestine or otherwise. In the case
of **Calèche** the perfume, those appointments today
may use other modes of transport but may be just as
secretive! It's that sort of perfume — seductive but
smart. It's composed of many, many lovely flowers —
principally gardenia, jasmine, ylang ylang, rose, orange
blossom, lily of the valley and iris — laid on a *chypre*
background of bergamot, lemon, vetiver, moss, green
leaves and sandalwood. There's a hint of spice and a
dash of pine to give added flourish and flair. But
although **Calèche** may be playful to the point of being
mischievous on its dazzling surface, beneath the fun
and games it's deadly serious about its intentions. It's
there to be noticed, to turn heads and charm with a
panache that can suddenly become an invitation to

more meaningful matters of the heart, for **Calèche** has a very warm heart indeed, and its targets might be taken totally by surprise. It is a wily, world-wise perfume, and has nothing to do with innocence, like the woman who has long since traded hers for the pleasures of civilised seduction. Taureans will love it for its elegance, while Geminis will instantly picture themselves being driven around Paris in a pretty *calèche*.

The Taurus male: down-to-earth gifts with class

The Taurus male is a fairly open, quietly passionate creature even though he might try quite vociferously to deny it. He has lots of practical commonsense, kindness, forthrightness, but doesn't usually brag about it. Some might confuse this natural modesty with dullness, but you know better than that. He just needs bringing out a bit, so his love of the outdoors, his appreciation of fine things, his good manners (especially toward women, as long as they don't try to take advantage of him) are the qualities you should complement and compliment him with when choosing a fragrance. He won't care for fiercely modern concoctions that blow their own trumpets loud and clear, or blatantly sexy numbers that will probably embarrass him. He'll be much more at home with quieter, more natural-smelling, close-to-the-earth fragrances. Remember, he's basically a nature

boy — not a flashy, fickle playboy.
- **Vetiver** by Guerlain
  Pronunciation: VETTY-vair/gair-LARN
  Type: green/woody
- **YSL Pour Homme** by Yves Saint Laurent
  Pronunciation: why ess ELL/eve sarn lor-ON
  Type: herbal/fruity
- **Safari for Men** by Ralph Lauren
  Pronunciation: saff-AR-ee for MEN/ralf lor-ENN
  Type: spicy/green
- **Tuscan**y by Aramis
  Pronunciation: TUSK-anny/ARRA-miss
  Type: fruity/spicy

Vetiver

This is a brilliantly refined concentration of vetiver which is the root of a highly aromatic grass grown in the Caribbean and the Far East. It has a very woody note with tinges of green and a certain subtle muskiness that Guerlain (masters in the art of male perfumery since the time of Napoleon III) have made even more bracing and dry with the addition of a little citrus, tobacco leaf and oakmoss. To achieve its famous smoothness (straight vetiver can be pretty over-powering), sandalwood and cedarwood are added, achieving a fresh but not strident exhilaration that appeals especially to businessmen or any man on holidays. You might even like **Vetiver** yourself for a change from all those flowers!

YSL Pour Homme

This has become almost a legend in a fairly long lifetime that shows no signs of visible ageing at all. It's one of those great 'reliables' — a fragrance most sophisticated men, and especially Taureans, like for its citrus fruitiness tempered with soothing, calming herbs like lavender, rosemary and thyme. **YSL**'s top notes are bracingly lemony, but a swipe of velvety oakmoss keeps this from being too acerbic along with a touch of exotic patchouli to give it a sensuous slyness that's kept tantalisingly just below the surface. It appeals especially to the young man about town and to young fathers. And it has such an urbane charm it can relax quite happily at dinner parties. **YSL**, however, is not much good in the boudoir. It's fresh in the wrong way!

Safari for Men

The spices in **Safari for Men** are a secret, but they're the lighter kind, such as cardamom and coriander, rather than heavies like clove and pepper. But there's an obvious bouquet garni of them, notably the aniseed tang of tarragon and artemesia. There's also a soft and haunting presence of cedar leaf and oakmoss to add to this refined silver-greenery, and finally a whiff of exotic patchouli to add a little sensuality to the trip. **Safari**, by its very name and nature, is an outdoorsy fragrance, but a thankfully civilised one that also caters to creature comforts —

which is why its urbanity and unusual restraint will appeal to the Taurus male, as will its very classy packaging. **Safari for Men** is an adventure minus the dust, danger and discomfort.

Tuscany

Tuscany is a very open and sunny fragrance full of gentle warmth and a certain dreamy quality as if high noon is not blazing but comforting enough to seek out a shady tree with a glass of good wine. It's unpretentious, uncomplicated but friendly with its orange and mandarin notes mixed with aromatic spices that aren't too fierce, plus a soothing whiff of lavender, all bedded down with oakmoss, patchouli and the earthy muskiness of geranium leaf. **Tuscany** has just about insinuated itself into classic male fragrance status simply because men find it non-threatening. It's like a little bit of solace to soothe the rough and tumble Taureans don't really care for. He'll dote on it — secretly, of course!

Who suits what, and when: getting the best out of your perfumes

Because perfumes become not only extensions of your personality but also give emphasis to the way you look and the mood you're in, naturally, to bring out their best, they should be treated with due understanding in regard to their characteristics and qualities. They too have limitations and strengths, just as we all have. So, the following table outlines when best to wear them (Day, Night), the age-group most suited to them (Young, Mature), the general complexion of the wearer (Fair, Dark), and the seasons they bloom best in (Spring/Summer – S/S, or Autumn/Winter – A/W). This table is meant only to be used as an approximate guide or reference point — it is not a hard and fast set of rules by any means.

rfume	Day	Night	Young	Mature	Fair	Dark	S/S	A/W
mme	•	•		•	•	•		•
ndi		•			•	•		
smir		•			•	•		
. 5	•		•		•	•	•	
. 19	•		•	•	•		•	
ma		•	•			•		•

YOUR SECRET WEAPONS

rfume	Day	Night	Young	Mature	Fair	Dark	S/S	A/W
ire	•	•	•	•	•	•	•	
cade	•		•	•	•	•		•
nzo		•	•	•	•	•	•	
atis	•	•	•		•	•		•
venchy III	•			•	•		•	
Aimant	•	•		•		•		•

TAURUS/GEMINI CUSPS

rfume	Day	Night	Young	Mature	Fair	Dark	S/S	A/W
nance	•	•	•		•	•	•	•
vy	•		•		•	•	•	
stalle	•	•	•		•	•		•
èche	•	•	•	•	•			•

ARIES/TAURUS CUSPS

rfume	Day	Night	Young	Mature	Fair	Dark	S/S	A/W
scany per Donna	•	•	•			•	•	•
tance	•	•	•	•	•		•	
rcisse	•	•	•	•	•			•
ean Dream	•		•		•	•	•	

MEN'S FRAGRANCES

rfume	Day	Night	Young	Mature	Fair	Dark	S/S	A/W
iver	•		•		•	•	•	
L Pour Homme	•	•		•	•	•	•	•
ari for Men	•		•		•	•	•	
cany	•				•	•		•

Gemini

The twins
May 21—June 20

John Paul Gaultier

You and the chandelier

Y ou're dotty about chandeliers or anything that twinkles, sparkles, glitters or dazzles. You want your life to be like one perpetual mirrored jazzball, twirling you away into giddy good times with lots of romance that doesn't even have to be serious. You *are* a serious creature, but that's private. To you, the world spins so you can spin with it — all glamour and glitz. And you do it so prettily! Along with Librans (another air sign), Gemini women are usually the most attractive in the zodiac. Beautiful clothes and fabulous jewellery seem made for them alone — and perfume is no exception. You gravitate like a firefly to the most magnetic, ravishing and enchanting of them.

Others might call you capricious, fickle and restless, but these are traits you treat as virtues. There's no room for pessimism in Geminis — not on the surface anyway. You live and love life to the hilt. You adore the buzz of big occasions and all the gossip that goes with it — yet you rarely use that gossip maliciously. Your nature doesn't stretch to deliberately hurting other people. You are by far the best communicators in the zodiac, and can be the soul of diplomacy (discretion is another thing altogether!). You are gifted performers and love the spotlight — cameras were invented just for you to seduce (think of Marilyn Monroe, the most celebrated Gemini of all!). You are inquisitive, adaptable, versatile and don't know the meaning of old age. Younger than springtime, you are!

Your basic problem is your inner soul. I know you don't like to admit it, but you can be in the utter depths of depression and would never show this dark and troubled side to anyone, except perhaps to another Gemini. You'd prefer to get out of it yourself. If you want help desperately enough, you'll ask for it, but you regard most voluntary and well-meaning advice as embarrassing and intrusive. This sometimes leads you to cover up your restlessness and instability to the point where you valiantly pretend it doesn't exist. But it always catches up with you, because you have such a personal regard for your conscience. Picking up the pieces, however, is not impossible, and it's amazing how you can resurface full of brightness and self-confidence once you've given yourself a good talking-to. This is where your appreciation of beauty helps you enormously. (I know one Gemini who swears by the miraculous effect of some very good champagne and a few hefty squirts of **Joy** — she says it never fails.)

Like your personal need for absolute freedom, you can be a bit demanding of others, but they usually give in to you. It's easier for them, because if you can't get what you want from one source you'll get it from another. However, you're not particularly choosy when it comes down to satisfying your desires. Sometimes you miscalculate and find that after you get what you want you don't really want it at all. This gives you your reputation for fickleness, and the only way out of this is the secret of your wonderfully generous and understanding nature. You love to give just as much as you love to receive. You will rack your brain until you think of the perfect present for a friend — you never give what you think they should be given, you give them what they really want. It comes straight from your genuine and thoughtful heart, and you don't give a damn about the cost.

Perhaps your greatest enemy is your desperation to be loved, which can sometimes lead you into being attracted to people who don't deserve you. Fortunately, your friends will stick by you until you wake up a little wounded but wiser. Maybe you'll never be able to accept advice, but at least you know it's there! And that's why you value your friends so fiercely and dearly. So, don't worry about sniping criticism, and don't ever take notice of people who call you shallow, two-faced, desperate and schizophrenic. Always have faith in your friends, the things you love and respect, and be as free-spirited and vivacious as you like. You are the zodiac's female equivalent of Peter Pan with a good dose of Tinkerbell thrown in, which is more than you can say for your glum (and possibly jealous) detractors! Just laugh at them and twinkle and tapdance your merry way through life.

Gemini style

You know very well you have heaps of it. It all comes naturally to you. It may not be the most sophisticated or refined style in the world, but it exemplifies your own world of bright and breezy, carefully casual, and almost always extremely expensive possessions. You like prettiness as long as it isn't too frilly, and insist on utter femininity and delicacy in your clothes, accessories and makeup. You don't usually go for the tailored, severe look and avoid clutter like the plague. You may find it difficult to settle on just one theme of expression and will chop and change things (especially furniture) until you think you have it just right. But you have been known to get up in the middle of the night to rearrange cushions or add another ingredient to a marinade. You just have to get things right!

Pastels, white, gold and silver are your reliables. Pink is usually the favoured colour — in any shade except puce. The glitter of gold and other metallics, the many-faceted brilliance of diamonds, sapphires and emeralds send shivers of lust up and down your spine, and you would walk through fire for anything from a jeweller like Cartier or Tiffany. You may not be a great cook, but you know how to assemble things to look terrific, and any party thrown by you will be a lavish and memorable one. (The thought of running out of champagne is like a nightmare!) So, with all this intense appreciation of beautiful and expensive things in your nature, choosing perfumes is not only a never-ending delight but an experience close to making love! You just have to have the best, the happiest, the most romantic, and the most effusive perfumes ever formulated, and in the prettiest boxes. The trick is to know which ones complement your social personality, and which ones will give you a credibility and unique subtlety even your best friends will be surprised at.

Your outer expression is *vivacity*. Your inner core is *generosity*.

Here's how you translate all of that into the best perfumes for you.

I have divided these perfumes into two sections:

1. *The big guns* — the all-important perfumes that should suit you best. They form the core of your perfume arsenal.

2. *Your secret weapons* — these augment the basics and are more daring and unusual, but still should suit you.

There is also a choice of perfumes for those of you born on the cusp of Gemini/Cancer, as well as a selection of men's fragrances suitable to give the Gemini man. (If you were born on the cusp of Taurus/Gemini see pages 95–100 for your further perfume choices.) I have given each perfume a category as well as a simple and easy guide to its correct pronunciation. At the end of the chapter I have summed all of the perfumes into a table that tells you whether they're best on young or mature women, in warm or cool weather, day or evening, for fair or dark complexions.

The big guns:
the indispensable basics

When Geminis are in the mood to party — clear the decks! It'll be laughs and bubbles all the way. Your capacity for gaiety, festivity and full-on fun is legendary (and a bit frightening for others who can't match your stamina). This is why I think your up-front perfumes, the ones that become indelible extensions of your most jubilant moods, are usually light-hearted and effervescent floral bouquets. Orientals are too deep and serious for you, and you think the warm fruity numbers are a bit on the dull side. You like greens as long as they're festooned with flowers — too much astringent sharpness goes against your insistence on utter femininity at all times, and you don't care all that much for the outdoors anyway (all those creepy-crawly creatures getting into your champagne flute are just not on). So, it's a case of the bubblier the better, and there are masses of perfumes that fill this bill with ease. Just be careful you don't swamp yourself in too many pretty perfumes — you have a reputation (mostly unfounded) for being a bit loose and coquettish, so it's a good idea to alternate these little caprices with one or two perfumes that have elegance and refinement on their side. It's not entirely coincidental that a couple of the perfumes that seem naturals for you come from famed jewellers who've extended their ranges to include a perfume or two. Your love of glittering baubles is, after all, not only famous but almost a fixation. But, with your unerring instinct in matters of self-adornment you have no rivals, so your choices will come with a minimum of indecision. Here they are:

• **So Pretty** by Cartier.
  Pronunciation: KART-ee-air
  Type: floral

- **Bvlgari** by Bvlgari
  Pronunciation: boulle-GAR-ee (or, as in Italy)
  BOULL-gar-ee
  Type: floral/spicy
- **Joy** by Jean Patou
  Pronunciation: zjharn PART-oo
  Type: floral
- **Yvresse** by Yves Saint Laurent
  Pronunciation: ee-VRESS/eeve sarn lor-ON
  Type: floral/fruity
- **Jean Paul Gaultier** by Jean Paul Gaultier
  Pronunciation: zhjarn-pole GO-tee-ay
  Type: floral
- **Champs-Elysées** by Guerlain
  Pronunciation: shom-ell-EE-say/gair-LARN
  Type: floral

So Pretty
— because it's endearing

Not that I suppose you need reminding, but Cartier is probably the most well-known jeweller in the world. Millions of women would give anything to possess even a trinket bearing this ultra-glamorous name (Geminis would, of course, prefer at least a bracelet bristling with big, dazzling diamonds). But it's nice to know you can at least own something created by Cartier, even if it's a perfume and not a precious bauble bearing the great name. And this new perfume seems to have been created especially with the

Gemini desire for loveliness in mind.

Legend goes that Louis, always considered by the Cartier family to be the greatest designer in the dynasty, had a particular nickname for his adored wife. He called her 'my so-pretty one' — hence the name of this prettiest of the Cartier perfumes. **So Pretty** is, however, not just a delicate and vulnerable creation for shy retiring violets or flibbertigibbets. Far from it — it has a spirit and attitude that make it quite outspoken and persuasive.

So Pretty is an intoxicating blend of lavish flowers — rich *rosa centifolia* from Grasse, exotic *rosa damascena* from Turkey, the glorious Papa Meillan rose, Florentine iris with its haunting violet-like scent, Tunisian orange blossom, Grasse jasmine, and that sensuous little Chinese flower called osmanthus. Then comes the unique addition of Brazilian Diamond orchid (used for the very first time in perfume), which gives a caressing softness, especially to the roses. Over all of this lushness comes a touch of Cartier finesse — a piquant dash of dewberry and the silky deliciousness of white peach.

Strangely enough, **So Pretty** smells anything but overblown. Instead it sings out with a brilliant many-faceted clarity that forms a delicious halo of its floral harmony underlined with a breath of muskiness which, for a refreshing change, does not come from musk itself but from the velvety depths of the three glorious roses that form its heart. **So Pretty** is an aptly named perfume —and who knows? — when you wear it, could easily become a term of endearment from someone who adores you.

BVLGARI — *because it's beguiling*

Don't twist your tongue trying to pronounce this as it's spelt — the 'v' is actually the 'u' of the medieval Latin alphabet, so just ask for 'Bulgari perfume' when you want to discover this wonderful liquid creation from one of Europe's most venerated master jewellers.

When it first appeared so splendidly in its dramatically simple chunky bottle of half-clear and half-frosted glass with an imposing stopper, word had leaked out that one of its secret ingredients was green tea. The media certainly got onto that and made a big fuss about how stunningly unusual **Bvlgari** was. Well, it was a bit of an anti-climax when women claimed it was a very lovely perfume, but where was the green tea component? Of course, as in most perfumes, such an uncommon ingredient is not used to assault your nose with its presence, but to give it a tantalising but subtle uniqueness. In **Bvlgari**'s case, it's merely used as a way to not only add a little orientalism to the basic harmony, but give it a mysterious undertone. It simply adds a whispered exclamation point. After all, in the tasteful hands of **Bvlgari**, you wouldn't expect a perfume to smell like a cup of jasmine tea, would you? It is interesting to add, though, that the tea association has caught on and an *eau parfumée extrême* strength has been introduced presumably to make a little more of this sub-theme. But tea's not really what **Bvlgari** is all about.

Bvlgari is based on very fresh floral notes — jasmine, mimosa, orange blossom, and the sumptuously rich Prelude rose (another perfume first!). But these are merely the backdrop for the unmistakably haunting scent of violet and the sweetness of freesia. Some Brazilian rosewood and musk deepen the bouquet, and then comes the *cause célèbre* — the tantalising green note of Sambac jasmine-scented tea. Thus the final accord is definitely floral but with the merest whiff of oriental redolence.

By having this enigmatic ambience to it, **Bvlgari** is bound to appeal to the curious Gemini. It's new, fashionable, enticing and very much associated with their strikingly modern jewellery. I see no reason why you wouldn't fall under the very alluring but subtle spell of this lovely perfume, even if the thought of vaguely smelling of green tea is not actually your bag! Believe me, it's a suggestion, not a deluge.

JOY — *because it delivers*

Once promoted as the costliest perfume in the world, **Joy** is still not what you'd call inexpensive. And neither should it be. Even when Patou introduced it (with the help of professional society hostess Elsa

Maxwell) in 1930 at the very height of his *couturier extraordinaire* fame, **Joy** was meant only for the very rich. And little wonder when you consider what went into its creation — a book could be written about that!

Jean Patou wanted the best — the absolute quintessence of luxury and extravagance to be epitomised in his new perfume. It had to be 'free from all vulgarity' as well as excitingly impudent and utterly unique. Cost was not of the faintest concern. (Miss Maxwell would have loved that brief!) Perhaps still smarting from the shattering success of his competitor Chanel's **No. 5** with its disdain for 'all-natural' ingredients, **Joy** used two of the most expensive natural components available at the time — *jasmin absolu* from Grasse, and Bulgarian roses grown in the fabled Valley of Roses in that country. What's more they were used in enormously high concentrations (each ounce of **Joy** is claimed to contain the essence from 10,000 jasmine flowers and over 300 roses, just for starters!). Over a hundred more ingredients were added to bring out the best in this mighty accord — peach, orchid, lily of the valley, ylang ylang, tuberose, musk, civet and so on — but that is all background murmur to the exultant shout of **Joy**'s two principal ravishments. **Joy** is pure joy to Geminis who have the *panache* and the *pizzazz* to relish every drop of its hypnotic ravishment. To put it bluntly, it never fails to deliver the goods. It is irresistible — and I'll bet if you fall under its dazzling and seductive spell you'll treat it with the same adoration and faithfulness you have for the man you love most in your charmed life. So who said you were fickle?

YVRESSE— because it loves luxury

Don't get too excited — it's not a new perfume from Saint Laurent, but the new name for his magnificent **Champagne**. Unfortunately, he finally lost the legal battle with the churlish winegrowers, and by law had to rename it. But, like a rose, **Champagne** by any other name still smells the same, especially when the name **Yvresse** is a clever combination of his Christian name and the French ivresse which means (appropriately) intoxication, pleasure and rapture!

Nothing else has changed, not the brilliantly original packaging that manages to be reminiscent of a champagne cork, and certainly not the fabulous perfume. **Yvresse** is still heady, delicious and daring. It doesn't make any attempt at imitating the wine, other than emulating its effect of making people happy to the point of euphoria. And it certainly succeeds there! **Yvresse** is one of the most ingratiating and gregarious of perfumes with a sophisticated sparkle and zing all of its own.

Appropriately, **Yvresse** boasts a completely unique composition. Having already said that Geminis usually find fruity perfumes a bit dull, I must say that **Yvresse** is quite fruity, but its fruits are anything but ordinary! There's nectarine — rich and ripe with its salivating citrus/peach tang — harmonised with Chinese lychee (now isn't that different?). It certainly is in this case, because **Yvresse** uses a new technique — the essence of the fruits is extracted just before picking-time to achieve a freshness not possible before. So both the nectarine and lychee notes are dazzlingly heady. To add to this extreme piquancy, a brilliantly imaginative alliance of mint and aniseed is added, along with some strong-smelling country roses, with dashes of oakmoss, patchouli and vetiver for airiness.

The effect of **Yvresse** is not only daring but strikingly sensual. It will appeal enormously to Geminis who like a little elegance, amusement and refinement with their fun. Giddy young sybarites expecting fizz and tickle might be a little disappointed with it, but the witty and worldly will luxuriate in its lilting lusciousness. What's more, **Yvresse** is dedicated to the real pleasures of celebration — an absolute priority with sophisticated Geminis. So, who cares if it's not called **Champagne** any more? It still has the same fabulous sparkle. And like all expensive sparkle, it lasts!

JEAN PAUL GAULTIER
— because it's sentimental

Couturiers, especially French ones, are often quite surprising when it comes to giving the nod to the creation of a perfume that will bear their name. And this once enfant terrible of non-conformist fashion probably delivered the greatest surprise of all. Everyone expected something bizarre and outrageous. But after a lot of secrecy and red herrings, **Jean Paul Gaultier** emerged as a sentimental, sweetly old-fashioned perfume. So, after all, he did manage to shock everyone, but in a typically perverse way.

Not that you'd suspect anything exactly virginal from the packaging, which begins with a silver tin can opened to reveal the corseted torso of a voluptuous woman (shades of Schiaparelli's legendary bottle for her **Shocking** perfume, which startled the world in 1937). This is a homage to Gaultier's beloved Madonna — the earthly, not the heavenly one — but the next surprise is the perfume itself. It's an almost homely mix of rose, orange blossom, orchid, iris, ylang ylang and tangerine, but spiked with ginger and star anise, then heavily saturated in vanilla and musk. It is sweet, pretty and quite disarming. 'But why?' you might ask. The answer is Gaultier's grandmother. He just loved to lose himself in her boudoir, which contained her lace-up corset, scented nail lacquer and pink face powder. The memory stayed with him, no doubt as a nostalgic antidote to all the bitchy, glitzy glamour he later found himself surrounded by.

Now you might ask if **Jean Paul Gaultier** is really a perfume you'd consider. The answer is yes, if you're a Gemini who loves sweet thoughts, pink powdery drifts of dreams, and losing yourself in poignant nostalgia.

Or if you simply can't resist the sensational packaging of this amusing and endearing *jolie folie*. You'll probably buy it for the glam bottle, anyway!

CHAMPS-ELYSÉES
— *because it's pure Paris*

I thought it would be unfair of me not to recognise your innate good taste with a Guerlain perfume in your galaxy. And **Champs-Elysées** came along just in time to cater perfectly for the Gemini penchant for prettiness and pleasure. It's a rather unexpectedly light creation from Guerlain. It is more flirtatious and vivacious than intensely romantic, but I think you'll like it for its breathless and intoxicating *joie de vivre*.

Champs-Elysées comes in a very impressive gold and bold pink box and a beautifully angular bottle that somehow suggests Parisian architecture without imitating it. The first whiff is glorious — it seems to whizz around you in an aura of brilliant light and sparkle. It couldn't be anything else but Parisian as it blossoms and bursts into the dizziness of springtime.

Its formulation, in true Guerlain tradition, is highly adventurous. It uses the haunting lilac-like scent of buddleia (known as the butterfly bush) as a counterpoint to an opening rush of mimosa leaves, blackcurrant berries, rose petals and almond blossom, followed by the sunniness of mimosa blossom, and an undercurrent of rich hibiscus seed and almond wood. The effect is startling, exhilarating and quite teasing with the beautiful heart of buddleia emerging to establish the softly romantic and totally feminine feel that gives **Champs-Elysées** its radiant freshness. It's playful and witty, elegant without being aloof, and best of all it has the ability to make its wearer seem extraordinarily young.

No doubt it was named either for the dazzling but over-crowded avenue that is synonymous with Parisian *chic*, or perhaps because the most beautiful of the Guerlain boutiques resides splendidly at 68, avenue Champs Elysées. But I like to think it harks back in history to the more elegant and ordered age of the seventeenth century when the original leafy avenue was on the outskirts of Paris, and was considered quite pastoral in its meandering way until it was formally landscaped in the eighteenth century. How blissful and truly romantic it must have been then without the rush, pollution and noise that can sometimes make the present-day Champs Elysées a nightmare! But it's nice to know you can always envelop yourself in this perfumed enchantment and imagine Paris exactly the way you'd like it to be. A truly intoxicating Gemini fantasy!

Your secret weapons: the surprises

Now let's turn to your quieter side, even though it

might be a minimal part of your hectic life. Geminis, as we know, are very prone to abrupt collapses in temperament. Suddenly the show's over, you've taken your last curtain call and put the roses in vases. Now what? Loneliness or being left alone for too long frightens you and you become morose and maudlin.

You have to sort if out for yourself, but a good way of doing that is to sublimate yourself by doing something for others. Call on the vast resources of your kindness and generosity. And, for a change, instead of adorning yourself with perfumes that smell like celebrations, turn to the less outspoken, the less dizzy and capricious. They don't have to be all that different from your big guns, but they won't make so much noise. In fact, they can become more than your second line-up — they can become saviours when the going gets gloomy. I've chosen them for their therapeutic effects as well as their prettiness and femininity. They're all lovely, but quite gentle, thoroughly charming and relaxed — just as you will be when you stop thinking about yourself and think of the ones you love. You always wanted to be an angel, didn't you? Here they are:

• **Extravagance** by Givenchy
  Pronunciation: zjhiv-ON-she
  Type: floral
• **Oscar de la Renta** by Oscar de la Renta
  Pronunciation: OSS-cuh dee lar REN-tuh
  Type: floral

- **Un Air de Samsara** by Guerlain
  Pronunciation: ern air duh SAM-surra/gair-LARN
  Type: floral/oriental
- **Moschino** by Moschino
  Pronunciation: moss-KEEN-o
  Type: floral/oriental
- **Grand Amour** by Annick Goutal
  Pronunciation: grand ar-MOUR/ARN-ick goo-TARL
  Type: floral
- **Muguet du Bonheur** by Caron
  Pronunciation: MEW-gay doo bon-ERR /KARR-on
  Type: floral

EXTRAVAGANCE
— because it's indulgent

Since the retirement of the great couturier Hubert de Givenchy and the taking-over of his crown (temporarily or otherwise) by the innovative upstart genius of Alexander McQueen, the fashion of the House has changed rather startlingly. Strangely enough, the new perfumes haven't. **Organza** and its spin-off **Organza Indecence** made an unexpected return to the classic style, and this delicious newcomer doesn't rock the boat either. It continues on in the Givenchy tradition of extreme good taste and a certain amount of indulgent luxury without ever forsaking style — style is and always has been everything at Givenchy!

Would the original Givenchy muse Audrey Hepburn wear something as flighty and deliberately pretty as **Extravagance** as she did the spicier but feminine **L'interdit**? More than likely, but not if she were being serious, because there's absolutely nothing remotely sober or sedate about this giddy and capricious charmer. It's been created for fun — and flirting, which it does quite outrageously.

Extravagance makes its joyous entrance in a flurry of green and gold with French marigolds, nettle leaves, green mandarin and a scattering of green peppercorns, before revealing its generous floral heart dominated by the sweetly romantic hypnosis of wisteria with jasmine and orange blossom all laced with wild strawberry and cooled with violet leaves. Purring underneath is a vibrant quartet of sandalwood, cedarwood, amber and iris to anchor its giddiness so it stays faithfully close to you and delicately reinforces your own radiance.

So you can see **Extravagance** is not out to make any deep and meaningful statement about you — heaven forbid! It's purely for pleasure, which it exudes with a light-headed and light-hearted frivolity that centres the attention on you — something a Gemini either expects or connives to achieve. It's rather like wearing one of McQueen's less outrageous but startlingly pretty and ultra-feminine creations and having a jolly good time while you're knocking 'em dead. **Extravagance** is that sort of perfume — arresting, vivacious, flirtatious and splashy. You'll charm the pants off anyone in sight.

Oscar de la Renta
— because it's like morning dew

This designer of wonderfully statuesque and richly flamboyant clothes that grace many of the fashion's most fastidious women, was born on the island of the Dominican Republic in the Caribbean. He grew up surrounded by its tropical charms and the varied passions of its multi-racial populace. His grandmother was a great influence in his early years, and it was in her rambling, wild garden that he was first captivated by the beauty and power of its lush flowers. Many years later, this garden was to inspire his first perfume with its profusion of extravagantly blended flowers, leaves and spices. It was an instant sensation and has become a genuine neo-classic.

Oscar de la Renta explodes in a tropical display of jasmine, tuberose, ylang ylang, orchid, gardenia and wild orange blossom. Its headlong rush is like smelling the dazzle of an unexpected garden discovered at dawn, the petals still dripping with fresh dewdrops. This is further accentuated by the pungent spiciness of coriander, basil, cascarilla (West Indian sweetwood bark), clove, myrrh and opoponax giving the perfume its intense piquancy, which is then tempered and tamed by the smoothness of peach, lavender, sandalwood, amber and patchouli (quite a dash of the latter!). It's all dazzlingly bright and breezy but rounded and diffused into a sensual femininity that breathes its message on an exotic trade wind. The beautiful bottle of undulating curves is topped with a glass flower in the centre of which lies a single sculptured dewdrop — nostalgia strikes again! And this is why it appeals to romantic Geminis in need of a little sparkle, a little flourish. **Oscar de la Renta** knows what women sometimes long for — a revival disguised as an exquisite fantasia.

UN AIR DE SAMSARA
— because it's insouciant

It's become fashionable for some big successful perfumes that might be too daunting for timid tastes to offer themselves in less explosive interpretations (usually with the rather lame excuse that they're lighter and therefore more modern — a questionable piece of perfume logic).

When Guerlain announced its new baby was to be born of the beautiful **Samsara** it would, of course, bear a natural likeness to its famous mother, but nevertheless would be a child of its time and nature. In other words, it was to be no weaker, watered-down youngster, but one with a mind and beauty of its own. Thus, **Un Air de Samsara**, right from its beginnings, promised to be of the Samsara bloodline but totally independent and unique. And that it is. The differences are considerable.

Samsara is basically an exquisite blend of the very best jasmine and sandalwood available, used in almost equal proportions to create an intensely haunting perfume. The formulation of **un Air de Samsara** uses both ingredients in a lesser concentration but bolstered with the daring freshness of mint and strong citrus notes. The difference is immediately apparent, and becomes more and more individual with heart notes of narcissus, violet-like iris and warm amber. A lei of green leaves is the final adornment — one I think you'll find a breath of fresh air.

Un Air de Samsara is deceptively light and fresh. It has an infectious tingle but quite unusual staying power for an *eau de toilette*. It is so much its own entity that layering or mixing it with its mother doesn't actually work — **Un Air de Samsara** is independent and outgoing enough to be the headstrong child that does not intend to exist in mother's shadow. That should appeal to freedom-loving Geminis needing a bit of a lift when the chips are down!

MOSCHINO — *because it's mischievous*

This is a sly little minx full of impudence and playfulness as you'd expect from its late-lamented, once-mercurial designer. To put it bluntly, if you like the idea of Guerlain's mighty **Shalimar** but find it too demanding for your own quicksilver moods, then **Moschino** will probably infiltrate and take you over with its slick mix of capricious charm and sexiness.

Moschino is nowhere near a copy, but it has a similar though less serious attitude than its inspiration. It is an oriental but a young and very modern one. And it has something of a split personality. Its very tenacious top notes are all spicy and hot — oregano, pepper, nutmeg, coriander and cardamom. These are infused with green galbanum and topped with dashes of patchouli and ylang ylang. It's a pretty torrid beginning. But when the smoke clears, **Moschino** has suddenly changed into something more sensuous and seductive — a simmering pot of roses, jasmine, carnation, gardenia and honeysuckle. This is serious business. Soothing notes of amber and musk are added to keep things just at the bubble — until a big dose of rich and sexy vanilla stirs up the potion to boiling point. **Moschino** has reached its goal — total captivation of the senses.

It's one of the most deceptive perfumes I know — full of titillation and flirtation on the surface but a calculating seductress at heart. Still, because of its mercurial recklessness, it's never heavy or sultry, but really just a mischievous little girl out to have a good, but not sinful, time. **Moschino** is the ideal accessory for you when you want to remind others (and yourself as well) that you've got what others envy — sassiness!

GRAND AMOUR
— because it's as passionate as Camille

Annick Goutal is a very rare woman. She is a *parfumeuse* — a female French perfumer with a collection of esteemed and exquisite creations adored by women fortunate enough to have access to them. Although distribution is still limited, I'm glad to say it's getting better with more outlets realising these are perfumes that women find highly irresistible. One look at their beautiful, baroque Baccarat bottles with the charming gold butterfly motif and you'll know what I mean. The latest of them is **Grand Amour**, a marvel of mysterious, heart-stopping femininity.

Grand Amour is meant to evoke memories, recall sensations, create new atmospheres that reflect the inner radiance a woman possesses when she is truly in love. Time has nothing to do with it. It could last only a day or perhaps an eternity. Only the indescribable passion she feels means anything. And Goutal's genius has managed to capture that fabulous *frisson* in **Grand Amour**'s mysterious and haunting *mélange* of lily, honeysuckle, hyacinth, heather, Turkish rose and Grasse jasmine given a warm intensity of musk, vanilla, amber, mimosa and balsam. It has an enchanting and enveloping sensuality that Geminis will take to their hearts — whether they be fickle or faithful. **Grand Amour** is too wise to draw lines on these delicate matters. It knows that 'Love is everything.'

MUGUET DU BONHEUR
— because it smells of spring

You might find this a little difficult to locate, but quite a few perfume boutiques have reintroduced some of the very extensive range of Caron perfumes, which are very famous indeed in Paris. Do persevere because it's one of the loveliest lily of the valley perfumes (if you draw a blank, both Dior's **Diorissimo** and Gucci's **Envy** are laden with it, but not as subtly, and there are also excellent lily of the valley fragrances from both Floris and Crabtree & Evelyn).

Muguet (which is French for 'lily of the valley') **du Bonheur** is a very delicate impression rather than a slavish imitation of the flower with its singing, piercing scent that has a surprising tenacity. Here it is used with great artistry and subtlety. The scent of the flower seems at first to be far away, but gradually it emerges quite shyly through a little tangled green glade, all trembling and innocent. Once coaxed from its hiding-place it sends out its lovely sweet radiance in a quietly enveloping aura. Around it like a halo are fresh touches of green leaves and a whisper of white hyacinth, but this is a tribute, first and foremost, to one of nature's sweetest creations. **Muguet du Bonheur** is not bold enough to be blatant about its presence, but it is a perfume that will have people around you mystified and sniffing the air with pleasure. Gradually it, and you, will fascinate them sufficiently to come closer.

The advantage of the cusp: taking your pick

It's not all confusion — being neither one star sign nor the other, or feeling you're partly both — if you were born towards the beginning of Cancer*. You can of course pick and choose from the perfumes suggested from both Gemini and Cancer, but be careful. Depending on your characteristics, they may not all sit easily on you. That's why I've come up with a selection of extras that might solve any perfume problems or indecision you might have. Anyway, the choice is yours, so have fun finding out! They are:

- **L'Air du Temps** by Nina Ricci
  Pronunciation: lair doo TOM/nee-nah REE-chee
  Type: floral/spicy
- **Beautiful** by Estée Lauder
  Pronunciation: ESS-tay LOR-duh
  Type: floral
- **Stephanotis** by Floris
  Pronunciation: steff-an-OH-tis/FLORR-iss
  Type: floral
- **So de la Renta** by Oscar de la Renta
  Type: fruity/floral

If you were born towards the very beginning of Gemini, you might like to check out the choices for those born on the cusp of Taurus/Gemini on pages 95–100.

L'AIR DU TEMPS — because it's rhapsodic
And also mysterious in at least one respect. No
breakdown of its ingredients has ever revealed what
the all-important spices are in its thoroughly
enchanting floral bouquet. I suppose that gives **L'Air
du Temps** its timeless fascination, its air of mystery.
Nina Ricci created it in 1948 when previously
unattainable ingredients became available again after
the war. Perhaps it was decided then the rarity of
these 'new' spices may as well form part of the
inexplicable magic this perfume has had for
generations of young and not-so-young women. And
since Gemini women adore secrets and Cancerians
love to use their imaginations, **L'Air du Temps** is the
perfect perfume to fascinate both signs. With its
glorious bouquet of gardenia, carnation, *rose de mai,*
jasmine and lily over a murmuring base of ylang
ylang, peach, moss and musk, plus the enigmatic veil
of spice notes enveloping it in its own world of
innocence and tenderness, **L'Air du Temps** is one of
those precious perfumes that has become a living
legend. I don't know of anyone who dislikes it —
especially in its fabulous Lalique crystal *flacon* topped
by a pair of frosted doves in an eternal embrace.

BEAUTIFUL — because it blushes
This must be the quintessential pink perfume. Its
packaging introduces it as such, and its flood of
flowers suspended in a breathless hush of soft, ripe

fruits gives the entire composition an appealing innocence that conjures up images of American Beauty roses, romantic summer nights swathed in pink tulle, and (of course) blushing brides. The Gemini love of smiling prettiness will give it the nod and I think the Cancerian love of sweet nostalgia will approve of its lyrical charm. It's also possible you could find it a bit cloying, unless used with discretion (in other words, don't be too lavish with it because it's quite tenacious). **Beautiful** could hardly be anything but beautiful with its opulent *mélange* of pink roses, lilac, violet, carnation, lily of the valley, jasmine, orange blossom and freesia whipped into a frothy flummery with lemon, bergamot, peach and blackcurrant, touches of sage, vetiver, vanilla and musk. And somewhere in that compelling deliciousness lurks the Southern Belle charms of white magnolia in full seductive bloom. It's described ecstatically by Lauder as 'smelling of a thousand flowers' which, in this case, is probably not an exaggeration. Just be careful of over-dosing and everything in your garden will be appropriately **Beautiful**.

STEPHANOTIS — because it's hypnotic
There was a time when this beautiful waxy white vine flower was the star of almost every bridal bouquet, but its Edwardian opulence has since gone out of fashion a bit with brides opting for more bizarre

arrangements. **Stephanotis** is too elegant and haughty a flower for that sort of nonsense, but thank heavens Floris of London still recognises its mesmerising beauty and has captured its majestic essence for women who appreciate really unusual scents that don't have to make their point by shouting.

Stephanotis is truly reminiscent of its origins and is complemented here by the subtle attendance of jasmine, carnation, orange blossom and a whiff of citrusy petitgrain. Magical when worn with soft, floaty creations in white or pastels, **Stephanotis** will melt Gemini and Cancerian hearts with its angelic grace and lingering sensuousness. What's more, you don't have to even consider a trip to the altar to wear it with hypnotic success!

SO DE LA RENTA
— because it's vivacious

Another very desirable designer name to have in your perfume wardrobe. Unlike his classic signature scent and the heavier **Volupté**, this sparkling new perfume is a delicious treat bursting with pretty flowers and succulent fruit. It's certainly not dramatic, but not frivolous either — it just makes you feel fresh, alive, and renewed, a pick-me-up perfume of great charm and vivacity. Its flowers come in a rush of clementine, peony, lotus, freesia, gardenia and a whiff of tuberose bolstered with Arabian jasmine. Then the fresh fruit salad perks things up with luscious mango, plum, citrus and pimento with a touch of cardamom to add spice to a bed of musk, vanilla and sandalwood.

It's a compelling confection and extremely wearable whenever you feel like a lift. For Geminis it's almost like a security blanket (which is always welcome in your hectic schedule!) and for Cancers it represents the comfort and serenity of a more ordered life that could do with a bit of a blast now and then. **So de la Renta** fills the bill perfectly with its delicious sparkle, its inherent poise and its balanced beauty. It has that unmistakable Oscar de la Renta quality that never fails — self-confident elegance.

The Gemini male: if it's not expensive, forget it!

It's not that the Gemini male is necessarily a snob, but he's certainly a peacock. Nor does that mean he's overly vain — he simply likes to preen in his best bib and tucker. It doesn't matter if he's dressed to the hilt or in casuals — you can bet they'll be the best he can afford. And if he's not paying for it, then any gift you bestow upon him had better reek of class — the more expensive and exclusive the better. He's a man of great refinement but not averse to splashes of bright colour, though never actually flamboyant. He spends his whole life either trying to party or at least being the most popular person in his group — he'll go to any lengths to impress. So, I'm afraid you will insult him deeply if you try to pass off something that doesn't measure up to his high standards. The only way you may get away with it is if it has a novelty value — he loves anything new, as long as he gets it first! He loves happy smells — preferably light and zingy, so avoid the big male classic fragrances — he'll find them too dull.

These four all have famous designer names (absolutely mandatory to fashion-conscious Gemini males, and impressive to those that aren't).

- **Égoiste Platinum** by Chanel
  Pronunciation: ee-go-EAST/shar-NEL
  Type: herbal
- **Insensé** by Givenchy
  Pronunciation: arn-sonn-SAY/zjhiv-ON-she
  Type: floral/fruity
- **Moschino pour Homme** by Moschino
  Pronunciation: moss-KEEN-o poor om
  Type: fruity/oriental
- **Jazz** by Yves Saint Laurent
  Pronunciation: eve sarn lor-ON
  Type: floral/spicy

Égoiste Platinum

A variation on the classic sandalwood formula of **Égoiste**, this Platinum version differs quite a bit from its mentor by being much fresher and lighter, but still quite substantial. Its fascinating formula of up-front lavender and citrusy petitgrain against a pungent background of minty clary sage and geranium leaf is given a foresty touch with cedarwood and treemoss. Sandalwood then smooths down the edges with its customary subtlety to give **Égoiste Platinum** a suave but quite shimmering and silvery presence. It has an obvious outdoors freshness but is refined just enough to be quite a sensation when it goes partying. It's no slouch when it comes to being noticed, but never smells raucous or over-the-top — that just wouldn't do for fastidious Geminis!

Insensé

This is a terrific fragrance for Geminis. It has the clout of the Givenchy name and its inherent sense of elegance and good taste, and backs it up with a highly original formula. Nothing else smells quite like **Insensé**, which makes it ideal for the male Gemini's love of elitism. **Insensé** is based on blackcurrant buds and leaves to give a strong head-start to a very unusual composition. Next up comes the unmistakable rich tang of Sicilian mandarin and a good whack of grassy vetiver from the West Indies. Then a surprise packet of flowers arrives — but don't let that put you off! They're played down to form a warm and pulsating heart with velvety oakmoss to give a dark green forest edge. The result is terrific, yet not too deep and meaningful. As to its name — well, I wasn't going to mention it knowing how sensitive Geminis are about being labelled as split personalities, but just for the record in French it means 'insane', but French insanity usually translates as 'I'm mad about you!'. He'd be mad if he didn't like **Insensé**, anyway.

Moschino pour Homme

The caravan of spices arrives at the disco end of the Silk Road in this over-the-top-of-the-world show-off. **Moschino pour Homme** is as impish as its female counterpart **Moschino**. It sends out vibes that are frankly insinuating but all in good fun. It's a very eclectic mix of coriander, nutmeg, pepper and tangerine, flashed with lavender and vetiver, and loaded with the sensual come-on of patchouli. Need I say more, except that it's a real party animal and definitely not to be trusted!

Jazz

He can play it cool in this classic from the master of all things tasteful but unconventional. **Jazz** has achieved its elevated status among men because of its free-wheeling ability to fit in anywhere but still emanate a certain unstated superiority. It's not by any means a snob, but it doesn't care for the pits or anyone in them. It's a benchmark composition of spices and juniper berries, Spanish rose geranium, a dash of cool lily and a good whack of pervasive incense. Men never feel obvious wearing **Jazz**, and women automatically gravitate towards its promise of fun times, being with a man who knows his apples and how to exploit them — and all that jazz! It creates the sort of ambience Geminis seem born to — the sheer brilliance of spontaneous improvisation.

Who suits what, and when: getting the best out of your perfumes

Because perfumes become not only extensions of your personality but also give emphasis to the way you look and the mood you're in, naturally, to bring out their best, they should be treated with due understanding in regard to their characteristics and qualities. They too have limitations and strengths, just as we all have. So, the following table outlines when best to wear them (Day, Night), the age-group most suited to them (Young, Mature), the general complexion of the wearer (Fair, Dark), and the seasons they bloom best in (Spring/Summer – S/S, or Autumn/Winter – A/W). This table is meant only to be used as an approximate guide or reference point – it is not a hard and fast set of rules by any means.

THE BIG GUNS

-fume	Day	Night	Young	Mature	Fair	Dark	S/S	A/W
Pretty	•	•	•		•			•
gari	•	•	•	•		•	•	•
			•		•		•	•
esse	•	•		•	•	•	•	•
n Paul Gaultier	•		•		•	•	•	
amps-Elysées	•	•		•		•	•	

YOUR SECRET WEAPONS

-fume	Day	Night	Young	Mature	Fair	Dark	S/S	A/W
travagance	•	•	•		•		•	
car de la Renta	•	•		•		•		•
n Air de Samsara	•		•		•	•		
oschino	•			•		•		•
and Amour	•	•		•		•		•
uguet du Bonheur	•		•		•		•	

GEMINI/CANCER CUSPS

-fume	Day	Night	Young	Mature	Fair	Dark	S/S	A/W
ir du Temps	•	•	•		•		•	
autiful	•	•		•		•	•	•
phanotis	•	•	•	•	•		•	•
de la Renta	•	•	•			•	•	•

TAURUS/GEMINI CUSPS

-fume	Day	Night	Young	Mature	Fair	Dark	S/S	A/W
mance	•	•	•	•		•	•	•
vy	•	•	•		•	•	•	•
stalle	•	•	•		•	•	•	•
lèche	•	•	•		•	•	•	•

MEN'S FRAGRANCES

-fume	Day	Night	Young	Mature	Fair	Dark	S/S	A/W
oiste Platinum	•		•		•		•	
ensé			•			•	•	
oschino our Homme	•		•			•		•
z	•		•		•		•	

Cancer

The crab
June 21–July 22

Romeo Gigli

You and the front gate

You've closed it securely behind you and wandered up the garden path admiring your daffodils trumpeting forth, your prize roses in bloom, the tibouchina has burst into purple splendour and the kids are safely at home. And even though you know when you walk through the front door of your haven it's all chaos and catastrophe, it is not going to faze you one bit. Somehow you assuage the kids, persuade the dog to stop barking, get the dinner going and maybe even arrange a bowl of your own home-grown flowers for the table. By the time hubby gets home, everything's organised and everyone's happy. They don't of course notice you're practically at screaming point under your cool, organised exterior. After all, this is what makes you tick. It's just that sometimes your clockwork goes off balance and starts telling you to wake up to yourself. You are not Florence Nightingale, Mother Courage and Joan of Arc all rolled into a nice, practical, unassuming and accommodating Cancerian. (They probably wouldn't notice if you were anyway!) But that's all perfectly normal to you, and you'd be lost without something to look after and people to care for. Home and family are everything. Everyone from the pooch up looks to you for comfort, sustenance and protection and they get it. Only the fact that it's often taken for granted nettles you, but after a slight blowing of the fuse (which they can't quite understand) you get your self-control and niceness back. Sometimes you might sulk a bit, but usually in silence. If you sulk, they either take no notice or steer clear of you. They know you are easily hurt and might get — well — crabby. And so you should. You have the inner strength to assert yourself, so use it, even if it puts other noses out of joint.

The over-riding principle in your life is honesty and straightforwardness. That's why you'll fight tooth and nail for a good cause, especially if it's limping a bit. Show you a sick animal or bird and you don't just feel sorry for it, you do something to fix it up, or bury it if necessary. And when it comes to justice — even in small matters — you can be a holy terror if it's not delivered with fairness and compassion. You hate cruelty as much as you hate crooks that get away with blue murder. There should be more women like you.

You make quiet assessments of things. You don't judge, you evaluate and make decisions that are practical and constructive. These are not made hastily but on those rare times when you can close yourself off into your intensely private world — usually after everyone's asleep at last. You should do more of it, because it regenerates you, and unleashes your creative forces and your insatiable thirst for knowledge and research — you love to delve into history, especially family history. You know your worth but tend to underestimate or sublimate it — your humility can sometimes be more of a hindrance than help. Do you sometimes forget just how clever you are at all sorts of things? You have a naturally enquiring and analytical mind which will atrophy if you don't use it. I mean it's all very well to be the safe harbour sheltering all those scared little boats from the raging storm, but not if they make too much a habit of it. Think of yourself for a change — think of your bright, intelligent brain! It's amazing how 'helpless' people can look after themselves when the crunch comes.

Most of you are basically shy but that shouldn't

stop you. Once this reticence has been overcome, Cancerian women usually manage to make successes of themselves in one way or another — if not on the domestic front, then in business — especially small business. They make great managers. They are very astute. They drive a hard bargain. They expect value for money. But they're polite and fair-minded about it. Only fools try to pull the wool over a Cancerian's eyes. So this is where your self-assessment comes in. Sometimes you might think it's too much of a battle to re-invent yourself, even for an occasion. Rubbish! You have so much potential and good taste in just about everything, make sure it extends to your personal image, even if it means a radical shake-up. You'll feel suddenly liberated, and the effect will not go unnoticed. Those that took you for granted will look at you with new eyes. They may even make surprising overtures.

But the smart Cancerian woman will merely thank them and let them know *she'll* call *them*, not the other way around. I'm not for a moment suggesting you do a Nora in Ibsen's famous play *A Doll's House* and slam the front gate behind you forever, but wouldn't it be nice to be offered a gentlemanly arm, and have the front gate opened for you where that big shiny limo awaits? Why not — you'd already arranged for the baby-sitter anyway!

Cancerian style

You have very definite tastes which don't run to prettiness or frills. Instead, you like classicism complemented with contrasting touches of pure imagination — like the antique mixed with the modern, a striking attempt at ikebana instead of a bowl of roses at afternoon tea, modest country furniture resting on fine Persian rugs and so on. It's your subtle way of being individual and unconventional — but not over-the-top (vulgarity has no place in your home). Everything must be practical and comfortable with a touch of discreet romanticism — just a touch! You can't live without flowers, the homelier the better, and you love colours that are chirpy without being blindingly bright. Cheery blues, yellows and warm ambery colours attract you more than imperious purples and hot reds. You're a very good cook, but not into nouvelle anything — your strengths are the staples of the kitchen, served with a creative flair all your own. You don't mind entertaining and can rise to the occasion, but you're much happier when they've all left saying what a nice time they've had. Then it's off with the heels, up with the feet, some calming music and something cuddly in your lap.

Comfort is bliss, but complacency isn't, and you know very well you're often in danger of being thought dull and even moody. Since the Cancerian craving for comfort can sometimes lead to throwing in the towel, it's important to remember just how adept you are when called upon to do anything. The same goes for your personal appearance. You're neat and dress carefully (you wouldn't be caught dead with a button missing) but you tend to get into a groove. Well, then it's high time to kick over the traces. Put colours together you wouldn't have thought of before, pamper yourself with a facial and a dramatic new hair style (a new shade will help too!), titivate yourself and try a new perfume or two — one you really honestly truly can't resist, and one that's so startling and un-you, it might give you a new perspective of yourself. And serve lots of sticky drinks after dinner. You might be surprised that another dimension of your style emerges and raises a few eyebrows — for a change.

Your outer expression is *compassion*. Your inner core is *surprise*.

Here's how you translate all of that into the best perfumes for you.

I have divided these perfumes into two sections:

1. *The big guns* — the all-important perfumes that should suit you best. They form the core of your perfume arsenal.

2. *Your secret weapons* — these augment your basics and are more daring and unusual, but should still suit you.

There is also a choice of perfumes for those of you

born on the cusp of Cancer/Leo, as well as a selection of men's fragrances suitable to give the Cancerian male. (If you were born on the cusp of Gemini /Cancer see pages 132–136 for your further perfume choices.) I have given each perfume a category, and a simple and easy guide to its correct pronunciation. At the end of the chapter I have summated all of the perfumes into a table that tells you whether they're best on young or mature women, in warm or cool weather, day or evening, for dark or fair complexions.

The big guns: the indispensable basics

There's no getting away from the fact that although Cancerian women may be too practical to be called romantic in the true sense of the word, they are nonetheless drawn to those types of scents that are labelled romantic for the sake of categorisation. Romantic perfumes usually are composed of flowers — lots and lots of flowers — which is probably why Cancerians are pushovers for them. Their imaginations conjure up lovely, hypnotic images of exotic gardens at twilight, or the exciting rarity of night-blooming beauties, as well as the simple, homespun and home-grown bouquets they might pick themselves. This is why you usually avoid dry, woody perfumes or those that are so modern in outlook their aggressiveness grates on you. Orientals of the full-on seductive persuasion you find clammy and oppressive, and pretty-pretty perfumes that are all giggles and no heart you find frivolous, and we all know you're not frivolous women! On the other hand, floral bouquets that are either given a fresh flourish of greenery, or warmed and softened with amber and musk attract you, as long as they're not too cloying. The qualities of lightness and airiness in perfumes you find comfortable and comforting. These will be your faithful favourites, the ones that don't scream and shout or try to be smarter than you are. But don't be reticent about using perfume with confidence — Cancerians are notorious for applying little discreet dabs so as not to offend. The fact is such pussy-footing won't make any impression at all — not even on you after half an hour or so. Do be a bit generous — don't be too self-effacing and understated — being lateral instead of liberal might put you out of the picture altogether. And you're too individual for that! Here are my choices for you:

- **Romeo Gigli** by Romeo Gigli
  Pronunciation: ro–MAY-o JEE-lee
  Type: floral/spicy
- **Amarige** by Givenchy
  Pronunciation: amma-REEZJHE/zjhiv-ON-she
  Type: floral/woody
- **Boucheron** by Boucheron
  Pronunciation: BOO-sher-on

Type: floral/fruity
- **Diorissimo** by Christian Dior
  Pronunciation: dee-or-ISS-immo/
  KRIST-ee-an dee -OR
  Type: floral
- **Cabochard** by Grès
  Pronunciation: CABBO-shar/GREH
  Type: floral/oriental
- **White Linen** by Estée Lauder
  Pronunciation: ESS-tay LOR-duh
  Type: floral/green

ROMEO GIGLI — because it's enchanting
I don't know of any woman who hasn't fallen in love
with this perfume once she's discovered it. It arrived
unheralded in the early '90s and remained a precious
secret to those who'd been told in advance about it.
They didn't want anyone raining on their parade. But
it's very difficult to keep anything great under wraps,
and the news about a ravishing new Italian designer
perfume eventually leaked out and it soon began its
inevitable conquest of hearts.

Its promotional slogan of 'A perfume that reminds
you of a woman that reminds you of a perfume' set the
ball rolling and, once hunted down at the more
exclusive perfume counters, women (and I suppose
men) found themselves completely seduced by the
fabulous little glass bottle with its swirl of a top that
looks a bit like a medieval banner flying (its inspiration

was actually Gigli's own antique inkwell!). And when they had their first whiff of it, its success was sealed.

Romeo Gigli is a truly romantic voyage that takes in bergamot, lime and mandarin from Sicily, marigolds from North Africa, basil from the Seychelles, Persian green galbanum, jasmine and mango from India, Turkish lilies and carnation, lily of the valley, blackcurrant bud from France and freesia from the English countryside. And that's just the head and heart notes. More exotic travel is required for Balkan oakmoss, Malayan patchouli and vanilla, some Arabian myrrh and a dash of Spanish mint to complete the base notes of this extravagant cargo. A touch overwhelming, you might think? Never. The blend is so beautifully harmonised you'd be hard-pressed to single out a single component. Everything melds into a dazzling, shimmering, incredibly fresh and vivacious intertwining that sends your head reeling, your senses senseless, and your heart melting.

Romeo Gigli is a masterpiece. It is youthful, outgoing and quite determined to captivate you. For normally cautious Cancerians it could open the door to untold daydreams of secret romance. I'll say this — if it doesn't have your current Romeo scaling your balcony to confess his undying love for you, then give him up as a bad job.

AMARIGE— because it's softly persuasive
The word is actually a charming anagram of the

French *mariage,* which of course means marriage, or at least an alliance. This doesn't mean that Givenchy created **Amarige** exclusively for brides to leave a fragrant trail of it walking down and up the aisle — indeed, he meant it to suggest 'mirages and magic — amorous and marvellous encounters' as well as marriage. **Amarige** does all that in many ways, but mostly in its wonderfully different composition.

The first alliance that sets **Amarige** apart from other florals with a marked individuality is its combination of gardenia and Brazilian rosewood — the opulently floral with a rich and resinous wood — quite daring when you think about it. But the uniqueness doesn't stop there. Along comes a bouquet of sumptuous flowers — mimosa, ylang ylang, neroli (which is the bittersweet oil from just-opening buds of the Seville orange tree) and jasmine all doused in a veil of musk and vanilla. Mandarin, tonka bean, violet leaves, red berries and other woods *simpatico* with the rich rosewood round out the exquisitely lovely procession.

Amarige is a like or don't like perfume, but don't be too hasty about making a decision against it. At first it may smell too deep and sonorous, rather like a saturated jungle after a downpour, but the dewy freshness, the lingering tranquillity of it will soon seduce most Cancerians. It is not playful, but mellow and glowing. It can waft you off into your private dreamworld, creating wondrous images of timeless peace and harmony that turn innermost thoughts to encounters and alliances that may not be fantastic mirages at all but something more definite and lasting (like a marriage perhaps?). If I were you, I'd give into it — with a satisfied smile.

BOUCHERON — *because you deserve it*

You honestly do. It's an extravagance that's worth its price — an extravagance you might have to rebudget to squeeze in, but what the heck? You can do without a few of the mundane things that seem to plague your life, and even though you might be a cautious, practical Cancerian doesn't mean you have to deny yourself every pleasure and secret desire, does it? I hope not. Cancerians deserve the best because they give of their best, so it's a fair trade.

Boucheron comes from those fabulous jewellers who pamper the rich and famous, but in their first foray into perfume, Alain Boucheron, the head of this elegant empire, insisted that it be nothing less than a priceless and precious jewel of a perfume worthy of the House of Boucheron. After years of perfecting a brilliant formula that defies description with its sumptuous originality, all was ready for his approval. But, just like most bosses, he had to have the last say and insisted that one of the top notes was not quite right, and had it altered. Now, as you know, a lot of these decisions from on high are made just for the sake of showing who's boss and can be very irksome, but in this case his unerring good taste and fastidious nose proved to be right. Thus **Boucheron** was born — corrective surgery already successfully performed!

With its avalanche of fruity splendour up-front (tangerine, apricot, bitter orange) forming a golden backdrop, a gigantic tumble of flowers arrives (orange blossom, tuberose, jasmine, ylang ylang, broom, narcissus), all of it then polished (just like faceting a jewel) with sandalwood, amber and tonka bean. The precious gem, sparkling with brilliance and revealing its pulsating inner depths, becomes **Boucheron**.

It's an overwhelmingly lovely perfume of great finesse and sophistication. It exudes splendour and refinement in its bottle shaped like a gold ring set with a huge blue stone. Most of all, it reminds you that luxury is not just indulgence but an affirmation of your own inestimable worth. So, save!

DIORISSIMO — *because it's lovable*

This is Dior's simplest and sweetest perfume, so much so it has no intentions of being anything other than a ravishing celebration of the beautiful little lily of the valley. Now this is a deceptive flower — seemingly shy and delicate, when actually it has a very outspoken, almost piercing and totally unmistakable scent. It is so strong that the Dior perfumers surround it with softness — lily, jasmine, boronia and lilac, then garland it in fresh green notes, and deepen it with ylang ylang and sandalwood. But that singing scent of lily of the valley triumphs over all.

Diorissimo is one of the freshest floral perfumes to grace a woman, and its innocent but eager flirtatiousness appeals to Cancerians who adore the euphoria of springtime flowers bursting into full-throated jubilation. It's a perfume that makes you blissfully happy, jaunty and optimistic. It's an optimism well-placed — most men swoon when it passes by. Bad news though for many Cancerians — **Diorissimo** is definitely reserved for the young. The more mature of you should resist its temptations — it tends to make you smell like mutton dressed up as spring lamb — sorry!

CABOCHARD — *because it smoulders*

You may think of yourself as too level-headed to fall prey to a seductive, sultry, suspiciously oriental perfume like this classic, but many women more conservative than you have. **Cabochard** is one of those wily but wise perfumes that keeps people guessing — yourself included. It was inspired by a cruise taken in the late '50s by Madame Grès to the Spice Islands, with a little side sojourn to India as well. Naturally, the sights and insights, the scents and the sensuousness rubbed off on her. On her return to France, she commissioned the perfumer Omar Arif to create an opulent oriental perfume that would not be out of place in the rarefied world of Paris. Thus, **Cabochard** emerged as a civilised and refined exotic beauty.

The word means 'impudent, stubborn, wilful' but in the less abrasive Gallic tradition of not calling a spade a spade, translates as 'charmingly persistent', which it certainly is with its lush fruity, spicy top notes that plunge without warning into a breathless splendour of jasmine, rose, spicy carnation and ylang ylang enveloped by oakmoss, green galbanum, geranium, patchouli, and embellished with the ambered suaveness of musk, tobacco leaf and leather. Then it's all left to simmer and smoulder before releasing its magic and mystery in warm waves of sensuality.

Now if you think this is all a bit much for the Cancerian sensibility, think again. **Cabochard** could be just the release you're looking for — a perfume of supreme elegance that lets people know there's more to you than just constancy and reliability. It might even get you smouldering with passion.

WHITE LINEN—because it complements you
Men always smile when they smell it on you, and even kids don't mind it at all. It fits in with your Cancerian image of niceness and unfailing geniality. Now that might sound like you're a leading citizen of Dullsville, but that depends on you. If you wear **White Linen** where and when it should be worn and with the correct clothes, plus the smiling demeanour it demands, then it can smell as if it were made for you and you alone.

White Linen has become a household word in perfume and that's because its success has been built on its breezy, midsummer casualness. It's clean and clear, happy and completely disarming. Irresistible might be too strong a claim, but its cheerfulness does make it hard to dismiss as merely reliable. Just learn to wear it quite lavishly — layer it if you like, from the bathroom onwards. Let it be an aura around you, not just a vague hint. Wear it all through the day, but put it away at night — it is not a party animal and smells distinctly countrified at big occasions. Don't expect it to perform miracles of seduction either — it is not a vamp (unless he's a farmer!). Flatter it with clothes that are zingy, sassy but simple. No, you *don't* have to twirl in a big cartwheel linen skirt, a button-through blouse and a straw hat with daisies around it! Don't take it *that* literally.

What's **White Linen** made from? It's more complex than you might think, but let's say it relies heavily on Bulgarian rose, vetiver grass from Reunion Island, lots of jasmine, lilac, honeysuckle, lily of the valley and hyacinth plus green leaves, moss, citrus oils, and spicy pimento from the West Indies. All of which harmonise beautifully to give it an open-air freshness that has a terrific buoyancy and crispness. So don't think of **White Linen** as old-fashioned — think of it as a reliable asset. Not all men like powerhouse women in powerhouse perfumes, you know.

Your secret weapons:
the surprises

I've already said that the expression of your inner self
— a part that you don't often expose for reasons only
you know — is the element of surprise.

Does this mean you suddenly spring shocks on
your unsuspecting family and friends, or you are
quite capable of surprising yourself with equally
sudden shifts of temperament? Well, it's both. And
both have far more potential for personal expression
and satisfaction than you might think. Because
Cancerians can get too comfortable and complacent,
they're open to criticisms of dullness or mental
lethargy. This in turn makes them resentful and
moody, so if it applies to you it's high time to catapult
yourself into action, to revitalise yourself. And the
best way to do that is by surprising *yourself*, which in
turn will surprise others. It will also bring your quirky
sense of humour, your razor-sharp and quite acidic
wit to the fore, as well as facing the facts in your
mirror. If what you see is what you don't want to,
don't give up the ship — relaunch yourself! A
second-string of perfumes quite different from your
mainstays will do the trick in a trice. The ones I've
selected for you are not exactly radical (which would
scare you anyway), but encompass a wide spectrum of
styles and personalities — yes, perfumes have
individual personalities or characteristics. They range
from the frankly seductive to the sophisticated to the

fascinatingly ambivalent. But they all contain surprises — not least the fact that they'll smell surprisingly effective on you. They are:

- **Volupté** by Oscar de la Renta
  Pronunciation: vol-OOP-tay/OZ-car de lar REN-tuh
  Type: floral
- **Venezia** by Laura Biagiotti
  Pronunciation:ven-ETZ-zee-uh/LOW
  (as in WOW) - ruh bee-adj-ee-OTTIE
  Type: floral/oriental
- **Tea Rose** by The Perfumer's Workshop
  Type: floral
- **Chamade** by Guerlain
  Pronunciation: shar-MARD/gair-LARN
  Type: floral/fruity
- **Y** by Yves Saint Laurent
  Pronunciation: EE (not WHY)/eve sarn lor-ON
  Type: fruity/floral
- **Opium** by Yves Saint Laurent
  Pronunciation: OH-pe-um/eve sarn lor-ON
  Type: oriental

VOLUPTÉ — because it's what it says
When this perfume hit the counters with a vengeance, there was a lot of accompanying publicity twaddle about what its name meant. Well, despite a lot of high-flying carrying-on of quoting the untranslatable poetics of its possessing Baudelaire's '*calme, luxe et volupté*' the French *volupté* simply translates as

'voluptuousness'. Which I'm sure is precisely what Oscar de la Renta had in mind when creating it.

He wanted it to be a return to elegance, and a reversal of the brash, brazen and aggressive perfumes that were striding rather offensively through the streets. So he went back to the opulent floral perfumes of the '30s — the ones that breathed, not bombarded, the senses with a sophisticated sexiness, but also managed to be light-hearted and joyous. Volupté was his very accurate, contemporary solution.

Its *mélange* of rich flowers — freesia, mimosa and osmanthus — are given an extra fidelity of scent through the new Living Flower technique and accented with jasmine, heliotrope, mandarin and melon, which in my opinion are all upstaged by the distinct smell of woody violets — a good thing too, since there are too few violet-laced perfumes around today. Anyway, **Volupté**'s success was immediately awarded top honours at the 1993 Fifi Awards of the Fragrance Foundation in America. And that success certainly made its hard-hearted competitors head for the hills for a rethink in terms of softer formulations.

You might find **Volupté** a little too voluptuous for you, but handled discreetly it is a very exhilarating and memorable perfume. Sure it wears its passionate heart on its sleeve, but maybe it's time you did too. At least you'll be noticed — **Volupté** cuts quite a heady swathe through crowds.

VENEZIA — *because it's adventurous*

That intrepid medieval traveller Marco Polo is credited with introducing to the West everything from spaghetti to fireworks, but one of the most esoteric and romantic of his seemingly endless list of oriental discoveries was the sweetly scented little flower from China called Wong-shi blossom. This gardenia-like bloom apparently captivated the hearts of high-born Venetian ladies, was dubbed *'l'elisir d'amore'* ('elixir of love') by local poets and an aphrodisiac by the jaded gentry. Its secret was also kept under lock and key by the avaricious and elitist Venetians, where it apparently grew in clandestine back gardens. Or so we're told. Truth or fantasy aside, it re-emerged in 1992 in this East meets West perfume from one of Italy's favourite home-grown designers.

To what effect, you might ask? Well, **Venezia** is a truly lovely and very haunting perfume and it certainly smells like no other. Its happy marriage of the Wong-shi blossom with jasmine works as the main theme, as does its capability to merge lusciously with oriental ingredients of mango, ylang ylang and that other fascinating Chinese blossom, osmanthus. The earthiness of blackcurrant bud and rose geranium are added, with some Spanish plum, a dash of fresh freesia, and to keep the perfumed potion at a high simmer, vanilla and musk. What emerges is a highly unusual, daring and dashing perfume — an *elisir d'amore* indeed!

Venezia is very rich, insinuating and highly

evocative of its romantic inspiration. It looks sensational in its Harlequin packaging, an indication of the fun, frivolity and fantasy it offers those Cancerians who need to throw caution to the canals and be impetuously adventurous.

TEA ROSE — *because life couldn't be rosier*

Chanel once declared that women don't want to smell like a bed of roses. Naturally she was, at the time, pushing her radical **No. 5** perfume at the expense of the pre–1920s fragrances, which were almost all based on heavy bouquets of flowers — especially roses. Well, she succeeded in changing the smell of perfume forever, but she forgot about those women who dote on single flower scents — especially roses. Decades later, dedicated perfumers sensitive to the needs of rose-starved women, returned to the rose's magical scent to create memorable perfumes composed almost entirely of them. The most outstanding (in more ways than one) is **Tea Rose**.

Tea Rose is mighty powerful. It will stand out in any gathering. You can see noses searching for the source of what smells like a rose garden in full bloom. In other words, be careful with its application. One squirt or two of **Tea Rose** in the right place will more than make your point! **Tea Rose** is pure, high-pitched, single-minded. It smells almost more like a rose than the real thing, which means it's been bolstered and intensified in the laboratory for heightened effect. It's a quite stunning scent and if you sniff deeply you'll detect the presence of a tea-like aroma, which is natural since tea roses were originally grown among tea-leaf bushes in China and India and absorbed the sharp tannin smell of them. That's why they differ from other roses quite markedly.

Of course if you're not keen on roses then **Tea Rose** will have no appeal to you. But if you're like a very glamorous Cancerian I know, you'll make it your signature perfume. I wouldn't make it your *only* perfume though — you might hear the ghost of Chanel laughing at you!

CHAMADE — because it's compelling

This is one of the most mysterious perfumes I know of. It is also one of the most sophisticated and insinuating. **Chamade** is a perfume whose message is so ardent no one within its orbit will be unaffected by it. It also happens to be a masterpiece of originality in the great tradition of Guerlain.

The word itself is ambivalent. It can mean the rapid beating of the heart as well as the total surrender of it. **Chamade** does both. It is a ravishing and sumptuous collection of lush and romantic flowers such as lilac, hyacinth, tuberose, rose and jasmine intensified with clove, blackcurrant bud and some richly exotic fruits that remain a Guerlain secret. It's these that give **Chamade** its throbbing undercurrents, its warmth and suaveness.

Chamade has that intensely intimate quality of seeming to be an intrinsic part of you rather than merely applied for effect. Supremely elegant but never haughty, **Chamade** is only for the worldly-wise and the audacious woman who would never think of overstepping the bounds of propriety — that is until she's made her conquest and is alone with the object of her desire. So, you Cancerians who might be a little reticent to follow up overtures might find **Chamade** an elegant curtain-raiser to a play that should only end with the total surrender to hidden passion. Don't say I didn't warn you!

Y — *because it emphasises your elegance*

I call this super-elegant classic from the great Saint Laurent a 'resurrection' perfume. Cancerians often suffer not so much from an identity crisis as an identity lapse. They become so immersed — bogged-down might be more accurate — with everyday affairs they almost forget who they are — they forget how individual and influential they can be.

Sublimation in others' lives is one thing, but drowning in it is another. That's when **Y** comes to the rescue. Its brilliant beauty and understated refinement are timely reminders that you are not just important, you're unique! It's the sort of perfume that can make you feel instantly self-confident — even dynamic! Suddenly you're someone to be reckoned with — a bit like the transformation of dull and dowdy Agnes Gooch in 'Auntie Mame' to a glamorous goddess — though you don't have to go *quite* so far as poor Agnes did to prove the point!

Y is an artfully balanced harmony of many flowers (all of them opulent) — gardenia, honeysuckle, jasmine, Bulgarian rose, ylang ylang, iris, tuberose and hyacinth, wedded to amber, peach, plum and patchouli, then topped with a sparkling green aureole of new leaves and oakmoss. The oakmoss note is particularly prominent — another daring stroke from Saint Laurent's never-empty bag of tricks.

Y is never to be underestimated. Created in 1964, it recently underwent a 'modern' re-orchestration in an effort to appeal to a 'younger, more modern' clientele. It made no difference. Only the packaging seemed to change — the exquisitely haunting elegance of its smell was so infinitesimal it didn't cause a riot among its ardent devotees. So all's well that ends well — a catch-phrase you might well be saying yourself when you let **Y** resurrect your individuality and set it back on the pedestal where it belongs. All too often, Cancerians sell themselves short. Y will take care of that — elegantly.

OPIUM — *because it unleashes you*

While we're on the subject of perfumes that can do extraordinary things to you, why not compound the 'resurrection' rescue operation of **Y** (see above) with another Saint Laurent temptress, the dazzling, dramatic **Opium**.

Now that the controversy over its name has long since become rather an old joke, **Opium** has the last laugh. It keeps on seducing women into wearing it and men falling for it (and hopefully refilling the bottle for you to keep the habit going). Yet **Opium** is not as *femme fatale* and vampish as its reputation. It is quite a lightweight in the sultry oriental stakes, avoiding the smouldering fleshpots and instead seducing in a much more subtle and manipulative way.

All the traditional oriental elements are present — carnation, cinnamon, myrrh, opoponax, amber, musk, incense, pepper, patchouli as well as roses, jasmine and orchid, but topped with hesperides (highly concentrated citrus oils), plum, coriander and vanilla to give a sparkling and sensual tang that gives **Opium** its shamelessly sexy sizzle.

Opium is the perfume you need to break out of your safe and conventional image — the one that nettles you. It's the perfume that can transform you into being desirable all over again. It's the perfume that practically forces you to kick over the traces and grab life by the throat.

It's not overpowering, but it's not subtle either. And it's very tenacious. Take it to bed and the body that lies beside you that night will be smelling of it in the morning. Straying partners beware!

The advantage of the cusp: taking your pick

It's not all confusion — being neither one star nor the other, or feeling you're partly both — if you were born towards the beginning of Leo*. You can of course pick and choose from the perfumes suggested from both Cancer and Leo, but be careful. Depending on your characteristics, they may not all sit easily on you. That's why I've come up with a selection of extras that might solve any perfume problems or indecision you might have. Anyway, the choice is yours, so have fun finding out! They are:

- **Chloé** by Parfums Lagerfeld
  Pronunciation: KLO-ee/PAR-foom LARGA-feld
  Type: floral
- **Theorema** by Fendi
  Pronunciation: tayor-AIM-uh / FEN-dee
  Type: floral/oriental
- **Dazzling Silver** by Estée Lauder
  Type: floral/oriental
- **Salvatore Ferragamo** by Salvatore Ferragamo
  Pronunciation: salva-TOR-ay ferra-GAR-mo
  Type: floral/fruity

If you were born towards the very beginning of Cancer you might like to check out the choices for those born on the cusp of Gemini/Cancer on pages 132–136.

CHLOÉ — because it's persistent

This was Lagerfeld's first foray into perfume and he got pretty excited about it. He also managed to make sure it hit the beauty headlines with its uncompromising approach, its insistence on a very heady floral bouquet with the emphasis firmly on the permeating scent of tuberose — a scent women either love to death or avoid like the plague. With his customary haughty disdain, he stuck to his guns and **Chloé** has survived a barrage of criticism from those who found it too overpowering. I think it's a terrific perfume — definite but romantically soft with its combination of tuberose and jasmine with orange blossom, ylang ylang and amber. But there's no doubt that tuberose emerges triumphant. Its floral theme will appeal to Cancerians — especially those who like to make their mark — which also falls right into Leo's lair. At least **Chloé** has the courage of its convictions.

THEOREMA — because it's rich

Wearing anything by Fendi makes a woman feel rich and pampered, even if she's not necessarily living in the lap of unlimited luxury. There's just something warm and comforting about Fendi, and this new perfume has that same air of casual but very aware privilege of owning the best there is.

In its handbag-shaped *flacon* that makes it seem like a necessary Fendi accessory, **Theorema** is a delicious and opulent mix of English eglantine rose, jasmine and citrus with a warm and glowing oriental interior of osmanthus (that intoxicating little Chinese flower that's reminiscent of jasmine, raisins and apricots all at once) plus cinnamon, sandalwood, pepper, and a lush topping of cream, would you believe! Yes, real, thick fresh cream, so it's no wonder it has such a smoothly rich finish. Well, you can always rely on something original from Fendi, and **Theorema** won't disappoint any woman who prefers luxury to self-denial. Cancers might have to throw their usual caution to the winds (and about time too!), but Leos of course won't even think twice about a bit of a splurge.

DAZZLING SILVER—because it glitters

This is the good-time girl of Estée Lauder's **Dazzling** sister-act. She's not nearly as opulent and dramatic as her **Dazzling Gold** sibling, but nor is she a reckless high-kicker out to shock and paint the town red. She prefers to shower it with a gentle glittering of sophisticated glamour, not vulgarity. She may be well-heeled but those heels are super-elegant, not tacky six-inch stilettos — **Dazzling Silver** is a well-bred, well-behaved Lauder lady, not a vamp! Apart from having orchid and passionflower in her make-up, she's quite different to **Dazzling Gold**. With the combined beauties of Monet lily, sunshine flower, lotus blossom, ginger lily and the voluptuous exotica of Japanese mountain orchid and rich purple vanilla orchid, she has a svelte and sparkling elegance that's nevertheless not too heavy for Cancers, but luxurious enough for Leos. Both will like the edge of carefree abandon she exudes and the delicious way she has of leaving a fascinating trail, not a heavy train, of follow-me fragrance behind her. She gets lots of attention for her sparkling good humour as much as for her playful sensuality. And in her smoothly sculpted modernist glass bottle, **Dazzling Silver** reveals she has impeccably understated taste as well

SALVATORE FERRAGAMO
— because it's gloriosa!

If you own a pair of Ferragamo shoes you know the expert craftsmanship, fashion innovation and sheer finesse that goes into making them, and wearing them is like walking on clouds. So, what's the new Salvatore Ferragamo signature scent like, you may ask? It's just as wonderful to slip into. In a word — glorious!

From the first spray from the statuesque bottle, you'll reel with delight in an unexpected fruit cocktail of orangey neroli, blackcurrant cassis and a dash of anise laced with pepper and nutmeg before you slip into the floral depths of iris, rose and peony swirled with almond, musk and raspberry. Different? You bet, but so cleverly harmonised you're never aware of any single ingredient standing out from the others. It's designed with the superb balance and artful elegance of a Ferragamo shoe — everything has its place in the overall grand design. That's why Cancers will like its seamless beauty and subtlety and Leos will go for its sensual glamour.

The Cancer male: bring him out of his shell

You may have noticed that Cancer men like to stick around the house. Sometimes they practically disappear into it. They have very hard-to-break habits which might include wearing old slippers past their use-by date, smoking pipes and grunting from the depths of a battered chair where they're immersed in a book or magazine. They tend not to respond readily to anything except a call to the dining table. Not noted either for their love of the outdoors, except in the garden, they tend to be sporting only if watching it in comfort. They are, however, lovable creatures — faithful, reliable and ever-helpful. They have a liking for water in general but are not intrepid sailors or white-water rafters unless pushed. Push is sometimes the operative word for them when it comes to grooming, so the gift of a manly fragrance will be appreciated, since they won't buy it themselves. Don't give them anything too trendy or highly charged with sexual overtones. Go for the more sophisticated but not too heavy numbers —

comfortable, refined, but with a little eccentric quirk that will fascinate them. After all, they are a little eccentric, aren't they?

- **Monsieur de Givenchy**
  Pronunciation: muh-SEE-yer duh zjhiv-ON-she
  Type: fruity/musky
- **Antaeus** by Chanel
  Pronunciation: an-TAY-us/shar-NEL
  Type: woody
- **Versus** by Gianni Versace
  Pronunciation: VER-sez/gee-ARN-ee vair-SAR-chee
  Type: fruity/spicy
- **Booster** by Lacoste
  Pronunciation: BOOS-tuh/lar-COST
  Type: green/herbal

Monsieur de Givenchy

There's nothing particularly eccentric about this masculine classic but its individuality will appeal to him instead. It doesn't follow the usual themes of male fragrances, which tend to go either for citrusy, fruity smells or woody, herby ones with soapy overtones. Coming from Givenchy you'd expect something elegantly different and far from the norm, and that's what you get. **Monsieur de Givenchy** is a super-suave charmer that comes on fairly strong and stays that way for quite a while, so if he gets a bit too lavish with it, for heaven's sake tell him or he'll wonder why people take a step back when he's around. Just a little is just the trick with this musky, lavender-laced smoothie. It has a citrus note of bergamot to give it its opening glow, a twist of lemon, a dash of sweet verbena and plenty of pungent lavender. Then musk makes its presence felt and creates a sort of olfactory osmosis to the composition. (If he shies away from the thought of wearing musk, tell him this is *French* musk and therefore very well, you-know-what — that ought to win him over!) He'll tend to use **Monsieur de Givenchy** for special occasions, and wisely so. It's very sophisticated and classy, but a bit too passionate for the office. You don't want him being charged with fragrance harassment, do you?

Antaeus

Tell him the legend behind this fragrance and surprising things could happen. In Greek mythology, Antaeus was a giant, the son of the sea god Poseidon and earth goddess Gaea. Anyone travelling through his territory had to wrestle with him. His secret strength was renewed each time he touched his mother (Earth) so if he was thrown to the ground he became invincible. (I won't tell you how he died!) Be that as it may, **Antaeus** is a pretty powerful interpretation from Chanel, full of rich sandalwood, cedarwood, clary sage (a minty herb), labdanum (a resin with a leathery smell), sensual patchouli and sweet myrtle. He'll like the heroic and classic implications of **Antaeus**, but don't tell his mother the legend!

Versus

Young Cancerians will think this is a bit of a rage, which doesn't mean it's outrageous, which it isn't. **Versus** is different but not threatening to a Cancerian's inbuilt conservatism, but it has plenty of vivacity and impact. It's a terrific mix of exotic things like papaya, nutmeg and tobacco leaf with high notes of sparkling citrus oils, the soft sensuality of jasmine and a sunset glow of amber. He might even think he's in Bali with the verve of **Versus**. Of course it's typical Versace — uninhibited and up-front, which might be a good way to get him mobile and in amongst the action (where he'll probably instantly find another Cancerian to marry and mother him)! Anyway there's Versace's **Versus Donna** for her, which has the same youthful dash and dazzle of **Versus**. They'll make a lovely couple!

Booster

In case you (or he) doesn't know, Rene Lacoste was a French tennis champ in the 1930s when he invented his famous shirt and put his nickname symbol of *le crocodile* on it to show it was like no other. Lacoste is an even more formidable name today and its crocodile signature is not only highly respected but jealously guarded from imitations. I don't think anyone will dare to knock off **Booster** — it's far too individual with its exhilarating clout of peppermint, basil, menthol, eucalyptol, citrus, tarragon, nutmeg, hot chilli and vetiver over a tangy green galbanum base. Okay, I guess it's mainly meant for sporting jocks, but a few short sharp bursts of **Booster** will make Cancerian couch champs feel like they're right in there amongst the action. **Booster**'s like a whack in the slats with a hockey stick, but much less injurious. It will not only appeal to his sense of eccentricity but make him think he's lifting his game to give his Personal Best.

Who suits what, and when: getting the best out of your perfumes

Because perfumes become not only extensions of your personality but also give emphasis to the way you look and the mood you're in, naturally, to bring out their best, they should be treated with due understanding in regard to their characteristics and qualities. They too have limitations and strengths, just as we all have. So, the following table outlines when best to wear them (Day, Night), the age-group most suited to them (Young, Mature), the general complexion of the wearer (Fair, Dark), and the seasons they bloom best in (Spring/Summer – S/S, or Autumn/Winter – A/W). This table is meant only to be used as an approximate guide or reference point – it is not a hard and fast set of rules by any means.

Perfume	Day	Night	Young	Mature	Fair	Dark	S/S	A/W
Romeo Gigli	•	•	•		•	•	•	
Amarige	•	•		•	•	•	•	
Boucheron		•		•	•	•	•	
Diorissimo	•		•		•		•	
Cabochard		•		•	•			
White Linen	•		•	•	•	•	•	

YOUR SECRET WEAPONS

Perfume	Day	Night	Young	Mature	Fair	Dark	S/S	A/W
Volupté		•		•	•	•		
Venezia	•	•		•		•		
Tea Rose	•	•	•	•	•	•	•	
Chamade	•	•		•	•			
Y	•	•		•	•	•	•	
Opium		•	•		•	•	•	

CANCER/LEO CUSPS

Perfume	Day	Night	Young	Mature	Fair	Dark	S/S	A/W
Chloé	•	•	•	•	•	•		
Theorema	•	•		•	•	•	•	
Dazzling Silver	•	•	•		•			
Salvatore Ferragamo	•			•	•		•	

GEMINI/CANCER CUSPS

Perfume	Day	Night	Young	Mature	Fair	Dark	S/S	A/W
L'Air du Temps	•	•	•		•			
Beautiful	•	•	•		•	•		
Stephanotis	•	•	•		•	•		
So de la Renta	•	•	•		•	•	•	

MEN'S FRAGRANCES

Perfume	Day	Night	Young	Mature	Fair	Dark	S/S	A/W
Monsieur de Givenchy		•		•		•		
Antaeus	•			•		•	•	
Versus	•	•		•		•	•	
Booster	•			•	•	•	•	

Leo

The lion
July 23–August 22

You and the throne

I don't know whether you should be told this, since Leos like to think they know things long before anyone else, but when you walk into a room it lights up! I don't know either if this incandescence comes naturally to you, or if you have to rehearse your illuminating talent before making your entrance. But it doesn't matter — Leo people, especially women, seem to glow with sunny radiance and *bon esprit* and thus are the envy of us all.

That's the good bit. The not-so-good is sometimes intense light can become blinding and you either overstay your welcome or, more in the case of Leo males, your light source suddenly snuffs it and the lion is left out of puff (or even asleep), which is an embarrassment they can live without. Loss of face or pride is a terrible blow to Leos.

But your virtues outweigh your faults as long as you're careful with your tongue (which usually means be careful of alcohol). Leos are naturally loquacious but if the hard stuff hits them they can become utter bores. Otherwise you make wonderful company, fabulous hosts who will make sure everything is ticking over perfectly, and are very witty to the point of being side-splitting. That's why Leos are always so welcome.

So what's this throne bit, you may ask? Well, it's the one you make a beeline for. You're convinced you were born to sit on it, and once you do, you rule like the regal creature you are. This rule can either be relentless and determined until you get exactly your own way in things, or it can be autocratic and bossy. A lot of people you wouldn't suspect call you 'She Who Must Be Obeyed' behind your back, and you do have a tendency to over-ride all other opinions and order people around like minions (even if you're not aware of it). But you mean well. There is not a nasty bone in your body. You are kindness and generosity personified — and honest.

The Leo woman is an ideal parent, fussing over her

cubs and making sure they are provided with everything they need (not want), and she is an ideal companion, be it wife or soul-mate, with her intense loyalty and willingness to make sacrifices. She is fearless and courageous, a bulwark, as long as she is not crossed. A crossed Leo is not a pretty sight. And dangerous as well. People usually end up going along with you, even if it is reluctantly and not necessarily sincere. It's because your anger or threats scare them, so they take the easy way out and give in to you. This is, of course, precisely what you had in mind. But it's also where the throne may start to wobble. A false sense of power leads to mistakes and grandiose ones at that, since a Leo never does anything by halves. You must watch yourself for signs of reckless over-indulgence — your own decisions are not always right and you should (in your own off-handed way) seek the advice of those who might have more experience than you and possibly even better taste. Leo taste can sometimes be a bit overwhelming — too much of too many expensive things — and this is where you falter. Try to be a bit humble (remember, all *really* regal people have humility) and listen to others who may know better than you. It won't kill you! It might save you from those stabbings in the back you will eventually feel.

Leos have a tendency to want to underline things, to make certain people know they are the ones ruling the roost — as if we could fail to notice! You surround yourself with splendour, the more extravagant the better. It's your fear that people might be missing the point, which of course is almost impossible. If you're not Queen of the Castle you tend to get sulky and growl a lot. This only reveals a chink in the royal armour — and a glimpse of your true feelings of insecurity — and must be covered up at all times. You don't have an inferiority complex, but sometimes even you may have second thoughts about your invincibility, so you get tetchy. The way out of this is to go somewhere private (like under a nice shady tree?) and lick your wounds. Only Leos can cure themselves — they hate people seeing them less than perfect. And there's nothing wrong with that. Soon you'll be prowling your jungle again, benevolent and proud.

But remember, there's always some pretender waiting to kick you off the throne while you're not looking, so make sure you choose your courtiers carefully — your craving for flattery can sometimes blind you to the insincerity of lesser individuals. So, when you enter that room and light it up (and everyone in it) keep a wary eye open. Not all people are as genuinely open-hearted and trusting as you are. Beware smiling hyenas!

Leo style

The phrase 'dress to kill' might have been coined for you. The personal presentation of yourself is deadly serious. You are not vain, but you spend whatever time and effort is necessary to make the big impression. You are meticulous, will try all sorts of combinations (even unlikely or unorthodox ones) until you get things looking just right. The thought of not looking your best is anathema to you — is this another interpretation of 'pride of lions'? You dream of, not covet, opulence, luxury and extravagance on a large scale. And if you can't actually have it, you'll strive to find its affordable equivalent. Nothing but the best, even if it isn't. At least it will look as if you've made an effort!

Your colours are gold and silver, red and black, purple and royal blue. Pastels don't do much for you. You will take accessorising to excess unless a restraining hand convinces you not to wear everything you own all at once. It's your love of flamboyance, of sweeping, dramatic ideas that dictates your taste — all you have to do is refine it somewhat. Once you're shown how, you do it with ease and aplomb — but there will always be a hint of the grand gesture lurking amongst the understatement. Naturally, your home is your castle and will always look stunning and immaculate (you are fanatically tidy), and since you treat everywhere else as if it were your castle anyway, you expect the same of others — if only out of deference to you (people who don't make an effort make you very angry).

When it comes to a complete understanding of

how to make the most of your best features you might tend to overemphasise, so a little (not a lot) of restraint is helpful. And that goes for your perfumes as well. Strangely enough you do not always choose what's best for you. You get sidetracked and fall in love with fabulous packaging, glitteringly different bottles and important names and all too easily dismiss things you might regard as pedestrian or even common! You often buy a perfume that is far too sexy for you. Leos are very sensual, even unrestrained, but they are not overtly seductive, so neither should they try to smell like vamps instead of the proud but incurable romantics they really are underneath their immaculately combed and coiffed manes. A purr is better than a roar.

Your outer expression is *openness*. **Your inner core is** *restlessness*.

Here's how to translate all of that into the best perfumes for you.

I have divided these perfumes into two sections:

1. *The big guns* — these are the all-important perfumes that should suit you best. They form the core of your perfume arsenal.

2. *Your secret weapons* — these augment the basics and are more daring and unusual, but should still suit you.

There is also a choice of perfumes for those of you born on the cusp of Leo/Virgo, as well as a selection of men's fragrances suitable to give the Leo male. (If you were born on the cusp of Cancer/Leo see pages 167–171 for your further perfume choices.) I have given each perfume a category and a simple, easy guide to its correct pronunciation. At the end of the chapter I have summated all of the perfumes into a table that tells you whether they're best on young or mature women, in warm or cool weather, day or evening, for dark or fair complexions.

The big guns: the indispensable basics

As I've more or less said without being too blunt, you tend to need a lot of guidance in the choice of perfumes that not only complement your personality but add to and emphasise its obvious qualities — which are your brightness, your flamboyance, your taste for luxury and your need to stand out (or even above). Taking guidance is not one of your obvious traits, which makes you even more vulnerable to making wrong decisions. You would never admit to making a mistake, so you just have to live with it even though you know it's just not quite you! So it's up to you — seek guidance on the quiet, or ask an experienced salesperson, even though this may be a bit beneath you — with a bit of luck she may even be a Leo! Or else do it by very expensive trial and error.

But I can make it easier for you by saying that voluptuously sexy perfumes are too obvious for you, and so are sweet romantic flutters. Outdoorsy perfumes don't go with your sophistication either, so it's best to stick to grand, elegant classics or multi-florals with a fascinating hint of spiciness — which doesn't necessarily mean the orientals. Don't be swayed by the look or name of a perfume — some of the less known ones have plenty going for them. And don't ever think a perfume can turn you into something you are not. People love you just the way you are, not the way you might like to fantasise about yourself. They look up to you, but, like royalty, you are open to scrutiny as well as admiration. So whatever perfumes you choose must be impressive but not at odds with your image. My choices are:

- **Coco** by Chanel
  Pronunciation: KO-ko/shar-NEL
  Type: floral/oriental
- **Knowing** by Estée Lauder
  Pronunciation: ESS-tay LOR-duh
  Type: floral/green
- **Gio** by Giorgio Armani
  Pronunciation: JO/JAW-gee-o ar-MAR-nee
  Type: floral/fruity
- **Donna Karan New York** by Donna Karan
  Pronunciation: DONNA KAIR-run or DONNA kuh-RAN
  Type: floral/woody

- **Dolce Vita** by Christian Dior
  Pronunciation: DOLL-chay VEE-tuh/KRIST-ee-an
  dee-OR
  Type: floral/fruity
- **Panthère** by Cartier
  Pronunciation: parn-TAIR/KART-ee-air
  Type: floral/spicy

Coco — because it prowls

Only Mademoiselle Chanel's most intimate friends called her Coco, so it's appropriate that the perfume named after her *sobriquet* will develop a very personal intimacy with the person who wears it correctly. She must be intense, passionate but sophisticated — a purrer, not a snarler. So if you're like that, **Coco** will intensify those traits with its permeating tenacity. It's a perfume with a pedigree and expects to be treated as such, so to wear it with less than your best is almost criminal. It might attach itself to you, but will not become a mysteriously disturbing part of you.

Coco has a warm and chocolaty smell, and there is some thought that a form of chocolate has gone into its very complex formula. On the other hand this could be due to the presence of benzoin, which is a rich vanilla/chocolate-smelling resin from Vietnam. The other dynamic note in its otherwise floral and ambery composition is the burnished, smoky smell of leather. These two highly distinctive and fascinating notes pulsate and throb under a beautiful bouquet of

Comoros Island orange blossom, Caribbean cascarilla (a sweet bark), Bulgarian rose, Indian jasmine, Javanese frangipani and mimosa from Provence. The spicy counterpoint of coriander, clove bud and angelica are then suffused with amber, sandalwood and overlaid with the velvety ripeness of peach — a mesmerising harmony that is slightly sweet, slightly woody, slightly spicy — and deeply mysterious.

Coco is dramatic and sensuous without being deliberately seductive. If it achieves any seductive victory it will be through the elegant *chic* with which you wear it. It is sinuous and insidious — very feline and feminine but never ferocious. It prowls around, staking out its territory and waits for those brave enough to approach. **Coco** will unflinchingly stand its ground with its haughty dignity. If it likes what it sees, it purrs.

KNOWING — *because it's super-smart*

The unique ingredient in the formula of this brilliant, showy perfume is none other than that sweetly hypnotic summer-night fragrance of pittosporum, here used in a dilution that won't knock you senseless to the ground! Wisely, it's been surrounded by less feral flowers such as jasmine, tuberose, ylang ylang, mimosa and rose, plus bay leaf, patchouli, amber and sandalwood. Lush, fruity notes of melon and plum deepen the message to something approaching seductiveness of the street-smart variety. **Knowing** is a very urbane temptress.

It has a brittle exterior — very New Yorkish — but if you're the right person to wear it, it will reveal its not-so-hard heart. It needs very tailored dressing of the boardroom or smart lunch variety to blossom with the right mix of sophistication and *panache*. It's uncompromising, edgy and flashy and has enormous self-confidence. In the evening, it can easily cope with glamour and glitz, but it's a very strong potion so don't overdo it. It has a habit of sticking to you with claws drawn.

Knowing is a good Leo-lady perfume as long as the action's witty and indoors. It does not take too well to the casualness of *al fresco* adventure. It's out to kill, or at least to score points on the board. **Knowing** is the sort of candid perfume you'll know immediately if you like or loathe. It will affect those within its orbit in much the same way.

GIO — *because it's the essence of Armani*

I don't quite know why this brilliant and haunting perfume hasn't achieved the success it richly deserves. Distribution may be the main factor (you'll more than likely have to go to perfume boutiques to find it), and if this is so, then it's a shame such a fabulously warm and bright perfume should be treated in such a cavalier fashion. It is one of my favourite perfumes and I think on Leo women (especially outgoing but sophisticated ones) it's a knockout! Much more than its older sister **Armani**, **Gio** epitomises the genius of its creator. It aligns itself perfectly with the simplified elegance, the casual daring and clean-lined classicism of his clothes. Most of all, it is generous, warm and happy. As Armani himself says of it, '**Gio** is not banal'. **Gio** comes from Armani's nickname, which should give you a clue to its intimate friendliness. It is extremely rich, very tenacious (don't overdo it) and full of *brio*. It couldn't be anything else but Italian. Its glowing fruity/flowery composition is dominated by tuberose, hyacinth and mandarin, perfectly balanced to achieve an instantaneous harmony of sweetness and light (but not of the sugary kind). There are underlying whiffs of green jasmine, gardenia, rose, ylang ylang and a lot of orange blossom to add to the al fresco headiness, plus clove, sandalwood, amber and peach to soften its vivacity — you might say that **Gio** glows!

Its ultra-simple but elegant packaging starts with a plain cardboard box with its name written in Armani's own hand. Inside is a beautiful no-frills broad-shouldered bottle with its tempting golden-amber liquid waiting to be unleashed. It's a great perfume to spray into the air and then walk into — you'll be enveloped in a halo of brilliance that is sensuous without being sexy, dazzling without being brash, and so joyous it ought to bring a big, broad smile to your face. **Gio** can lift you out of the glummest mood into the happiest in a blinding flash.

I think it's just perfect for Leos who honestly love

life (and it's very rare to find one who doesn't). It will add generously to your good-natured warmth and broad sense of humour. **Gio** is not just the quintessence of Armani, but of Italy itself. Just try resisting its bravado!

DONNA KARAN NEW YORK
— because it's svelte

Three of her favourite things, she says, are the smell of Casablanca lilies, the warmth of cashmere and the scent of suede. New York designer Donna Karan has managed not only to include the evocation of them in her first perfume, but also given it a unique and alluring *luxe* that might take you by (pleasant) surprise.

It's been a successful perfume with its beautifully curved black and gold bottle designed by her sculptor husband, and its air of casual Manhattan sophistication. But I think the most remarkable thing about **Donna Karan New York** is its haunting impression of suede and cashmere using woody, leathery ingredients to simulate them — plus the wonderful top notes of exotic Casablanca lily with the golden warmth of apricot. Under these comes a most imaginative bouquet of cassia flowers, ylang ylang, jasmine, rose and heliotrope — the latter suffusing its cherrywood sweetness into the secret ingredients that constitute the suede and cashmere accord. Amber, sandalwood, cinnamon and a hint of patchouli add a little orientalism, and the smooth, sensual and spicy harmony is complete.

Although a soft, caressing perfume, **Donna Karan New York** is quietly persistent. It has both depth and edge. It makes its presence felt but doesn't swamp its surroundings in an attempt to impress. I think Leos will be drawn to its air of *luxe* tinged with vivacity. Once it settles in on you, you might find noses sniffing the air for the source of such a pleasant and unusual scent. If you want to keep its name a secret, just say you're wearing suede underwear!

DOLCE VITA
— because you love the sweet life

Leos work hard (or at least appear to) to achieve the finer things in life. You will be the first to say what a dreadful day you've had but no one will believe you because you never show it. Being immaculate and fresh at all times is part of your nature — like cats constantly cleaning themselves. But when it comes time to enjoy, you are no slouch. Suddenly you're all vim, verve and vigour — and centrestage of course. And no other perfume can make your star shine brighter than this dazzler from Dior.

Dolce Vita is not Italian, but may as well be. It shimmers, sparkles and shines with good humour and a zest — even a lust — for life! It's hedonistic, sensual and exuberant with its barrage of magnolia blossom, white lily and roses doused in cinnamon, cardamom and clove, dried with cedar and sandalwood, and anointed with sensuous dashes of vanilla, patchouli and vetiver, before being crowned with a sunburst of luscious peach and apricot. It's like a joyous hymn to the sun, and about as uninhibited.

Dolce Vita is not so much a tribute to Fellini's bizarrely brilliant film as it is to the city that inspired it — Rome in all its sun-swamped, laughter-laden enthusiasm and generosity. One look at its brilliant yellow packaging and its fabulous-to-hold globular bottle tells you that. Which is why it is so gravitational — especially when you're recharged and ready for anything marvellous. It's like having a Roman festival in a bottle just waiting to be exposed to the sweet life, with you shining at its centre.

PANTHÈRE
— because it's stealthy

Being the proud Leo you are, I suppose you expect at least one perfume to epitomise your jungle cunning and prowess in practically anything you undertake. **Panthère** therefore sounds like it might be just the thing — especially because it was created by one of the world's great jewellers with a reputation for opulent luxury. It also helps that Cartier have been jewellers to some of the great royal families of Europe, past and present. That alone should set your regal claws ready to possess **Panthère**.

But hold on. If you imagine **Panthère** is poised to leap out from nowhere and attack its hapless victim with *femme fatale* ferocity, then think again. **Panthère** is almost the opposite. But it is as far from being a cub as it is a lethal predator. Instead, it is sleek and sophisticated, highly civilised, and far too well-mannered to snarl. It purrs, but purrs seductively.

It is based on the theme of tuberose spiked with ginger and pepper — very powerful indeed. Then an exotic host of jasmine, narcissus, gardenia, carnation, rose and heliotrope, with the inevitable jungle note of ylang ylang, bolster it with an intricacy of floral beauty that is breathtaking. The usual underpinnings of woods and mosses are there throbbing like tom-toms in the background, and over everything comes the wildness of blackcurrant bud, coriander, and the deliciousness of peach and plum. But tuberose, although somewhat refined from its usual lushness, hovers hauntingly over the entire harmony. **Panthère** is a triumph of wild extravagance tamed. It's a well-bred feline, not a wildcat. **Panthère** captures by stealth, not by savagery. In its captivation, your admirers will be licking their lips, while you're licking your pretty paws.

Your secret weapons:
the surprises.

A few of these suggestions for your second line-of-attack might seem a bit too low-key for flamboyant and outspoken Leos, but they cater for what is probably an underlying trait you might not like others to know about or even face yourself. There's nothing wrong with being restless, impatient or bored, but it does become tiresome when these very un-Leo things nag at you. So, rather than get yourself all het up and grumpy, make the best of it by calming yourself down. Surprisingly, perfume can be a great help. Think of the beneficial delights of aromatherapy for instance. Well, perfumes, being far more complex and lasting, go one better at soothing and assuaging ruffled manes and tetchy claws. They are far more personal and intimate, and if appreciated for their worth can be a welcome change (maybe even a welcome relief) from your up-front arsenal of brilliant fireworks. Not one of them is remotely wimpish or ephemeral. Each one stands firmly on its feet and makes it own statement quite emphatically — it's just that they're perfumes that might not have occurred to you to try because you're naturally drawn to those big beauties in the fabulous bottles. They range from the frankly romantic to the highly individual — some calmly beautiful, others highly original. But I think they'll help you cope with that side of your nature even you sometimes have trouble coming to grips with — regal restlessness. They are:

• **V'E Versace** by Gianni Versace
  Pronunciation: VAY vair-SAR-chee/gee-ARN-ee
  vair-SAR-chee

Type: floral
- **Angel** by Thierry Mugler
  Pronunciation: arn-JELL/teery MOOG-luh
  Type: fruity/oriental
- **Safari** by Ralph Lauren
  Pronunciation: saff-AR-ee/ralf lorr-EN
  Type: fruity/floral
- **Infini** by Caron
  Pronunciation: arn-farn-EE/KARR-on
  Type: floral
- **Alchimie** by Rochas
  Pronunciation: al-KIM-ee/hro-SHAR
  Type: floral/fruity
- **Quadrille** by Balenciaga
  Pronunciation: kard-REEL/bal-en-see-ARGA
  Type: floral/fruity

V'E VERSACE
— because it's a celebration of life

The very much-missed Versace is said to have once shouted '… we should have the courage to declare *Libertà del Profumo*! This expression allows us to break away from rules and regulations we set ourselves.' He was as good as his word, and promptly created this dazzling all-white floral perfume, with his shorthand signature of **V'E**. And what a fabulously exultant perfume it is.

The reason I've put it in as one of your secret weapons is that it is precisely the sort of opulent but outgoing floral you might usually baulk at — too light, too bubbly, too flowery, I can hear you say. Which is exactly the sort of role-reversal you should play now and then. Okay, **V'E** is not dramatic, couldn't be bothered making a grand entrance, and certainly is not out to do a heavy seduction scene. Let's face it, you'd be a bit boring if you were *always* onstage, which is why it's a good idea to take off the crown now and then and join the throng — you'll stand out, don't worry. And **V'E** will help you with its vivacity and heady intoxication.

It's a delicious cocktail of lily of the valley, white rose, jasmine, lily, narcissus, orange blossom and hyacinth, played over notes of zingy bergamot, Florentine iris, incense, musk and sandalwood. Stunningly contained in a modern crystal cube that isn't exactly cubic (it was inspired by Versace's inkwell), **V'E** is as sparkling, brilliant and breezy as the Mediterranean on a good day. It's a perfume to enjoy — not to trot out as a lethal Leo weapon. So bend the rules a little — be frivolous!

ANGEL — *because it's ambrosial*

Mugler, like his Parisian colleague Jean-Paul Gaultier, went back to his childhood as inspiration for his first perfume, which appeared in a fabulous star-shaped bottle of quite heavenly brilliance in 1993. It created the controversy he wanted. The shock of what was inside the innocent little star caused immediate schisms in both the perfume industry and those to whom it was offered — an unsuspecting (though rarefied) public. Nobody had smelt anything like it before, but the cries of both outrage and praise put a smile on the naughty boy's somewhat seraphic face.

Angel is composed almost entirely of things you eat. There are fruits both fresh and sun-dried, honey, dewberry, a water-growing herb called helonial, vanilla and (wait for it!) caramel and chocolate. Also present are coumarin (a vanilla-like scent derived from the tropical tonka bean and lavender) and that good old sexy standby, patchouli. Not a flower in sight!

Mugler intended **Angel** to be the harbinger of a new olfactive universe which presumably excludes any flowers or trees, but relies heavily on your salivating taste-buds to get the message to the nose. Some women adore it, while others reel back in horror from its surprisingly sweet but soft onslaught. But it has a curious calming effect — rather like sitting down and wolfing back a forbidden box of chocolates in blissful secrecy. For that reason alone, you may find it irresistible. Mugler says he called it Angel because it brings about mysterious dreams and soft imagery. The dreams are certainly sweet ones, but don't overdose on sugar-spun flights of fantasy that might be nothing more than chocolate pie in the sky.

SAFARI — because it's a change of scenery
This sun-splashed perfume from a very urbane

designer is not only an original idea but an original perfume. It's all adventure without the hardships and discomforts. It's a natural habitat for Leos but one you don't have to travel to be in. When you buy **Safari**, you buy an all-inclusive ticket to the great outdoors and take it as your only luggage.

It's an extremely civilised adventure in putting together a multiplicity of international ingredients, mostly fruits and flowers melding perfectly into a finish that is both smooth and exciting. Plum, peach, blackcurrant and raspberry notes come laden with heady orange blossom to start the journey, then joined by a plethora of rich flowers — gardenia, tuberose, magnolia, jasmine, carnation, heliotrope and lily of the valley. Then the animalic notes come on board to give **Safari** its dryness and sparkle — oakmoss, amber, sandalwood, cedarwood and tonka bean. It's a well-packed carry-all.

Lauren says of **Safari** that he sees it as a world without boundaries with the ideal **Safari** woman (that's you) yearning for adventure, romance and intrigue. In this state of mind, **Safari**, he says, gives her the impression she is surrounded by her innate need for luxury — and the experiences that stimulate her. This is publicity talking, but it's fairly spot-on. **Safari** is good-natured, outgoing and quietly self-assured. It won't make you go fearlessly into the world of danger and discomfort, but it will coax you out of your restlessness and get you going somewhere!

As a lure to your love of beautiful ornaments, **Safari** is contained in an elegant hip flask to see you perfectly equipped for your sojourn through the Great Safari of Life.

INFINI

— because its possibilities are endless

This is one you will definitely only find in perfume boutiques, unless of course you're in France. Respect and love for the Caron perfumes still flourishes there, and should here. They are all magnificent creations of striking uniqueness and beauty, and **Infini** is one of the most beautiful — even ravishing — examples of them. I remember when it first appeared (in big department stores at that!) in its fabulously asymmetrical *flacon* with a diamond-shaped cutout in its centre — immediately giving an almost surreal look into the future from an essentially classic point of view. Which just about summates what **Infini** is all about. (It's a bit of a come-down to now find it mostly available only in very straightforward, functionally simple bottles — but at least it's still with us.)

Infini is a mesmerising journey through formal gardens of roses, lily of the valley, jasmine, carnation, iris and ylang ylang to an orchard of orange blossom and peaches, attended by coriander, sandalwood, vetiver and musk. Over this goes the orange-lemon pervasion of bergamot and a touch of exotic tonka bean. This may sound like a classic French formulation, but the basic melody is then formed into a fugue by the mystery of aldehydes. What emerges is polished, assured, yet meltingly lovely (I know a woman who dotes on it to the point where she says she'd like to swim in it stark naked!). It is a very alluring, enticing perfume.

I think you'll find **Infini** a secret source of joy you won't want to reveal the name of. It has that air of being created especially for you alone with its calm, almost ethereal beauty. So, let it be your infinite secret.

ALCHIMIE— because it's modern magic

From the glorious fruity depths of **Femme** to the feminine chic of **Madame Rochas** and the lusciousness of both **Byzance** and **Tocade**, the House of Rochas has always created perfumes of stunning refinement rather than outspoken non-conformity, yet each one is a priceless jewel in itself. Now comes the precious gold in the crown — **Alchimie**.

Once upon a time alchemy was the dubious art of turning base metals into precious ones, and was the province of medieval sorcerers and magicians. Well, today the magician is the perfumer Jacques Cavallier, the man who created **Poême** for Lancôme. And what he's done with a list of ingredients, a lot of which are barely ever used in perfume, is nothing short of sorcery. What about this for an unlikely line-up for starters — lilac, cucumber, pear, mandarin, hyacinth and blackcurrant? What looks like a mish-mash actually comes together perfectly to sound out the triumphant top note of **Alchimie** — one whose sheer boldness automatically leads you further into its romantic heart notes of wisteria, jasmine, mallow flower, acacia, jasmine and a delicious surprise of fresh coconut. Even the warm and glowing base of sandal-wood, musk, amber, vanilla and a touch of tonka bean adds another clever twist with cherry pie-like helio-trope. Now, that's what I call sleight of hand, and it all works magically. **Alchimie** emerges as a magnetic and imaginative *tour de force* Leos will automatically warm to.

It's a perfume that appeals to the woman who expects luxuriousness around her but doesn't make a fuss about it. Any well-bred Leo will purr contentedly while she basks in the rich golden warmth of **Alchimie** — there's no need to bare her claws or go on the prowl — the magic of this perfume will bring it all to her very civilised den.

QUADRILLE — *because it's breathless*

You'll only find this gem now in boutiques and duty-free outlets, and even then it might be elusive. It is part of that greatest of *couturiers*, Cristobal Balenciaga's perfumed legacy, being created in 1955 as a total contrast to his enormous success with the elegant **Le Dix** in 1947. It all seems so far away now, but **Quadrille** (and **Le Dix** for that matter) has not diminished one bit in its brilliance and beauty. Like

Balenciaga's *couture*, it is blissfully timeless.

Wearing **Quadrille** is reminiscent of being at a glittering and extravagant ball, all lightness, laughter and scintillation. It was designed specifically for the younger of Balenciaga's clientele but was so captivating, their mothers took to wearing it with brave abandon. The same holds true today, so it doesn't really matter what age you are, as long as you don't feel it!

It's a giddy, entrancing harmony of greengage, peach and lemon flitting brightly over jasmine, rose, honeysuckle and Florentine iris (which has a rich, violet-woody scent), then touched with the spiciness of nutmeg and cardamom, cloves and coriander. It is then warmed with seductive whispers of amber and musk and a hint of sandalwood. The result will make you feel like dancing — elegantly, not wildly.

Quadrille is impetuous, impudent and infiltrating. It spins its feminine web of silken threads far and wide to trap the unsuspecting. Yet it is always refined (or aims to be). A dash of it will give prowling Leos a different slant on how to captivate — and charm, rather than charge!

The advantage of the cusp: taking your pick

It's not all confusion — being neither one star nor the other, or feeling you're partly both — if you were born toward the beginning of Virgo*. You can of course pick and choose from the perfumes suggested from both Leo and Virgo, but be careful. Depending on your characteristics, they may not all sit easily on you. That's why I've come up with a selection of extras that might solve any perfume problems or indecision you might have. Anyway, the choice is yours, so have fun finding out!

They are:

• **Dazzling Gold** by Estée Lauder
Type: floral/oriental

•**Sunflowers** by Elizabeth Arden
Type: fruity/floral

•**Parfum Sacré** by Caron
Pronunciation: par-FOOM suk-RAY/KARR-on
Type: floral/oriental

•**Birmane** by Van Cleef & Arpels
Type: floral/oriental

DAZZLING GOLD — because it's alluring
This is the warmer, more intimate and slightly more-grown-up half of Estée Lauder's **Dazzling** duo. It's not so much about having a good time as its **Dazzling Silver** sister — **Dazzling Gold** is more like one of those amazingly assertive supermodels

---

* *If you were born towards the very beginning of Leo you might like to check out the choices for those born on the cusp of Cancer/Leo on pages 167–171.*

striding down the catwalk, all pouts and drop-dead looks of superiority — quite intimidating, except you know it's all a put-up job carried off with tongue-in-cheek. Behind the scenes she's a sensible, down-to-earth girl with plenty of ambition and all the right ammunition to get what she wants, but in a very lady-like way. Leos are naturals at this sort of thing, and so are Virgos once they lose those silly little inhibitions that get in the way. **Dazzling Gold** is just that sort of ice-breaker — vibrant, svelte, sophisticated but never snooty or aloof. How could it be with its extravagant collage of passionflower, ambrosial fig, orchid and white lily intertwined with frangipani, amber, vanilla and sandalwood? That's a sure-fire recipe for luring the desired target well within manipulative range. It's a perfume that slinks and shimmers rather than makes waves. It's suprisingly subtle and just tenacious enough to keep its velvet tentacles caressing and not strangling. And it all looks so innocent in its fashionably minimalist sculptured glass bottle!

SUNFLOWERS — *because it shines*

Perhaps Leo ladies will never need the 'open up!' reminder that this perfume practically shouts at you, but Virgos being more reticent and discreet will. **Sunflowers** begins with an exultant shout to wake and take the day in your hands with its bright, ripe notes of honeydew melon and peach joined by jasmine, tea rose, osmanthus and the elusive but sweetly spicy scent of cyclamen. A little velvety moss, sandalwood and musk serve only to intensify the happy, splashy ambience of this innocent little charmer. **Sunflowers** is no classic, but it will give you a feeling of renewal, of pitching in to enjoy the pleasures of life lived simply and with gusto. Virgos might be unnecessarily sceptical, but Leos will rush in, not like fools but like the sun-worshippers they are. And so they should. A good time will be had by all in **Sunflowers**.

PARFUM SACRÉ
— because it's rich and rare

It is not only rare to find this rhapsodic perfume, but to know it is to love it for its rare embodiment of rich, dark roses, hallowed incense and precious spices. **Parfum Sacré** is almost like a religious experience in its intense and smouldering serenity. It is a perfume created in the Grand Manner of Caron, and is a modern hybrid of two of their past glories (**Poivre** and **Fête des Roses**) now considered too uncompromising for today's cut-and-dried, matter-of-fact market.

Parfum Sacré has a throbbing heart of roses — big velvety ones — anointed with musky myrrh and olibanum, another name for frankincense. There are also strong notes of pepper and cinnamon, with orange blossom and mimosa adding warmth to this mysterious, veiled perfume. You'll find it in good perfume boutiques and some duty-free shops — your perseverance will be rewarded. Leos will love it for its unconventionality, Virgos for its mystic beauty. A rarity like **Parfum Sacré** deserves to be loved and cherished.

BIRMANE — because it's a rare jewel

This has to be one of the most beautiful new perfumes in years! It joins **First** and **Van Cleef** in the hallowed halls of one of the world's most revered jewellers. And what an unexpected treasure it is. Named after the country once called Burma and now named Myanmar, it harks back to the great days of Burmese royalty in all its bejewelled splendour — the times when precious rubies and emeralds were treated like trinkets and opulence taken for granted. We may never see that sort of regal largesse again, but we can relive it in **Birmane**. It's been created from flowers and fruits that are anything but exotic in the eastern sense with a main accord of all-white jasmine, freesia, rose and lily tempered with ripe white peach and cumquat. The orient makes its appearance with white musk and cedarwood, with a hint of tonka bean to give it a jungle feel. **Birmane** is unashamedly opulent yet it settles on the skin as if you deserved such riches — and why not? Leos will just love its sybaritic luxury (not to mention its credentials) and Virgos will have a great time feeling terribly guilty about such wanton extravagance!

The Leo male:
gifts to get the royal nod

The difference between Leo males and females in the fragrance department is that the ladies adore to wear perfume at all times (especially to please their consort and their subjects at large) while the men tend to get embarrassed about the whole un-butch business of smelling sociable and nice and rarely can be persuaded to use them, unless bluntly blackmailed into it! You can go to no end of trouble choosing the right one for him to preen and prowl around in, but after he admires the fittingly rich and luxurious packaging — which is absolutely mandatory — he'll grunt his thanks and hope you'll forget you've given it to him. *He* will!

I have no idea why they react this way — perhaps out of some atavistic shyness, or maybe they just like to be perpetually in the natural state they were born in. But the situation is not hopeless. You can always shame or persuade Leo men into doing anything that will increase their importance in the eyes of others. They consider themselves as being very superior beings even if they're actually not. We all have to play the royal game, don't we? So, if you think you're fighting a losing battle, you could take the line of least resistance and choose the grandest and most impressive packaging without much though to what's in it (which is a needless waste of your money) or tackle the situation head on and give him a suitably subtle male fragrance that at least has a hope of being used without any fuss and nonsense. He'll never swamp himself in it anyway. Just refuse point blank to accompany him anywhere until he smells like the king, emperor, tsar, celebrity or whatever he likes to think he is. Try these very up-market selections and you might get the roar of royal approval!

- **Eau Sauvage Extrême** by Christian Dior
  Pronunciation: o sor-VARHJE ex-TRAIM/
  KRIST-ee-an dee-OR
  Type: fruity
- **Boss** by Hugo Boss
  Type: spicy/floral
- **Égoiste** by Chanel
  Pronunciation: eeg-o-EAST/shar-NEL
  Type: woody/oriental
- **Van Cleef & Arpels Pour Homme**
  Pronunciation: van KLEEF and ar-PELL poor
  OMM
  Type: oriental

Eau Sauvage Extrême

This is pulling a swiftie on him. He may even have heard jungle rumbles about the existence of this extremely popular scent (sorry, men's cologne!) that's been around for so long it must have something going for it. He has probably smelt it time and time again on other, more grooming-conscious males, and perhaps even on you! After all, there was a serious female attempt to purloin **Eau Sauvage** out of the wetpack and into the purse. That's why you should sneak up on him not with the original **Eau Sauvage** but with **Eau Sauvage Extrême** — the newer, stronger version! It's almost exactly the same formula of lavender, rosemary, petitgrain (very intense citrus notes), and oakmoss, except the **Extrême** version goes one brave step further by adding genista (a powerful, raisin-like extract from broom bushes) and cistus, which has a rich leathery smell. Anyway, if he turns his finicky nose at it, use it yourself — it's terrific!

Boss

I haven't deliberately chosen this for its name and the way he'll chuckle smugly over its aptness to himself, but it helps! Once he's got over liking the thought of being recognised personally for his leadership, he might actually get to like what he smells. If one wants to be literal about it, **Boss** does carry the leader-of-the-pack theme through with a terrifically assertive scent of earthy marigold aligned with tangy mandarin, jasmine and a garnish of strong spices and sandalwood that will carry him to the seductive arms of the Orient. And you might as well let him think he's the boss on special occasions when his ego needs to be stroked a little.

Égoiste

It sounds like you're pandering to his ego yet again, but a lots of men's fragrances have these fearless leader, king of the castle names. So let's concentrate on what **Égoiste** actually offers him. If he likes the creamy, woody smell of sandalwood he'll be halfway hooked because there's a big concentration of it here, along with coriander and cardamom. Then rich rosewood and glowing tangerine appear, along with a touch of Damascus rose and a sexy dash of vanilla. **Égoiste** is very sensual and stealthy. It's meant to pander to him of course, but you might be surprised at just how much it becomes a habit — especially if you purr kittenishly at him.

Van Cleef & Arpels Pour Homme

This is pure royal ritz and glitz on the palace prowl, and very sneaky when it comes to the big kill in the boudoir. Mind you, it's a pretty crafty beast in the concrete jungle as well — all cool elegance on its charming surface with its sunny alliance of bergamot and ylang ylang, but growling under its breath with a hotbed of patchouli, moss, tobacco leaf, forest woods and leather. **Van Cleef & Arpels** means business and it doesn't take too long for its smoulder to ignite and pounce. This time Leo really means it, and I have witnessed many a pretty, wide-eyed gazelle come to grief when this particular lethal weapon is used by the usually lethargic but often chest-thumping King of the Jungle. Mind you, if he overdoses on **Van Cleef & Arpels** he may just put himself quietly to sleep!

Who suits what, and when: getting the best out of your perfumes

Because perfumes become not only extensions of your personality but also give emphasis to the way you look and the mood you're in, naturally, to bring out their best, they should be treated with due understanding in regard to their characteristics and qualities. They too have limitations and strengths, just as we all have. So, the following table outlines when best to wear them (Day, Night), the age-group most suited to them (Young, Mature), the general complexion of the wearer (Fair, Dark), and the seasons they bloom best in (Spring/Summer – S/S, or Autumn/Winter – A/W). This table is meant only to be used as an approximate guide or reference point – it is not a hard and fast set of rules by any means.

rfume	Day	Night	Young	Mature	Fair	Dark	S/S	A/W
co		•		•		•		
owing	•	•	•	•	•	•	•	•
o	•	•	•	•	•	•	•	•
nna Karan New York	•		•	•		•	•	
lce Vita	•	•	•	•	•	•	•	
nthère		•		•	•	•		•

YOUR SECRET WEAPONS

rfume	Day	Night	Young	Mature	Fair	Dark	S/S	A/W
E Versace	•	•	•		•		•	
gel		•		•		•		•
fari	•		•	•	•	•		
ini		•	•	•		•		•
chimie	•	•		•	•	•	•	
adrille	•	•	•	•		•	•	

LEO/VIRGO CUSPS

rfume	Day	Night	Young	Mature	Fair	Dark	S/S	A/W
zzling Gold		•		•		•	•	
nflowers	•		•	•	•		•	
rfum Sacré		•		•		•		•
rmane		•		•		•		•

CANCER/LEO CUSPS

rfume	Day	Night	Young	Mature	Fair	Dark	S/S	A/W
loé	•	•	•	•	•	•		•
eorema	•	•	•	•	•	•		•
zzling Silver	•		•		•		•	
vatore								
rragamo	•	•	•	•		•		•

MEN'S FRAGRANCES

rfume	Day	Night	Young	Mature	Fair	Dark	S/S	A/W
u Sauvage trême	•		•	•		•	•	
ss	•	•	•	•	•	•	•	•
oiste		•	•	•		•		•
n Cleef & Arpels Pour Homme	•	•	•	•		•		•

Virgo

The virgin

August 23–September 22

You and the blackboard

Depending on your age, it could be 'you and the whiteboard', but the colour is immaterial. What I mean is that you are a natural-born teacher even if that's not your job. Virgos see the world as their classroom and their place in it is not only to teach but to advise and help. You are the true givers of the zodiac. You never think twice about personal sacrifice or sharing even your most private and precious possessions. This is not true, however, of your private and precious thoughts, which you consider not for public consumption or exposure. This makes you the most discreet and secretive people in the zodiac. You dislike any invasion of your territory, especially if it's uninvited (drop-ins are regarded with stern disapproval) simply because you hate being caught at less than your best — and your best beats most other people's standards hands down.

Taking this one step further, it also reveals that insecurity is a constant *bête noir* — your deepest fear — and must be disguised from discovery or scrutiny at all costs, since it's hard enough for you to cope with, and you never want to burden others with your own shortcomings. Shortcomings to you are admissions of either failure or not handling things properly to better yourself — and you are the most ardent pursuers of perfection, wisdom and truth. You will dissect yourself with merciless self-criticism to get to the bottom of your self-dissatisfaction. It's all think think, worry worry, probe probe, until you've got to the bottom of the problem and worked it out. Then, as if the shackles have been miraculously unlocked, you are free to face the world with the solution.

This is all very well for you, but it can annoy the hell out of others who find themselves shut out of your life until you've got it back on track again. You might suffer in silence, but you inadvertently make others suffer too! And then of course, from your elevated (and sometimes smug) position from on high, you begin to criticise others — mercilessly. You don't do it nastily or hurtfully, and you tell yourself it's all for the good of those concerned, but boy, do they cop it! Worst of all for them, you don't see it as anything else but helping them solve their problems, in the nicest and most constructive way. And to rub salt into the wound, you're usually right!

Poor misunderstood Virgo — it's just as well you are such beautiful people nobody likes to offend you and tell you to mind your own business. You put yourself in a cleft stick — if they don't agree with you, you lose faith in their intelligence, and if they do, you want to take it upon yourself to fix up everything for them as a big-hearted personal favour. You just don't give people room enough to move, and they're usually too polite to tell you to back off!

But all is not lost. Victory (or at least success) comes your way because of your honesty, your sincerity and the kind and compassionate way you go about actually doing things for people. You are not windbags. You are practical and realistic (a little too practical perhaps?). You find it hard to take thanks without feeling acutely embarrassed and almost shy, but inside you are flushed with the pride of success. And success means everything — it is the reward for your hard work, diligence and altruism.

Just look at your circle of friends — they adore you, and you them. To lose one would be like losing a limb! You dote on them, and you would go to the ends of the earth for them. If something awful happens and there's a fall-out or misunderstanding, you worry and fret, but you never give up hope of rectifying the situation (even though a few pithy remarks might fall from your usually discreet lips — you'll regret them later anyway). You know they'll eventually come back into your fold. It's the schoolteacher in you again — determined to get the best out of your most recalcitrant pupil!

You make wonderful mothers, even better grandmothers, and can sometimes go on to become a saint! Of course all saints suffer, but you know that's your lot in life — and anyway you always thought a halo would look good on you! Actually, there is a saintly aura about you! It might come from your fanatical attention to detail — especially in your personal appearance, which is never anything less than immaculate — or it might come from your utter devotion to whatever field you work in. This makes you envied and admired by those not quite up to your standards — I doubt if there is another sign in the zodiac that is more looked up to.

Just remember though — a black- or whiteboard can be a very instructive tool, but a harping, carping teacher in front of it is a pain in the neck! And nobody likes the cane, so be a little lenient sometimes. Not everyone can aspire to your ambitions and ideals, nor can they be so tirelessly aspirational as you. Take care that halo doesn't slip a little and end up choking you.

Virgo style

You are probably the most truly tasteful people in the zodiac. You don't divide things into 'good' or 'bad' taste. You see taste as a natural extension and expression of your recognition and respect for the finer, more creative things in life. You are usually understated, but never conventional — observant people will find you quite quirky in many ways. You add small but surprising touches to your basic love of classicism and unity — imaginative, eclectic and amusing contrasts that easily give away your love of making small things as meaningful as big statements — it's your wonderfully offbeat, quietly pixilated sense of humour speaking volumes for you.

You can be so darned creative it makes others sick. They look at your home environment and cringe with feelings of inadequacy. For instance, if invited to one of your legendary dinner parties, they'll be greeted by a vision of ordered, unflustered beauty (you) looking (and smelling) stunning, then walk into your living room and be flattened by what you've done to it (wonderful flowers wonderfully arranged), and when ushered to the table, they'll be falling over themselves burbling compliments about the fabulous setting and almost speechless as the procession of amazingly imaginative and perfect food arrives. You've done it again, Virgo, and manage to look as if it's nothing, even though that sensitive stomach of yours is fluttering with butterflies and you're terrified you've forgotten some tiny detail you're convinced will wreck the whole effect! Of course you'd be the only one to notice it if you had.

But if your friends looked deeper into all this seemingly effortless display of perfection they'd see another side of you. (Don't panic, it rarely happens!) What is in there is someone else screaming to get out. They might get clues from the way you dress neatly but in colours that almost tip over the edge into flamboyancy. Being an earth sign, Virgos gravitate towards rich reds, copper colours, oranges, gold, but most of all blues. The use of blue is almost biblical to you — the more vibrant and intense the better, which is why you usually also have a passion for purple. You are not a pastel person. But it's how you use these favoured colours — in striking contrasts, almost wildly — that more incisive people will realise the inhibition that lies within you. It can be so strong it almost blinds you — hence your reputation for extreme order and primness. The fact is that underneath all the cool, calm, collected exterior lurks a creature so passionate and unorthodox it frightens the daylights out of you. This is why when, more by circumstance than design, you let yourself go, you shock everyone in sight! All your inhibitions, self-discipline and practicality go flying out the window. This is the Virgo that wants to wipe all those rules and regulations off the blackboard and with a big sweeping scrawl write something wickedly whacky! A breakthrough at last! Of course it won't last long and you'll soon be back to your lovely, angelic self, but at least you've damned well done it! The tongues and telephones of your friends will be in a frenzy for days, and they'll never look at you the same way again. At least you've taught them not to underestimate your powers of suddenly doing the unexpected, unconventional — even wild — thing.

The same goes for your perfumes. You choose the loveliest and most flattering with painstaking evaluation (indeed, sometimes you go nearly mental trying to make up your mind!), that might drive both the salesperson and you up the wall, when all the time you desperately want to buy the most unlikely ones — the rebels, the renegades, the grand seductresses. You should. It's all very well to conform and be admired for your exquisite taste, but it can also lead people to pigeon-holing you into the box marked 'nice', when all the time you'd rather not be in a box at all but flying about free as a bird of paradise in some magical and dangerous jungle. Your wings aren't really clipped. Spread them and take off. You might never come down to earth ever again!

Your outer expression is *altruism*. Your inner core is *wildness*.

Here's how to translate all of that into the best perfumes for you.

I have divided these perfumes into two categories:

1. *The big guns* — these are the all-important perfumes that should suit you best. They form the core of your perfume arsenal.

2. *Your secret weapons* — these augment the basics and are more daring and unusual, but should still suit you.

There is also a choice of perfumes for those of you born on the cusp of Virgo/Libra, as well as a selection of men's fragrances suitable to give the Virgo male. (If you were born on the cusp of Leo/Virgo see pages 201–205 for your further perfume choices.) I have given each perfume a category as well as a simple and easy guide to its correct pronunciation. At the end of the chapter I have summated all of the perfumes into a table that tells you whether they're best on young or mature women, in warm or cool weather, day or evening, for dark or fair complexions.

The big guns:
the indispensable basics

Just because you might finally come to realise that you're not as conservative and predictable as you think, you might not be comfortable or game enough to really kick over the traces and go for really radical perfumes. Not every day anyway — it would be tiresome if you did. You feel you must maintain that cultivated charm and coolness, that sleek and smooth *savoir faire* people indelibly associate with you. The perfumes that extend and emphasise your ordered personality can be very individual without being the least bit safe and predictable. In fact, the ones I've chosen as your up-front arsenal are very striking and singular — some of the greatest and most dynamic perfumes available! Each one is a knockout for its ability to flatter yet move with your air of graciousness and elevate you to elegant heights. The thing they have in common is their classicism, but a classicism overlaid with unexpected flashes of daring to make them rare but unconventionally refined — like you, beautiful but enigmatic. Here are my choices:

- **Mitsouko** by Guerlain
  Pronunciation: mit–SOO-ko/gair–LARN
  Type: green/oriental
- **Arpège** by Lanvin
  Pronunciation: ar–PAI-zjhe (as in 'beige')/lon–VAN
  Type: floral/fruity
- **Amazone** by Hermès
  Pronunciation: AMMA-zone/air–MAZE
  Type: floral/fruity
- **Parfum d'Hermès** by Hermès
  Pronunciation: par–FOOM dare–MAZE/
  air–MAZE
  Type: floral/oriental
- **Sublime** by Jean Patou
  Pronunciation: soo–BLEEM/zjharn PART-oo

Type: floral/fruity
* **Nahema** by Guerlain
  Pronunciation: nar-HEEM-uh/gair-LARN
  Type: oriental

MITSOUKO — because it's peace on earth

Lucky Virgo! A lot of other signs would give their eye teeth to have this cool beauty as theirs, but it really belongs most of all to gentle, unpushy Virgos who nevertheless want to make their mark with an intense expression of their love of beauty. **Mitsouko** is a great and grand classic in its own quietly persuasive way. Jacques Guerlain created it in 1919 as a salve to alleviate the dreadful upheaval and tragedy of World War One and as an expression of oriental serenity and peace. The colours, clothes and artefacts of the Far East, especially Japan, were then the height of fashion (they represented the complete antithesis of European decadence) and **Mitsouko**, with its almost inscrutable bewitchment and its extraordinary other-worldliness, became a raging success.

Mitsouko, which in Japanese means 'mystery', is so haunting it almost defies description. It was the first in a line of great green perfumes, yet its main note is peach blended with soft lilac. But then a gentle green wave of *chypre* notes washes over this loveliness — bergamot, oakmoss, vetiver, *fougère* (fern) — followed by jasmine, ylang ylang, amber and patchouli. The final accord is then emphasised with the blush of more peach. It is also refined with what has now become the Guerlain trademark of 'Guerlainade' — the secret house formula at the base of their perfumes that gives each one its indefinable but unmistakable individuality.

Mitsouko's initial popularity was further heightened by a French novel called *La Bataille*, which told the sadly romantic tale of an ill-fated love affair between an English naval officer and the entrancingly beautiful wife of a Japanese ship's commander. Her name was, of course, **Mitsouko**, and thus the perfume was enshrined as a memorial to their love. Rather like the love story of *Madame Butterfly*, the embodiment of this doomed oriental/occidental liaison lives on in **Mitsouko**. Virgos are not usually romantic in an overt or sentimental way, but are pushovers for the discreet subtlety of idealised love. I think you'll treasure the understated yearnings of **Mitsouko**'s mesmerising message, and might even find yourself feeling quite uncharacteristically vulnerable to the gently sensual stirrings of this spellbinding perfume — if you already haven't.

ARPÈGE — *because it's rhapsodic*

If ever there was proof that tampering with a classic is not only irreverent but disastrous, **Arpège** is it! Created in 1927, it became an instantaneous success with women of taste and refinement. Everything about it was adored — from its evocatively musical name suggested by Jeanne Lanvin's daughter Marie-Blanche, to its dramatically feminine round black opaque glass bottle with gold embossing, and its fabulous formula of extravagant flowers married to fruit and deepened with patchouli. Alas, in 1993, the powers-that-be that came into possession of **Arpège** after Madame Lanvin passed on, inevitably wanted to 'modernise' it to appeal to a younger, mainly American, market. Not only did the black orb bottle disappear to be replaced with a truly ugly asymmetrical outrage, but the scent's formula was changed from a classic romantic to something so zingy and zappy it smelt more like flyspray than perfume! Faithful **Arpège** devotees complained bitterly. They would, of course, have nothing to do with this fabricated and artificial upstart, and stayed away from it in droves. The whole pointless exercise was doomed to deserved failure, and pretty soon **Arpège** magically reappeared in its original form and presentation. Millions of women breathed a sigh of relief, and **Arpège** not only recaptured its former market but was discovered by a new generation of young sophisticates. Of course it will never be a perfume for the very young, but those burgeoning into womanhood, especially uncompromising Virgos with a love of the classically daring, should be drawn to its many surprising delights.

Arpège begins with the time-honoured accord of roses and jasmine, but veers away from this traditional path with dashing notes of orange blossom and bergamot, peach, patchouli and lily of the valley firmly based on sandalwood, musk and vetiver all interlaced with fascinating but elusive aldehydes to form a bouquet so synergised it is impossible to identify one over-riding influence. Like the fabulously thrilling, rapid succession of musical notes it is named after, **Arpège** goes trilling and soaring off into its own ecstatic rhapsody.

It's a perfume to be trusted and treasured for its prowess and power to create around you an aura of sensuous elegance. It stirs your emotions yet gives very little of your intentions away, except your air of waiting to be approached. Your response may be guarded or deliberately enigmatic, but eventually the warmth and radiance of this wonderful perfume will find you with your guard down. You're on your own then!

AMAZONE — *because it beckons you on*

Sometimes Virgos need to be prodded into another, less familiar direction. You know the feeling — you feel as if your dogged dedication to teaching or advising other people leaves you no avenue of your own to explore. You might feel guilty about abandoning a cause to indulge or pamper yourself, but eventually you feel so trapped and frustrated, a complete change of course is prescribed. And this fascinating perfume is your release. **Amazone** is a ticket to an earthly paradise.

I'm pleased to say it has nothing to do with those single-breasted warrior women of ancient times. It has much more to do with the great and leisurely river. It is a perfume that captivates you then meanders its own spectacular but wayward way to an eventual delta of untold possibilities and far horizons. **Amazone** is not so much an adventure, but a catharsis!

Your exotic journey begins with a cargo of fruits — the most dominant being blackcurrant bud, which becomes the travelling theme, plus orange, lemon, bergamot, tangerine, grapefruit, peach, raspberry and strawberry garlanded with green galbanum, before a floral barrage of hyacinth, lily of the valley, narcissus and jasmine comes on board. To give even more weight to this glorious collage, there's ylang ylang, oakmoss, vetiver and orange blossom softened with cedar and sandalwood. What a privileged passenger you are to be wafted along in all this Amazonian opulence!

Amazone will be a departure for most Virgos. It's usually available at perfume boutiques, duty-free outlets and exclusive Hermès boutiques, but is such an exclusive and first-class ticket to a well-deserved freedom, you'd be mad not to immediately embark on its wildly unpredictable journey.

PARFUM D'HERMÈS
— because it's beautifully bred

More than any other perfume, this one defines your acute sense and appreciation of heritage and pedigree. It is, more or less, the spokes-perfume for the House of Hermès and its reputation for the finest in luxury leather and silk goods, most of them with an equestrian motif. It is even encased in a stirrup-shaped ringed bottle with silver hoop strap as a stopper. And this well-bred image extends to the complex and luxurious harmonics of the highly unusual perfume itself.

Basically a sumptuous floral bouquet, **Parfum d'Hermès** has been more than passingly influenced by the mysterious and seductive Orient. The basic theme of jasmine, hyacinth, iris and rose is infiltrated by a rare ylang ylang called Nossi-be, incense, spices, myrrh and vanilla backed with the tang of bergamot and the smoulder of vetiver and amber. Sparkling aldehydes create a background of fireworks to ignite **Parfum d'Hermès** into a display of vivid but cultivated celebration.

It's not by any means a powerhouse perfume and never descends to mere showiness, but it has hidden depths that suddenly detonate into excitement and splendour. **Parfum d'Hermès** is compelling to you and magnetic to others who enter your field of attraction. But it is always slightly aloof from action that might not meet its high standards. **Parfum**

d'Hermès is a perfume for mature Virgos, not young neophytes. It knows the rules of the game and never bends them. Nor does it necessarily play to win. **Parfum d'Hermès** is the coveted prize, not the desperate-to-win competitor. Mere competition is beneath it!

SUBLIME — *because it soars*

This is another triumph from the House of Patou, created in 1993 as a lasting tribute to some of the now long-forgotten masterpieces of Patou perfumes. **Sublime** lives up to its ecstatic name, yet never tries to be as devastatingly feminine as **Joy** or as extravagantly opulent as **Patou 1000**. **Sublime** is its own world of quietly-spoken passion and delicious delights. It is a golden and glowing evocation of sunlit warmth and subtle beauty — it always reminds me of the perfumed equivalent of Grand Marnier!

Its overture is one of mystery as it draws you closer into its depths on a wave of brilliant and sparkling orchard notes of mandarin and orange accented with sultry whispers of ylang ylang and jasmine. Nuances of rose and lily of the valley, drifts of orange blossom and sandalwood float by until a glorious accord of ambery warmth gilded with shafts of sunlight creates a quietly pulsating dazzle. It all evanesces in a veil of powdery gold.

Sublime mesmerises rather than manipulates. Whether you're attracted to its dappled light and shade is entirely up to you. It makes no effort at all to seduce you, yet on a Virgo possessing wit and warmth, gentleness and enigmatic allure, **Sublime** positively shines. It is as radiant as you can be capable of, so don't think it's too reticent to be noticed. It makes its impact in softly-spoken whispers and murmurs, in trills of laughter, in cascades of eloquent cheerfulness. It unwinds you so all the frowns and furrows that too often unnecessarily cloud your attractiveness, simply evaporate to be replaced with that sunny smile and kindness you are noted for but sometimes get too frazzled to use. **Sublime** is sheer serenity.

NAHEMA — *because it's provocative*

Virgo women are a lot of fascinating things, but being provocative isn't usually one of them. Kicking over the traces, non-conforming, playing up and showing off are not your usual behaviour — even if you'd like them to be. On the other hand, you can be so strikingly individualistic, you may have dropped the safety net and are quite happy performing brilliantly without it. If that's the case, then **Nahema** is your trapeze, ready to let you fly high and not drop a spangle!

I have to warn you about two things, though. It is notoriously difficult to find. You may have to have it specially ordered in from Guerlain, but sleuthing is second-nature to you, and you'll enjoy the hunt and the success it eventually brings. The second is

Nahema is a like or loathe perfume — it polarises women, although I can't recall ever seeing a man recoil from either its onslaught or its wake! **Nahema** could very well be a heart-breaker as well as a rule-breaker.

It certainly broke new ground when Guerlain introduced it in 1979 complete with its exotic story inspired by a tale in Scheherazade's *Thousand and One Nights* about the fates of two abducted princesses. The fierce one of the two was called **Nahema** (which means 'daughter of fire') and was ruled by passion. So, what does **Nahema** the perfume feature in profusion but passionfruit! Plus the whole oriental caravan of rose, ylang ylang, jasmine, lily, benzoin, sandalwood, vanilla and vetiver, plus a hefty dose of Peruvian balsam (a warm and sweet resin). **Nahema** is nothing if not original — and sexy with it. But it's a great perfume and can do wonders for you with its penetrating and passionate wildness. You may well ask yourself — do I really need that boring old safety net anyway?

Your secret weapons: the surprises

The following six perfumes have one thing in common, and it's the thing that bedevils many a Virgo woman — the niggling thought that she might be too practical, too pedantic, too discreet, and it's slowly choking all the other intensely emotional feelings that have been submerged or controlled for far too long. So, the suggestions were chosen with one goal in mind — breakout!

It's all very well to do things by the book, but not if you disappear into the print and become a principle rather than a person. And you have to admit on those rare occasions when you let everything rip, didn't you have an impish and satisfied smile on your face — even if it was in the dark? That's precisely what you need more of to fulfil and develop your hidden qualities, and you can achieve that with ease. Go out and buy clothes that are more daring, more unconventional but still follow the rules of classicism (in other words, nothing tarty, or you'll be laughed at) and explore the infinite possibilities of perfumes that were never meant to be anything but sensational! You'll be amazed at the result. You'll not only enjoy a new freedom of expression, you'll also realise it's a great way of relaxing the sternness and inhibitions that straiten you. To hell with the black- or whiteboard, and to heck with the pupils. Start learning to enjoy yourself! Here they are:

- **Dioressence** by Christian Dior
  Pronunciation: dee-or-ESS-ense/
  KRIST-ee-an dee-OR
  Type: oriental
- **Van Cleef** by Van Cleef & Arpels
  Pronunciation: van KLEEF ar-PELL

Type: floral/fruity
- **Parfum d'été** by Kenzo
  Pronunciation: par-FOOM det-AY/KEN-zo
  Type: green/floral
- **Gardénia Passion** by Annick Goutal
  Pronunciation: gar-DEEN-ya PASH-un/ANN-ik
  goo-TARL
  Type: floral
- **Rumba** by Balenciaga
  Pronunciation: RUMM-buh/bal-en-see-ARGA
  Type: floral/oriental
- **Boudoir** by Vivienne Westwood
  Pronunciation: BOO-dwah
  Type: floral/oriental

DIORESSENCE
— *because it throws down the gauntlet*

Despite its maker's ultra-feminine reputation, this one is an out-and-out vamp. If it had been around when Mata Hari was plying her trade, she'd have been awash in it. It was not made for shy, retiring violets.

Dioressence looks starkly different from its more ladylike sisters with its swirly black and blue packaging and the deep, dark amber of its liquid. In fact it's even startlingly different from other orientals — it has far more panache than most. But you know right away you're not in for a picnic and neither is anyone within your orbit when you wear it. Just make sure you can back up its seductive intentions by being in something dramatic and daring — dirndl skirts are definitely out!

Dioressence sets its trap with top notes of pungent green geranium, clove and cinnamon laced with mysterious aldehydes, before big drifts of jasmine and patchouli add their oriental clout along with the almost-mandatory sensuality of vanilla and tuberose. But the overwhelming floral presence is carnation — spicy, rich and piquant. As you can see, there's not much sweetness and light in this powerhouse perfume.

It is very warm, sultry and penetrating — certainly not reticent about announcing its presence and intentions, but far from vulgar or blatant. With the inimitable elegance of Dior to keep things sensuously simmering and not boiling over, **Dioressence** manages to be both opulent and smouldering. It may not immediately appeal to the more pure-minded and straight-laced Virgo, but if you're adventurous and ready to change your image (even if only temporarily) from violet to vamp, **Dioressence** is your visa. And although this may all sound highly serious, it isn't really. The pedigree of Dior's name and finesse gives you the reassurance of knowing it's never sluttish or common — just a little bit sly and wicked. Any other passionate approaches are entirely up to you.

VAN CLEEF — *because it announces you*
At first you may think this blazingly brilliant perfume is just a little too much for your tastefulness. Not a bit

of it! It offers you presence and pizzazz and expects you to follow through with your own incandescence.

Van Cleef, like the fabulous jewellery institution it comes from, is grand and glorious. It recognises no competitors and holds itself far above the madding crowd.

This is a big league perfume that knows no boundaries to its adventurous allure. **Van Cleef** is not content with staying nicely in the background — it's out there pushing your personality with so much self-assurance you'll barely need to muster up your own. It literally sweeps ahead of you with a brilliant fanfare. You have no choice but to bravely follow.

It breezes in with defiant top notes of raspberry and sharp green leafy galbanum backed by orange blossom and bergamot. Then the curtain opens further to reveal the broad and heady sweep of tuberose, Bulgarian rose, jasmine and exotic caramel notes of tonka bean and creamy vanilla. This is all played at top volume, all stops out, no holds barred. You're definitely on the roller coaster and there's no going back!

But, above all the blaze and bravura, **Van Cleef** has the refined clout of richness. It was born and bred in luxury and does not appreciate being seen in anything less than the best. It's unashamedly elitist, opulent and almost outrageous. And completely irresistible. It has exactly what a lot of Virgos need — daring! (As if you already didn't know that.)

Parfum d'été
— because it is reflective

Now for something completely different. Of course not even newly liberated Virgos can go rushing around shocking (or at least surprising) people all the time with their new-found expressionism. Even your most faithful friends would get tired of that, and so will you. So it's time to sit back, unwind, contemplate and reflect on your outlook on life. **Parfum d'été** provides the atmosphere for that respite and re-appraisal of yourself.

It is one of the most serene and hypnotic of all perfumes with its seamless harmony of the fresh and lively green notes with the gentlest and most sentimental flowers, all seen from an oriental point of view. It is tender, murmuring and languid. Parfum d'été ('summer perfume') begins its poetic ode with notes of green sap and grass that seem to be growing in cascading water. On the banks of the brook are hyacinth, freesia, white narcissus and a mysterious secret flower. Soft notes of rose and jasmine glide in to be gradually surrounded by velvety oakmoss, sandalwood and violet-like hints of iris. Kenzo wanted it to express the journey of a calm summer's day from dewy dawn through noon haze and afternoon tranquillity to the nostalgic hush of dusk. With his Japanese eye for harmony and Parisian romanticism he has succeeded charmingly and unforgettably.

Parfum d'été is an idyllic unfolding of awakened

senses, subtle interplays of rhythm, and a glorious poignancy that most Virgos will recognise as the peace and quiet they need — no questions, no arguments, not even any answers. Just detached enchantment. In its beautiful frosted glass bottle resembling a leaf, **Parfum d'été** is your means of escape to another world. Just for a change, give in and take it. You may wake up a new woman.

GARDÉNIA PASSION
— because it's single-minded

Unfortunately not every retailer who should, carries the enchantingly presented and delicately formulated collection of perfumes created by the famed French parfumeuse, Annick Goutal. In France they are treated as the exquisite treasures they are. The rest of the world has been a bit slow to realise their beauty and potential, but some far-seeing exclusive perfume boutiques now stock them as very special rarities.

Gardénia Passion is one of the most adored of them. It is also one of the strongest in the collection, concentrating almost exclusively on capturing the essence of the gardenia as faithfully as possible. Gardenia has always been not only an elusive scent to concentrate in an essence and still retain the essential heady glory of the flower's perfume, it has been the downfall of many a perfumer over many years of trial and disappointment. I'm glad to say that Annick Goutal seems to have solved it most successfully.

Is it really gardenia? Is it natural or synthetic? Has there been a bit of laboratory wizardry going on to produce its miraculously faithful-to-the-flower fragrance unhindered by any other ingredient? Its creator is not saying, for obvious reasons! But it has been put around perfume circles that **Gardénia Passion** is the pure, unadulterated scent, even though doubters insist it is the result of a careful blending of tuberose and jasmine with not a gardenia in sight. Who knows? Who cares, when the resultant perfume is so sweepingly gorgeous and captivating? Even the most probing and analytical of Virgos might as well give up and give in to this ecstatic and passionate triumph. Instead of wasting all that time working out its mysteries, perhaps you should be devoting it to tracking down this marvellous and enigmatic beauty. And how nice to know it can be your personal secret.

RUMBA — because it's tempestuous

If your heart doesn't respond to the sensual and insistent rhythm of a rumba, a tango or a samba, then this fiery fandango of a perfume will do nothing but scare the living daylights out of your gentility! I'm not sure what the austere but innovative Balenciaga himself would have thought of it (it was created in 1989, long after his death) but I'm sure he would have been highly amused at its uninhibited raunchiness. **Rumba** is not for the faint-hearted or the discreet.

The first whiff of it will not just carry you away, it will scoop you up and hurl you into a frenetic and fabulous world where only passion rules. It comes on strong with dramatic sweeps of luscious, almost over-ripe mirabelle plum, peach, raspberry and orange blossom quickly joined by the sexiness of magnolia, orchid, tuberose, gardenia, jasmine, carnation and heliotrope whirled into the exotic depths of tonka bean, styrax, vanilla and musk. And lurking like shadowy partners in the background are Spanish geranium and basil. The rumba begins, but don't be at all surprised if it suddenly turns into the flashdance of a flamenco!

Rumba is not recommended for older Virgos prone to heart palpitations, or teenaged ones with no experience in wild and worldly matters. In fact, if your own emotions can't stand the sudden jolt of a perfumed electric shock, I'd avoid its dangerously dizzy dance steps and sit it out. On the other hand, Rumba does at least promise you nothing but fireworks and torrid possibilities, so if, for once, your heart can rule your head, then the dance floor is all yours. Who wants to be a wallflower anyway? Olé!

BOUDOIR — because it's lusty

Everyone in the fashion world kept wondering why The High Priestess of Eclecticism didn't have a signature perfume to go with her (admittedly unpre-dictable) collections. But despite her often-bizarre but always amusing antics Vivienne Westwood's developed a recognisable style almost in spite of herself — and it's a style that's easily translatable into a perfume. And at last she's come up with the goods, and it's a knockout!

Boudoir burst on the scene with all the oohs-and-aahs and hysterical screams of delight and derision you'd expect. And just what sort of scented outrage has she pulled on us? She hasn't. Instead of some far-out, smack-in-the-chops anti-perfume, she's come up with one so lovable you could almost call it old-fashioned — old-fashioned in the nicest possible way.

Before you even allow yourself a whiff of the stuff, take a good look at the bottle it comes in. That's about as outrageous as **Boudoir** gets. If a mish-mash of ideas and symbols can have a style, this has it. Designed by Fabrice Legros, it's a chunky glass pedestal filled with juice, gold-sealed in the classic French manner, and stoppered with a regal golden orb around which one of Saturn's rings seems to have escaped, complete with what look like wanna-be Crown Jewels, and all of it majestically topped with a glittering Maltese Cross. Easily the best bottle any English perfume ever had the luck to find itself in!

So, what's in it? Well, for starters it's the very first perfume to feature the heady, spicy-sweet scent of viburnum as its top note (achieved by the miracles of head-space technology). This clout is followed with French marigold, rose, orris (a violet-like essence), orange blossom and the tang of Indian cardamom. Then there's the usual base notes of sandalwood, patchouli and vanilla, plus another surprise — the nocturnal sweetness of tobacco flower that delivers the powerful punchline. It all sounds a touch much, and for timid creatures it probably is. But for fearless perfume buffs who like a busty, lusty seductress with open arms, **Boudoir** is very accommodating. Neither bizarre nor raunchy, it's a sweet old-fashioned thing with more than a touch of the good-natured bawd about it!

The advantage of the cusp: taking your pick

It's not all confusion — being neither one star nor the other, or feeling you're partly both — if you were born toward the beginning of Libra*. You can of course pick and choose from the perfumes suggested from both Virgo and Libra, but be careful. Depending on your characteristics, they may not all sit easily on you. That's why I've come up with a selection of extras that might solve any perfume problems or

*If you were born at the very beginning of Virgo you might like to check out the choices of those born on the cusp of Leo / Virgo on pages 201-205.

indecision you might have. Anyway, the choice is yours, so have fun finding out! They are:

- **Miss Dior** by Christian Dior
  Pronunciation: miss dee-OR/KRIST-ee-an dee-OR
  Type: floral/green
- **Hugo Boss Woman** by Hugo Boss
  Type: green/floral
- **Bellodgia** by Caron
  Pronunciation: bel-ODJ-ee-uh/KARR-on
  Type: floral/spicy
- **Le Dix** by Balenciaga
  Pronunciation: luh DEESE/bal-en-see-ARGA
  Type: floral

MISS DIOR — *because it's ageless*

It doesn't really matter whether you're young and want to smell more grown up, or mature and want to smell like many springtimes ago — this enduring beauty will do it for you with the most elegant ease. More to the point, Virgos will adore it for its style and finesse, while Librans will love it for its teasing and mischievous charm.

Miss Dior was Dior's first perfume, created just after World War Two, and it came as a feminine celebration of joy and freedom, as well as the perfume that epitomised his revolutionary New Look in fashion, with all its flair and extravagant use of materials. It was la nouvelle belle époque. Every woman fell in love with **Miss Dior**, and every man loved to smell women wearing its tantalising mix of rose, jasmine, lily of the valley and gardenia, its spicy top notes of patchouli, nutmeg, vetiver and clary sage topped with fresh green notes. Now, after all those years, it has made a new resurgence to remind devotees just how lovely it is, and to introduce its fascination and spontaneity to a new generation. All I can add is — voilà!

HUGO BOSS WOMAN
— because it infiltrates

This is a perfume that doesn't presume to automatically open doors, get you through that glass ceiling or even trap a gorgeous hunk. But it sure helps you if you have the style to understand its gentle, almost subversive tactics. **Hugo Boss Woman** belies its rather strident name — it's one of the most feminine and subtle calculators around the traps. It fills the air with cooling swathes of green papaya flowers, green apple, jasmine, white lilies and river moss, spreading its magnetism with a luminous serenity that camouflages its strategy — it's that sort of slowly-slowly-catchy-monkey type that gets results without having ever to reveal its hidden agenda. Perfect for sly or shy Virgos and for Librans who play their cards close to their chests — and isn't that all of them?

BELLODGIA
— because it's mellifluous

This delectable and haunting perfume is named after a little island in Lake Como in Northern Italy. I don't know if it still is, but the island was famous for its fields and hillsides of pink carnations with their sweet and clove-like scent. And carnation is most certainly the dominating theme in **Bellodgia** along with the romantic duo of roses and jasmine, the sweet penetration of lily of the valley and a scattering of spices to give depth and accent to its unmistakable carnation theme. It's a peaceful haven to hard-working Virgos and a feminine lever to flirtatious Librans. No other floral perfume is quite as heart-achingly and sweetly nostalgic.

LE DIX — because it's aspirational

This great classic had the unqualified approval of Balenciaga himself, since it was his first perfume and named after his revered salon at No. 10, avenue Georges V, the address of the world's most sophisticated and awesomely elegant clothes. In every way it epitomises his style, his philosophy and his supremacy in couture. Introduced in 1947, it had to compete with Dior's New Look and his new **Miss Dior**, but succeeded easily with its heady harmonies of jasmine, rose, lily of the valley and lilac pulsating warmly under bergamot, peach, lemon and coriander. Interlaced through this lovely *mélange* are murmurs of sandalwood, vetiver, tonka bean and amber fused with the modern artistry of aldehydes to give **Le Dix** its svelte and scintillating sensuousness. Yet it never stoops to either presumption or pretence. It remains highly sophisticated and discreetly beguiling. Vestal Virgos will be drawn to its hauteur, while Librans will see it as a means to cloak themselves in its sophisticated chic. Both will benefit from its patrician air of being aloofly above it all.

The Virgo male: gifts for the cut and dried

He is usually so neat, spruce and meticulous you have to curb a strong desire to throw a mud pie in his smug face. The phrase 'cutting edge' might have been invented for him. Nothing ruffles him, and nothing must spoil his aura of methodically achieved perfection. The face a Virgo male shows to the world is the result of rigid self-discipline and carefully considered effect calculated within an inch of its life to impress — the fact that it might not necessarily include good taste is neither here nor there, because whatever he chooses to appear in will undoubtedly be thought by him to be the absolute pinnacle of perfection! So now you know what you're dealing with — it isn't vanity, it's self-possession!

Fortunately he is a pushover for fragrance and will

actually use it religiously and not always sparingly either. He is one star sign that likes to alter his presentation with the appropriate male scent, so you can't just give any old smell to him. He'll turn up his cultivated nose if it's beneath him and his standards. Of course he'll have already chosen for himself what he thinks complements him (he's not after accents or surprises, he's after definition — that cutting edge again) so you'll just have to give him more of what he already has or somehow sniff out a new fragrance that will be worthy of admission to his considerable line-up of grooming aids. If that sounds daunting, it isn't. He likes types of smells that add to his aura in a crisp but sophisticated way. What he loves is clout and classicism — which means it must carry a very famous designer name!

- **Heritage** by Guerlain
  Pronunciation: air-it-ARJZHE (or HAIR -it-idge)/
  gair-LARN
  Type: herbal/oriental
- **Fahrenheit** by Christian Dior
  Pronunciation: FARRAN-hyte/KRIST-ee-an dee-OR
  Type: floral/woody
- **Tsar** by Van Cleef & Arpels
  Pronunciation: ZAR/van KLEEF and ar-PELL
  Type: spicy/floral
- **Chanel pour Monsieur** by Chanel
  Pronunciation: shar-NEL poor mers-YEER
  Type: fruity/woody

Heritage

This is what you might call a Class Act. The latest creation in the very formidable male Guerlain stable, **Heritage** is a scent to be taken seriously. It is extremely cultivated and one of the few new male scents that does not outstay its welcome with that awful clinging tenacity so common to its lesser rivals. Its effect is immediate but not rapacious, and it unfurls like a proud flag into three distinct phases until its unnoticed fade-out. It begins with a marvellous accord of lavender and bergamot, then spikes it with coriander and pepper and just a dash of vetiver, then adds exotic tonka bean and patchouli. Finally, deep velvety greens smooth it out to a refinement that is masculinely elegant but singularly individual. Lots of women will be drawn to **Heritage**, and the slightly superior male wearing it. Then it's up to you to blunt his cutting edge.

Fahrenheit

There is something remote and intensely private about this fragrance, launched with a lot of expensive hype, that seems to have worked judging by its popularity with men who consider themselves a cut above the rest, both personally and business-wise. It's a very definite and almost challenging fragrance that's quite out of the ordinary with its unique mix of hawthorn and honeysuckle giving it a very airy sweetness that is then brought down to earth with strong woody notes of cedar and sandalwood, all of which is fixed with incense-like resins that add a sense of mystery as well as giving **Fahrenheit** its famous tenacity on the skin. If he's a Virgo with very definite ideas about himself, then **Fahrenheit** will convince him he's very cool at raising female temperatures.

Tsar

He'll feel as if he's 'Puttin' on the Ritz' in this sparkling, outgoing mix of lavender and jasmine, oakmoss and sandalwood, subtle Eastern spices and the happy zing of lily of the valley. Sounds a bit flowery, but it isn't in the master hands of Van Cleef & Arpels who turn the whole thing into a dazzling, though gentlemanly brilliance he'll feel extremely confident wearing. The name might give him grand and superior ideas, but **Tsar** is no Ivan the Terrible — it's more like Ivan the Smoothie!

Chanel pour Monsieur

There is a vast legion of men professing to have impeccable taste in gentlemanly things who wear no other fragrance than this to establish and affirm their unassailable self-confidence — so you can see it's more than an option for Virgo males at the top or on the way up. Discreet, warm, refined and urbane, **Chanel pour Monsieur** is definitely not for the crass or vulgar with its haunting mix of citrus oils, orange blossom, woody cedar, soft oakmoss and lemon-spicy cardamom, topped with a brilliantly subtle *coup de grâce* of clove-scented carnation, which gives it its ultimate polish. If that doesn't impress him, having Chanel in his bathroom will.

Who suits what, and when: getting the best out of your perfumes

Because perfumes become not only extensions of your personality but also give emphasis to the way you look and the mood you're in, naturally, to bring out their best, they must be treated with due understanding in regard to their characteristics and qualities. They too have limitations and strengths, just as we all have. So, the following table outlines when best to wear them (Day, Night), the age-group most suited to them (Young, Mature), the general complexion of the wearer (Fair, Dark), and the seasons they bloom best in (Spring/Summer – S/S, or Autumn/Winter – A/W). This table is meant only to be used as an approximate guide or reference point – it is not a hard and fast set of rules by any means.

Perfume	Day	Night	Young	Mature	Fair	Dark	S/S	A/
Mitsouko	•	•		•	•	•	•	
Arpège	•	•		•	•	•	•	
Amazone	•	•	•	•	•	•	•	
Parfum d'Hermès	•	•		•	•	•	•	
Sublime	•	•	•	•	•	•	•	
Nahema		•		•		•		

YOUR SECRET WEAPONS

Perfume	Day	Night	Young	Mature	Fair	Dark	S/S	A/
Dioressence		•		•		•		
Van Cleef	•	•		•		•		
Parfum d'été	•		•		•		•	
Gardénia Passion		•	•	•	•		•	
Rumba		•	•	•			•	
Boudoir		•		•		•	•	

VIRGO/LIBRA CUSPS

Perfume	Day	Night	Young	Mature	Fair	Dark	S/S	A/
Miss Dior	•	•	•	•	•	•	•	
Hugo Boss Woman	•	•	•	•	•		•	
Bellodgia	•	•	•	•	•		•	
Le Dix	•	•		•	•		•	

LEO/VIRGO CUSPS

Perfume	Day	Night	Young	Mature	Fair	Dark	S/S	A/
Dazzling Gold		•		•	•		•	
Sunflowers	•		•		•		•	
Parfum Sacré		•		•		•		
Birmane		•		•		•		

MEN'S FRAGRANCES

Perfume	Day	Night	Young	Mature	Fair	Dark	S/S	A/
Heritage	•	•		•	•	•	•	
Fahrenheit	•	•	•	•	•	•		
Tsar		•		•	•		•	
Chanel pour Monsieur	•	•		•		•		

The Perfume Zodiac

Libra

The scales

September 23–October 22

You and the mirror

Librans, on the whole, can be a pretty lethargic lot — even to the point of indolence. Although you pretend to be fiercely independent you actually rely on other people to do things for you, especially providing your creature comforts and security. This gives you plenty of time to do what you do best — romanticise about the achievement of perfect luxury. Yours might be the star sign of harmony and diplomacy but this harmony and diplomacy is always carried out (especially by Libran women) hand in hand with your trump card — charm. This is no ordinary charm. It's the one that 'charms the birds right out of their trees' — in fact, you have so much of it you could open a Charm School and make a fortune! It's not manipulative but it comes with all the trimmings of flirtatious femininity and outright seduction. It will get you anywhere and anything you want. Of course to achieve all this you have to look your best, and Librans always make sure they look nothing short of sensational. To put it bluntly, you are more than inclined to be secretly vain, even though you might call it 'having an eye for beauty'. Which is right in a way, because that eye is never far away from a mirror.

Having said that, you are beautiful people — attractive, refined and witty with a marvellous, pixilated sense of humour, a mischievous and wandering eye and enough good taste to make others grind their teeth with envy at your cool and calm collectedness. This inevitably leads to success, and you're usually very successful once you've defined your goal and go for it. You might be a bit scatter-brained about trying this and that, but once you set your sights and pull out that famous charm of yours, there's no stopping you. And you love the material rewards of success.

Librans are very good with money, and extremely careful with it. You are not spendthrifts (except on yourself, where expense doesn't come into it at all) and although you are generous, you do not give with extravagant spontaneity. You figure the money could be spent better on improving your surroundings and, of course, yourself. Selfish? No, but very prone to self-indulgence. It's the vanity factor again.

You love art and beauty around you, and yourself at the centre of it. Of all the star signs you are usually the most well appointed and well groomed. As I said, you would never dream of setting foot out of the house unless you looked just right! You have a tremendous zest for life and your vivacity allows you to sparkle and shine while you're quietly achieving exactly what you want. You are great strategists and therefore are considered sensible, fair-minded, rational (which you're not!), clear-headed and co-operative. You are supposed to be great mediators, but I think there is a lurking sense of righteousness in your makeup which makes you able to forgive someone only after having put them through the horrors of hell. You like to discipline others but never yourself. Your compassion is exhibited in an altogether different way — you offer an understanding shoulder to cry on and plenty of advice, which you expect to be taken. You figure your point-of-view is not only wise but the only one.

But, stern as you can be, you relent when tears start to flow. You can't stand the sight of anyone crying or being unhappy and your understanding heart melts — though your mascara certainly won't!

This is why you make wonderful wives and mothers. You quietly run the house, repair bruised egos and disillusioned dreams with a success that borders on efficiency. You are absolutely adored by your family, who take your word as Law. You may not be the world's tidiest person (except with yourself) or its best cook, but you give them what they want without even thinking of yourself as a martyr. Martyrdom is not your style — it's adoration and adulation you're after!

But do people, apart from your family, take you as seriously as you wish they would? Do they value your real worth? Or are you still taken at face value? You're not certain, so it's back to the mirror again. You know you can win anything if you look your best, so naturally you flutter those pretty eyelashes and smile innocently, and it's yours for the taking. But it's all too easy — too facile. Your intrinsic longing to be wise and intellectual still hasn't been convincing. This is your dilemma and there are only two ways to solve it. One is to forget it altogether and concentrate on your wit, charm and effervescent company. In other words, romanticism is preferable to failure. So, if you're blessed with more beauty than brains, then thank your lucky stars and take advantage of it. The other is to put vaseline on the mirror and thus give people a less perfect but far more human impression of yourself. If you are highly intelligent and want to prove it, then try thinking less about your image, and more about others. You'll be amazed how self-fulfilling it can be. You might even be admitted into deep discussions and deeper relationships. So let the mirror crack — you'll still be charming, and charm doesn't need a mirror.

Libra style

As I've already said, Librans love the art of beauty. What's more you *understand* how to achieve it in practical terms. You have an unerring eye for detail as well as the overall effect. For instance, you'll stand in front of a great painting and see all the marvellous little elements that make up the whole, then stand back and judge, usually in its favour — especially if it's romantic. You go beyond liking mere prettiness right into the heart of loveliness. Your idea of beauty is a careful and imaginative assemblage to form an idealised world of artistic expression, although you never lose sight of the impact of simplicity.

You surround yourself with as much comfort and luxury as you can, and make this the backdrop to your own carefully collected image. To look serene in your own environment is vital — you picture yourself looking as beautifully arranged as the flowers you've taken so much trouble with. Flowers, books, glossy magazines, romantic music are not just props — they're part of your wish for a charmed and balanced life. They also guard against that gnawing Libran fear of being alone — you must have the things you love around you so you can attract others and avoid loneliness. You're not usually over-gregarious, but you are a thoughtful and successful hostess. You plan carefully so that everything will be harmonious, and you'll work overtime to see nothing goes amiss — after all, it would be a bad reflection on your taste and grace. Librans don't take failure too well.

When it comes to clothes, you are meticulous and will never throw anything together and hope it works. You'll work at it until it's perfect.

You love style, but you also must have comfort and fluidity of movement at all times, without sacrificing elegance. You're inclined to tear your hair out finding the right combination of comfort and style — but you always find it. This quest for harmony is reflected in the colours you like — you rarely wear one colour and find contrasts and unusual combinations far more interesting. It's your innate desire to stand out without saying 'Look at me!'. And you do stand out, especially in blues, greys, pinks and neutrals — soft colours that flatter you. In fact, it's only in bright, vibrant colours you feel uncomfortable — you'd hate to be considered even slightly vulgar.

I always think of roses when I think of Librans — those lovely old-fashioned country ones with big velvety petals and heady, sweet perfumes. Cold-blooded, scentless hothouse hybrids are not your idea of romance. This comes right into the perfumes that express your love of beauty. A Libran in anything but a full-on romantic, or at least sensual perfume smells off-key and trying too hard to be outstanding. Femininity mixed with a little mischief will get you anywhere, so why bother trying to smell like someone you aren't? Fall back on your powers of sweet, disarming seduction — you'll charm more than birds out of that tree!

Your outer expression is *romance*. Your inner core is *seriousness*.

Here's how to translate all of that into the best perfumes for you.

I have divided these perfumes into two categories:

1. *The big guns* — these are the all-important perfumes that should suit you best. They form the core of your perfume arsenal.

2. *Your secret weapons* — these augment the basics and are more daring and unusual, but should still suit you.

There is also a choice of perfumes for those of you born on the cusp of Libra/Scorpio, as well as a selection of men's fragrances suitable to give the Libran male. (If you were born on the cusp of Virgo/Libra see pages 239–242 for your further perfume choices.) I have given each perfume a category as well as a simple and easy guide to its correct pronunciation. At the end of the chapter I have summated all of the perfumes into a table that tells you whether they're best on young or mature women, in warm or cool weather, day or evening, for dark or fair complexions.

The big guns: the indispensable basics

Although I said Librans reminded me of roses, I certainly don't mean you should be enveloped in rose-dominated perfumes. But since roses are almost synonymous with ideas of romantic attraction and everlasting love, the sure-fire perfumes that will complement you are those that have a lovely, lilting and lingering quality, with or without the help of roses. I don't think very dramatic or demonstrative perfumes suit you — they go against your ability and determination to be feminine to the point of fragility at all times. Even when you want to de-emphasise your feminine elegance, there's no need to go to great lengths to smell startlingly different or even outlandish — that isn't the subtle way you go about things. Subtlety of approach and finesse are your natural attributes, and accompanied by perfumes with the same admirable qualities, can do wonders for you — they let your love of beauty blossom and shine. They don't need to be fussy or frilly, but flirtatiousness is never far away from their evocative and enchanting wiles. They are seductive but not in an obvious or blunt way. Like you, they are suggestive — suggestive of romance that could very well lead to something more serious. It could even be sexual provocation — and you, dear ladylike Libran, are not averse to that, are you? Anyway, here they are for your delectation:

- **Dolce & Gabbana** by Dolce & Gabbana
  Pronunciation: DOL-chay ay gabb-ARNA
  Type: floral/oriental
- **Cabotine** by Grès
  Pronunciation: CAB-o-teen/GREH
  Type: floral/green
- **Paris** by Yves Saint Laurent
  Pronunciation: pah-EE (or PARR-iss)/
  eve sarnlor-ON
  Type: floral
- **Organza** by Givenchy
  Pronunciation: or-GARN-zuh/zjhiv-ON-she
  Type: floral/oriental
- **24, Faubourg** by Hermès
  Pronunciation: varn-KARTRE FO-boorg/
  air MAZE
  Type: floral
- **Deci Dela** by Nina Ricci
  Pronunciation: deh-SEE deh-LA/neena REECHee
  Type: floral/fruity

DOLCE & GABBANA
— because it has savvy

It also has clout, which you'd expect from this Italian design team whose trademark is dynamism and dash. Their perfume was supposedly inspired by the likes of Loren, Mangano and Lollobrigida when they filled screens with lusciously sensual glamour before turning to more serious cinematic intentions. So was it created for the new league of lean and leggy glamour girls? Not really. It's far more sophisticated than that, although in an off-handed, carefree kind of way. Certainly not for empty-headed bimbos. In fact, I know women of quite advanced years who wear it with great aplomb and panache — and they're definitely women of taste and intelligence.

What **Dolce & Gabbana** needs is a woman who knows what she's about — cool and confident and romantic, not reckless and dizzy.

It has a complex formulation that goes through unexpected nuances from its volatile top notes of tangerine, freesia, coriander, ivy and basil through to a floral invasion of rose, carnation, lily of the valley, jasmine, orange blossom and marigold that is then plunged into oriental fleshpots of musk, tonka bean and vanilla. There's a softening with sandalwood, but by now the caper's up — **Dolce & Gabbana** has revealed itself to be a mischievous little minx! It winks and sparkles, insinuates and invites, yet knows exactly what effect it has — light-hearted and capricious seduction. It's an elegant ally for ·those witty and savvy enough to wear as an extension — not as a weapon. Men seem to drool over it and have been known to present extravagant bottles of it to their seductresses. Isn't that where you come into the picture?

CABOTINE — *because it's breathtaking*

Sorry, but if you're over the quarter-century mark, I'd advise you to give this a miss. It's strictly 'younger than springtime' territory, and good on it!

There are so few perfumes created specifically for the young end of the market — poor teenagers and coming-out twenty-one-year-olds find themselves all at sea in a plethora of super-sophisticated or deep and meaningful scents that mean nothing to them! Too young for **No. 5**, too innocent for **Poison**, too grown-up for giddy trifles like **CK One**. Cheer up — here comes **Cabotine** in its resplendent lime green bottle complete with cute matching glass bow. And it smells like heaven!

The exotic headiness of ginger lily is the launching pad. It zings and zaps, hurling you into a blissful disarray of sweet wild hyacinth, sexy ylang ylang, tangy mandarin, heady orange blossom and lots, lots more — like tuberose, rose, jasmine and coriander before the full-on exotics of cassia, green galbanum, vetiver and vanilla get a whack of ginger to ensure **Cabotine** makes its point. If it reminds you of nights in a wild tropical garden under a silvery full moon, then you've got the message.

Cabotine is described by its makers as '*un parfum presque innocent*' — almost innocent — which says it all. It's not delicate, and certainly not shy, but urges you to wear it with your most beguiling dress and most disarming smile. It adores to flirt, to be sassy and tantalising without ever smelling anything less than gorgeous! And what does **Cabotine** mean? Mischief! (Which is why you should keep it locked away from your mum — she won't be able to resist its oh-so-young magic, although she should, poor old thing!)

PARIS — *because it takes you there*

Years and years ago, François Coty created a very popular perfume called **Paris**, and although it was light-headed and coquettish, it nowhere approaches the dizzy heights of Saint Laurent's intoxicating concoction that was launched with as much celebration as Bastille Day, in 1984.

Saint Laurent wanted it not just to epitomise Paris itself but the flower most synonymous with his beloved city, the rose. Not the newly cultivated and over-sophisticated varieties — he wanted it to be reminiscent of the big, full-throated country beauties of *La Belle Époque*. No scentless, tortured mutants for him! Thus **Paris** was created as a celebration of nostalgically beautiful roses and all the romantic joy they've come to symbolise.

Paris is unmistakable. Not only is it almost overloaded with the wildly sweet and musky headiness of its old-fashioned roses, it gathers other scintillating flowers into its lush bouquet — most notably the strong and haunting scent of violet, which acts as a catalyst to send the roses into paroxysms of ecstasy and impact! Hawthorn (another YSL favourite), mimosa, orange blossom, hyacinth and even nasturtium turn up to add emphasis, but it's definitely a rose-and-violet spectacular when the fireworks clear to reveal the zing and zip, the almost drunken splendour of this irresistibly lovable Parisian beauty.

Paris is a very strong perfume, so do be your usual discreet self with its usage or it will become overbearing in its effort to radiate its reckless giddiness. It is indeed the essence of Paris in spring — and the perfect way to look at the real world through dazzling rose-coloured glasses.

ORGANZA
— because it's in the grand manner

Who would have thought the first new perfume to come from the re-structured House of Givenchy after the Master retired and the iconoclastic Alexander McQueen took charge, would be a perfume as classic as **Organza**? There is nothing remotely revolutionary or perverse about this perfume which, in fact, goes way back to the grand tradition of highly charged but feminine perfumes with a very definite point of view.

One thing must be said for **Organza** — it's not low-key! It is outspoken but tremendously elegant. I think even the discreetly non-committal Monsieur Givenchy himself may even approve of its emphatic stance.

So what is its claim to neo-classic superiority? Certainly not subtlety. At first it may seem to be rather too strange and overwhelmingly sweet, but once it settles a more enigmatic sensuousness appears. So if the top notes of intensely green leafiness full of astringent sap make a startling assault, wait until they meld into a rich garden of gardenia, tuberose and ylang ylang whose sweet opulence is then tempered with some exotic spices, the warmth of amber, the softness of cedarwood and the sexiness of vanilla, before you pass judgment. No perfume has ever carried the Givenchy name until it has achieved an elegant luxe and well-bred refinement, and **Organza** is no exception. Its dynamic beaten gold and scarlet packaging, its imperious frosted glass column that looks like an asymmetrical, tall female form topped with an arabesqued scroll is *très formidable*! This is an awesome perfume, not a pretty put-on. **Organza** is like a modern goddess — statuesque, elegant, tenacious and undeniable. It is She Who Must Be Obeyed, but put ever-so-nicely with true Libran tact and persuasion.

24, FAUBOURG
— because it's a very select address

This is a perfume that breathes good taste with a faint but tantalising suggestion of romance — alluded to, not promised. It is one of those serene and inviting perfumes that makes a fascinating impression on contact and departs with a beckoning wake.

It is named after the address of the House of Hermès in Paris, so you know immediately it carries pedigree credentials *sans pareil*. The elegance you'd expect is certainly there, but accompanied and made more approachable by a very warm and expressive friendliness. This is the result of its accord of white flowers — orange blossom, Sambac jasmine and the magical little Tahitian gardenia-like flower called tiare. To add a dash of exotic colour, what else but the sensuality of ylang ylang and the sultriness of patchouli? Breaths of amber and sandalwood, a waft of vanilla and the violet-like mystery of Florentine iris complete the perfect harmony of controlled emotion. **24, Faubourg** would never be guilty of overstatement and prefers to be vibrantly lovely rather than voluptuous.

Does this make it sound a bit dull? Well, it isn't. **24, Faubourg** sets out its own standards and adheres to them to produce something very rare in modern perfumes — a complete lack of blatherskiting pretension. Instead it has a lovely, lilting and light radiance that is quite infectious. And, to make it thoroughly memorable, that ravishing and unfamiliar smell you will detect once it settles in on your skin, is the charming tiare flower. Not very many perfumes have discovered its haunting but elusive power, but after its long journey from Tahiti, it's made itself right at home at its fashionable new address. So, I think, will you.

DECI DELA — because it's a born flirt

The charming name means 'here, there, everywhere', just like you when you're out looking for fun and flirtation — two things you enjoy immensely. Librans adore to be unfettered, liberated and on the loose (or, if you like to be more discreet — potentially available). Wear **Deci Dela** when you're out on the town and there's no telling what may eventuate! Not as romantic as its lovely sister, **L'Air du Temps**, or as madcap as **Les Belles de Ricci**, **Deci Dela** is the gadabout in the Ricci family — not rebellious but a little bit reckless. It's a scintillating cocktail of fruits and flowers thoroughly in love with each other. It kicks off deliciously with raspberry, peach, redcurrant and watermelon, then rushes headlong into fields of fresh freesia, sweet pea and that little French powerhouse of penetrating scent, *rose de mai*. But its main floral note is none other than Australian boronia, all wild and honey-sweet. Some oriental influences slink in — mainly Sumatran balsam and Cambodian agarwood, patchouli and cedarwood, plus the soft green of oakmoss. Then, to top off the concoction, a slice of ripe papaya! All that's missing is a maraschino cherry and a paper umbrella!

So that's the dizzy, devil-may-care recipe for uninhibited *joie de vivre*. **Deci Dela** is deliciously French but, like good wine, travels well. It's a perfect perfume to take on holidays — companionable and daring. It adores being introduced to perfect strangers and will burble and bubble on as long as you can. Its creator for Ricci, Jean Guichard, was told to go for broke — to come up with a completely different and audacious perfume. The owners of **Deci Dela** have been laughing all the way to the bank ever since!

Your secret weapons: the surprises

Librans love being asked to adjudicate. An internal pleasure suddenly radiates from within you in waves of satisfaction at having your intelligence called upon to make an important decision. At last your serious side has been recognised, and you can leave all that flirting and feminine frippery behind and don the cape and cap of wisdom! Suddenly you see yourself as Portia in *The Merchant of Venice* — wise, canny, learned and beautiful all at once. You can be for the defendant or the prosecution, judge and jury all at once. Your fingers itch for the gavel and the moment of ultimate truth! But you have to project an entirely different side of you — not the romantic and narcissistic, but the balanced and analytical. You doubt that you can achieve this in a fabulously floral or seductive perfume, and so you should. This calls for an almost radical change in looks and the scents that will reinforce your sober new appearance. Frills are out, and finesse is in. The perfumes I've suggested for this exercise in public relations are far from severe, though — in fact they're all very beautiful. They just happen to be a little more restrained and complex than your normal arsenal, and any one of them could be elevated to big gun status quite easily — it depends on what stage of your Libran life you've reached. And since Librans make excellent, efficient and attentive businesswomen, they are very wearable on your way up. Here they are for your learned consideration:

- **Vanderbilt** by Vanderbilt
  Pronunciation: VANDA-bilt
  Type: floral/spicy
- **Eternity** by Calvin Klein
  Type: floral
- **Blonde** by Gianni Versace
  Pronunciation: gee-ARN-ee vair-SAR-chee
  Type: floral
- **Je Reviens** by Worth
  Pronunciation: zjher rev-ee-ENN
  Type: floral/spicy
- **Nocturnes** by Caron

Pronunciation: nock-TURN/KARR-on
Type: floral
•**Magie Noire** by Lancôme
Pronunciation: mah-ZJHEE NWAH/LARN-kom
Type: woody/oriental

VANDERBILT
— because it smells rich

Since it was created under the auspices of one of America's richest heiresses, Gloria Vanderbilt, you would expect this perfume to exude the trappings of wealth and luxury. And so it does, but not quite in the flamboyant way you might expect. Like anyone seriously rich, it is at great pains to be well bred and understated. This is not the crass showiness of the *nouveau riche*, but the smell of old wealth. It's all heritage and subtlety, class and refinement. Just what you're looking for to go with that new tailored suit and cashmere coat! **Vanderbilt** will underline rather than emphasise your poise. It's a like or dislike perfume, but if you're fascinated by unspoken depths and mysterious smoulder, you'll swan through any situation with dauntless grace in **Vanderbilt** — which is fitting, since its logo image is a swan etched ever-so-nicely on the severely elegant bottle.

As to the smell itself, it's a complex accomplishment based on top notes of orange blossom, apricot, coriander, basil and bergamot, which give way to the floral depths of tuberose, jasmine, narcissus and mimosa, before being deepened even further with chocolaty benzoin, musk, vanilla, incense and some rich woods to give it an earthy edge. It's the woody, spicy notes that dominate, giving **Vanderbilt** its unique smoky sultriness.

Vanderbilt could easily become your signature fragrance if you're cultivated, reposed and given to emotional nostalgia at dusk and twilight — or wishing you were filthy, but quietly, rich. It's a very languorous and warm perfume in a quietly assured, rather snooty way. Not exactly for those born with a silver spoon in the mouth, but more for those that think they should have been!

ETERNITY — because it's neo-romantic

Apparently Calvin Klein realised in the late '80s that women's attitudes to romantic commitment had changed — not necessarily for better or worse. But the mood now seemed to be one of sobriety, commonsense and self-awareness in place of ecstatic mistakes in the love stakes. So, **Eternity** was planned with that newly-awakened woman in mind — still very feminine but not dizzy or glamorous. Just the sort of woman who'd wear his pared-down, no-frills clothes and the perfume to match!

Eternity was born in a blaze of publicity that showed a man and a woman imitating the notorious surf scene from the film *From Here to Eternity* which, after it had made mouths drop too much, was replaced by more healthy and loving couples looking ultra-trendy but oh-so-natural and apparently quite happy to be locked together forever. Women seemed to swallow this notion because they certainly lapped up **Eternity** and it has become a household name in American perfume. I can understand why.

It's awash with fabulously fresh white flowers (the wedding bouquet of freesia, narcissus, lily of the valley, lily, rose and jasmine) which then mingle with fruits (the honeymoon of mandarin, bergamot, lemon) and then deepen (the commitment of sandalwood, sage, amber) to love everlasting (the sexuality of patchouli, musk, meadow wildflowers). Get the drift? **Eternity** kept its promise. Love it and it will love you back.

It's a wonder no other perfume had been called this wonderfully evocative name before, but it all came to pass when Calvin gave his bride Kelly (who'd been his principal designer) a ring once owned by the Duchess of Windsor. Lo and behold — inside was inscribed the magic word! That aside, it's nice to know that **Eternity** is one of the few very successful perfumes entirely formulated by a female 'nose', Sophia Grosjman — so it certainly has the stamp of feminine approval all around. **Eternity** supposedly has its feet firmly on the ground, but I think it's also left room for just a little old-fashioned romance to sneak through.

BLONDE — *because it's a standout*

Created before Versace's untimely death, this blonde bombshell is dedicated to his beloved (and very blonde) sister Donatella, whose favourite floral scent is the heady and pervasive tuberose. And I must say straight away that if the seductive sweetness of tuberose is too much for your olfactory senses, then tough luck! Because there's not all that much more in **Blonde**. And I wouldn't go so far as to say that **Blonde** is exclusively for blondes either — brunettes, redheads, even brownettes have a perfect right to wear it successfully too!

So why am I prescribing this firecracker for your more serious side? Because it's subversive, sly and sinuous. **Blonde** certainly has a great whack of tuberose, but it's softened a little with smouldering gardenia, spicy carnation, a spike of raspberry, a dash of cinnamon and a hint of sandalwood to keep it from going way over the top. And once the fusillade has stopped, the after-effects are surprisingly lovely — almost serene!

Worn with due discretion and not sprayed with wild abandon over every inch of you, **Blonde** is very user-friendly. It's warm, it's pulsating, it's vibrant. It can't be taken entirely seriously, but it will certainly brighten any ambience that looks like turning dull. It likes a good hearty laugh as much as an intimate suggestion. And you can certainly handle that!

JE REVIENS — because it's unforgettable

This classic, created in 1932, is still forever-young. No fad or fashion has been able to dim its light, bright sparkle and its inimitability. No other perfume smells remotely like it, probably because its incredibly complex and expensive formulation would be almost impossible to duplicate with the same fidelity and finesse.

From the year of its creation, villagers from the tiny but hilly hamlet of Lozere have collected each springtime the blooms of the wild narcissus flowers that grow in profusion practically from the rocks, as well as irises whose roots will be stored underground until they exude their precious orris oil, which is used as a likeness to violet, a flower notoriously difficult to capture in perfume. These two priceless ingredients are then fused with the heady blooms of jasmine and orange blossom, rose, lilac, ylang ylang and hyacinth, then given an incredibly piquant pungency with clove, moss, vetiver and incense, before a halo of amber and sandalwood gives the entire harmony its glorious *joie de vivre*.

Traditionally, **Je Reviens** has been promoted as a youthful and innocent perfume that causes young hearts to open impulsively and become very vulnerable. It's true that **Je Reviens** does attract the inexperienced and adventurous, but it also makes more worldly Librans feel strangely spirited and uninhibited, usually through the sentimental nostalgia of past romances or long-gone giddy flings.

But don't think for a minute that **Je Reviens** is mushy and oversweet. In fact it's a pretty tough-minded little concoction designed for optimism, not regret. And it's so unique that even though you might ignore it for a while, one day you'll wake up and need its fresh and cheerful exhilaration. It works like a tonic! Suddenly the tired world looks young and frivolous again.

In case you don't know, *je reviens* means 'I will return'— and it's not General MacArthur talking, it's your incurably romantic, easily bruised heart!

NOCTURNES — *because it's tranquil*

Another one of Caron's beautifully composed and elegant perfumes only found now in sensible and imaginative boutiques, unless you're in the vicinity of their fabulous boudoir-like boutique at 34, avenue Montaigne in Paris! **Nocturnes** is one of their more recent glories (created in 1981 — very youthful when you consider that Caron has been going strong for almost a century!).

Nocturnes is a glorious composition of rose and jasmine, ylang ylang and tuberose, stephanotis and lily of the valley, violet and cyclamen played ecstatically around green and citrus notes, while the base fingers through a mysterious, murmuring chord of vanilla and vetiver, musk and amber, benzoin and sandalwood. It forms a heady but haunting theme that goes off into romantic rhapsodies. But a Caron perfume never wanders off into uncertain territory — this is definitely a nocturne worthy of Chopin's intense romanticism or Debussy's impressionistic imagination.

Nocturnes has a sophisticated but not slavish elegance. It's more at home when you want to make an indelible but subtle impression — something to remember you by. Despite its name, it's quite lovely as a floral daytime accessory, but it really shines in the evening with its sparkle and wit, its charm and beguilement. A little night music perhaps, instead of a climactic symphonic blast? Definitely in the case of **Nocturnes**.

MAGIE NOIRE — *because it's deceptive*

Level-headed Librans into witchcraft? Surely not. Unless it's Lancôme's smouldering siren, **Magie Noire** (which translates simply as 'black magic'). Not as forbidding as it sounds, this dark jewel is certainly bewitching but in the most seductively subtle way. Black cats won't run screaming from you, and nor will anyone avoid you — especially not the opposite sex who seem to be drawn to its powers by some magical magnetism.

Heavily influenced by the mystical Orient, **Magie Noire** is nevertheless bursting with opulent flowers — hyacinth, jasmine, ylang ylang, rose, narcissus and tuberose interwoven with raspberry, bergamot and blackcurrant bud before a Far East avalanche of spices, cedarwood, mosses, musk and leather culminate with the sensual earthiness of patchouli. The resulting potion is thrilling, smoky, peppery, and almost volcanic!

So why should a well-mannered, well-bred Libran sink to dark and dangerous depths when she's trying to make herself a respectable reputation as a nice girl? Because through some unfathomable Parisian osmosis, **Magie Noire** emerges not as an oriental sexual threat but as a worldly, witty, French enchantment that's not the least bit wicked. **Magie Noire** is, in fact, highly sophisticated and very, very friendly.

It's certainly not for young Librans, but if you're over twenty-five or so and willing to throw a little caution to the winds of change, then **Magie Noire** will convince you there's more to black magic than voodoo. It's as smooth as velvet, dark as midnight — it has true magic that comes from a fearlessly romantic heart bent more on illumination than mumbo-jumbo. But I warn you, **Magie Noire** can become highly addictive if you get to like it.

The advantage of the cusp: taking your pick

It's not all confusion — being neither one star nor the other, or feeling you're partly both — if you were born toward the beginning of Scorpio*. You can of course pick and choose from the perfumes suggested for both Libra and Scorpio, but be careful. Depending on your characteristics, they may not all sit easily on you. That's why I've come up with a selection of extras that might solve any perfume problems or indecision you might have. Anyway, the choice is yours, so have fun finding out. They are:

- **Loulou** by Cacharel
  Pronunciation: LOO-loo/kash-ar-EL
  Type: floral/oriental
- **Tabu** by Dana
  Pronunciation: tar-BOO/DARN-uh
  Type: oriental
- **White Jeans** by Gianni Versace
  Pronunciation: jee-AR-nee vair-SAR-chee
  Type: floral
- **Trussardi Light** by Trussardi
  Pronunciation: troo-SAR-dee
  Type: fruity/floral

LOULOU
—, because it's a vamp in the making

The cusp of Libra/Scorpio is a thrilling but difficult one, especially for the young. It is the slide from the light-hearted, romantic flirting of Librans into the deeper waters of Scorpio sexuality. This smouldering little teaser certainly has all the right ingredients to

If you were born at the very beginning of Libra you might to check out the choices for those on the cusp of Virgo/Libra on pages 239–242.

project the image of the child/woman legend of Lulu, and her heartless seduction and rejection of lovers. Needless to say, **Loulou** is crammed with seductive ingredients from the caramel/marzipan sweetness of tonka bean, incense, vanilla and ylang ylang, to the exotic gardenia-like scent of Tahitian tiare flowers. Its sultriness and enticing overtures are something of a Pandora's Box, so be warned. Young players might find themselves swamped by **Loulou**'s outright ravishment.

TABU — because it knows all the tricks
Don't underestimate the power of this worldly wise oriental that shocked the perfume world in 1930 with its claim of being 'the forbidden fragrance'. Over the years **Tabu** has caused many an outraged feminist affront, and even today where it's one of many similar perfumes, it can still teach its imitators a lesson in survival tactics as well as the artful tricks of making its wearer highly desirable. Loaded with the exotic earthiness of patchouli, **Tabu** blends orange blossom, jasmine, clove, oakmoss and bergamot and then adds an animal-attraction note of civet (the synthetic kind) to really warm things up. Librans who have tipped the scales a touch in the direction of sensuousness will learn a lot from it, while Scorpios will merely use it to underline what they already know in the seduction stakes.

WHITE JEANS — because it's uplifting

The Versace 'Jeans' perfume collection is remarkable for its carefree and casual attitude — uncomplicated, undemanding, adding an aura of easy-going vivacity and versatility — qualities both Libra and Scorpio have heaps of. **White Jeans** is the new girl next door — and one to make a friend of. It's as light as laughter, as soft as twilight and as open-hearted as a posy of flowers. If you're getting the blues (very Libran) or working up to a storm (very Scorpion), **White Jeans** will quickly dispel the nasties with its romantic barrage of white flowers — jasmine, soft rose, carnation and lily which emerge from a dazzling opening gambit of ylang ylang, gardenia, orange and a dash of green galbanum, all softened with cedarwood, sandalwood and a hint of patchouli, giving **White Jeans** its subtle whisper of orientalism. It's an absolutely lovable, uplifting perfume with that typical flash of Versace finesse and brio! Above all, it's blissfully unpretentious. It'll easily get Librans laughing again and lower the Scorpio blood pressure. Too goody-goody you may think? Never. There's always a wicked twinkle in a Versace perfume, and **White Jeans** is no exception!

TRUSSARDI LIGHT
— because it's liberating

This is the light, bright and lovely spin-off from that

classic for grown-ups, **Trussardi**, and it's certainly not a teenaged lightweight. In fact, a woman of any age can wear it — it's not just for eager young cusps! It's sassy and sexy, but doesn't like to be too serious about it. It's more substantial than a flirt, but can't be bothered with dull company even if they look like big, gorgeous hunks. Like you, **Trussardi Light** is basically out for a good time, and its zingy, zesty make-up makes that quite clear with jazzy top notes of Yozu lemon, Jamaican lime, nectarine and quince blossom dancing happily along with drifts of wisteria, rose, lotus and waterlily, cyclamen and a mini-barrage of berries and apricot, plus a sensuous whiff of that reliable old favourite that sends out pretty definite vibes, Indian patchouli. **Trussardi Light**'s open-faced freshness and innocent playfulness are certain to attract as you sashay by — it's up to you if you want to make something of it. Basically though, it lets you feel free and easy, which will appeal to Librans who don't like to be pinned down too early in life, and even Scorpios might find it a welcome change from all those sexual heavies they're supposed to seduce the world with!

The Libran male: gifts for his balancing act

Fastidiousness is both the benchmark and the bane of

the typically urbane Libran male. He would not leave home without it, yet sometimes he wishes he could replace it with something less inhibitive. Unlike Libran women who want to be taken seriously, he has already achieved that but with the lurking suspicion that though it might make him look supremely confident, he might be considered deadly dull as a result. He has balanced every aspect of his life to such a perfect standstill he sometimes resembles a stone statue! Of course, what he desperately needs is a little less balance and a daring (but not heroically hazardous) dive into the vague area of desire he wistfully calls 'something a little bit different'. What he needs is a good shove! And there's no more challenging way to deliver this friendly push than a new fragrance to upset his applecart. But not any old fragrance — it must have good credentials and cost a lot. That part will appeal to his vanity at least. And it also has to persuade him it's better than the 'old faithful' he seems almost married to. But you don't have to worry about that — just tell him he's never smelled sexier than in the new one, and he'll begin his peacock act, preening his pants off. Flattery, with Librans, will get you everywhere! Naturally, there's no need to buy him something overtly raunchy — Librans like being seductive but not vulgar or loutish. That 'something a little bit different' he pines for is usually just a dash of derring-do, not self-destruction. And it must always remain reasonably within the bounds of his good taste — which he usually has plenty of. So, just niggle him a bit with a challenging new smell to push him off his precious perch!

- **L'Eau d'Issey pour Homme** by Issey Miyake
  Pronunciation: lo DISS-ee poor OM/
  ISS-ee mee- AR-kee
  Type: herbal/fruity
- **Xeryus Rouge** by Givenchy
  Pronunciation: ZEER-ee-us HROOzjhe/
  zjhiv-ON-she
  Type: green
- **Black Jeans** by Gianni Versace
  Pronunciation: jee-AR-nee vair-SAR-chee
  Type: oriental
- **Équipage** by Hermès
  Pronunciation: air-kee-PARZJHE/air-MAZE
  Type: woody/spicy

L'Eau d'Issey pour Homme

What a departure! What he did for women in his clean-and-clear-as-water women's perfume, Issey Miyake does for men — and without smelling remotely oriental at that. His male fragrance is a stunningly smooth and serene liquid sculpture of citrus zest, aromatic seaweed, classified 'secret' herbs and soft blue waterlily, spiked with nutmeg and tobacco leaf with a whisper of musk to set the deeper senses pulsating. It's light and lilting, but masculine in the New Age way — putting subtlety ahead of bombast. But it has presence — like its famous female counterpoint. Its clarity and stimulus give the wearer an air of serene ease. So, if he prides himself on being a man of the world, business or otherwise, **L'Eau d'Issey pour Homme** might soften that stitched-up smugness he often gets.

Xeryus Rouge

Probably named after some Ancient Persian king or warrior, which will appeal to his sense of appreciating history while trying to make his own mark on modern times. The Libra male just adores the thought of contributing something meaningful to Life (usually his super-ego), and **Xeryus Rouge** will certainly announce his heroic individuality. Its terrific onslaught of cactus greens, the aniseed pungency of of tarragon, peppery red pimento and cedar leaf might sound a bit too outdoorsy for his indoor charm, but it's all smoothed down with a very sexy stroke of soft Tibetan musk. The trouble is that women are often tricked by its disarmingly fresh impact, and suddenly find themselves lured into the seductively velvet trap **Xeryus Rouge** and the Libran Lothario have laid for them.

Black Jeans

This no-holds-barred dazzler will test the Libran swagger and ruffle his feathers. **Black Jeans** makes no bones about its bravado, and doesn't give a hoot about subtlety. It's a potent blast of citrus petitgrain, vervain (a piquant smell like verbena), rosemary, and those wonderfully pungent juniper berries they put in proper gin. This is laced with Spanish geranium, spiced with nutmeg and ginger, bedded down with vetiver, oriental agarwood, super-strength musk and poured into a very macho frosted black bottle. **Black Jeans** is definitely not for wimps. It's a high-flying trapeze act, and in the Versace tradition, takes the plunge without a safety net. If he suffers from vertigo or has dicky ticker, don't tempt fate!

Équipage

Warning — the name alone might go to his head. **Équipage** comes from a House that symbolises equestrian-inspired elegance. It carries with it an image of fast horses, faster cars and laurel wreaths around the neck — his! Just stand back and look at his amazement when he smells its assertive stamp of the well-heeled gentry! Not quite what he had in mind, although he'd never admit it. **Équipage** is so original it's breathtaking — a complex medley of cinnamon, clove buds, clary sage, incense, sandalwood and patchouli. Its sheer classiness is daunting and uncompromising, but — you watch — he'll soon get its message and start thinking about things like owning the horse that will win him his first Melbourne Cup!

Who suits what, and when: getting the best out of your perfumes

Because perfumes become not only extensions of your personality but also give emphasis to the way you look and the mood you're in, naturally, to bring out their best, they should be treated with due understanding in regard to their characteristics and qualities. They too have limitations and strengths, just as we all have. So, the following table outlines when best to wear them (Day, Night), the age-group most suited to them (Young, Mature), the general complexion of the wearer (Fair, Dark), and the seasons they bloom best in (Spring/Summer – S/S, or Autumn/Winter – A/W). This table is meant only to be used as an approximate guide or reference point – it is not a hard and fast set of rules by any means.

			THE BIG GUNS					
Perfume	Day	Night	Young	Mature	Fair	Dark	S/S	A/
Dolce & Gabbana	•	•	•	•	•	•	•	
Cabotine	•	•	•		•	•	•	
Paris	•	•			•		•	
Organza		•		•		•	•	
24, Faubourg	•		•		•		•	
Deci Dela	•		•		•	•	•	

			YOUR SECRET WEAPONS					
Perfume	Day	Night	Young	Mature	Fair	Dark	S/S	A/
Vanderbilt		•						
Eternity	•		•		•	•	•	
Blonde	•	•	•		•	•	•	
Je Reviens	•		•		•	•	•	
Nocturnes		•	•	•	•		•	
Magie Noire		•		•		•		

			LIBRA/SCORPIO CUSPS					
Perfume	Day	Night	Young	Mature	Fair	Dark	S/S	A/
Loulou		•	•			•		
Tabu		•	•	•		•		
White Jeans	•		•	•	•	•	•	
Trussardi Light	•	•	•	•	•	•	•	

			VIRGO/LIBRA CUSPS					
Perfume	Day	Night	Young	Mature	Fair	Dark	S/S	A/
Miss Dior	•	•	•	•	•	•	•	
Hugo Boss Woman								
	•	•	•	•	•	•	•	
Bellodgia	•	•	•	•	•	•	•	
Le Dix	•	•	•	•	•	•	•	

			MEN'S FRAGRANCES					
Perfume	Day	Night	Young	Mature	Fair	Dark	S/S	A/
L'Eau d'Issey pour Homme	•		•		•		•	
Xeryus Rouge	•	•	•		•	•	•	
Black Jeans	•	•	•		•	•	•	
Équipage	•	•		•	•	•	•	

The Perfume Zodiac

Scorpio

The scorpion
October 23–November 21

Shalimar

You and the losers

Y
ou must be sick and tired of being circled with
apprehension and suspicion when others find
out you're born under this highly respectable
and perfectly nice star sign. Scorpions (the infamous
arachnid with the sting in its tail) have suffered much

unwarranted fear and loathing for centuries, and for no good reason. They actually prefer to retreat rather than fight and will only use their venomous sting if so provoked — they have no other choice! If they do sting, they reckon their enemy deserves it. Scorpios are such fierce fighters that if *they* look like losing, more often than not they'll turn their sting on themselves! Doesn't this apply to you as a human Scorpio? Being a loser is for others, not you.

The thing is you poor Scorpios aren't really understood at all, unless intelligent people put their trust in you. They might never fully understand you because Scorpios play their cards very close to the chest and absolutely hate their territory being invaded — their private secrets are theirs alone! That's why you'll rarely be caught suffering in public. You'd much rather cope with it yourself — loss of face or image is something you'll avoid like the plague. No one is going to call you a loser and get away with it! The thought of being belittled behind your back is just not on.

Do you *really* put on a fearsome and threatening exterior? Well, own up, you *can* be ruthless, overbearing, melodramatic, conniving and vindictive, with a moodiness like thunderclouds around you, although there's rarely any thunder and lightning. It all becomes introverted, bottled up to be used later when you can't resist a little sweet revenge. It is true you might forgive, but forget? *Never!* You forget nothing and you strike with deadly precision. You have no feelings of remorse. You figure it's deserved retribution, and therefore fair play.

Those, however, are your extreme characteristics and not every Scorpio has them (or at least uses them). In the main, you are a bit of a softie, but a shrewd one. You do face people from a fairly superior position and can't tolerate stupidity or failure in anyone. You do not fall for flattery, and too many compliments become not only annoying but embarrassing. You expect to be respected, but not fawned on. This comes from your incredible and admirable sense of loyalty and compassion. You will have the patience of Job with those you like or love, and will protect them ferociously. To have a Scorpio for a friend is to be very lucky indeed.

But if there's something important to be thrashed out you'll grapple with it and not let go until it's solved. Sometimes this tenacity can be seen as preachiness, but it isn't always — it's your incurable desire to make sense of things, and to show yourself (and others) how intelligent you are.

But you have a wonderfully light side as well. You might not be as mercurial as the star signs either side of you, but you know how to enjoy life to the hilt. You dive into it — no matter how deep and dangerous the water — and splash around having a great time. Nothing daunts you, nothing upsets your natural poise. Consequences don't interest you at all.

But now to that part of your reputation that

fascinates people to the point of being presumptuous about you, which you hate. Everyone thinks you're a sex fiend of some sort, that your entire life revolves around your lower abdomen (just because this is the area that's supposed to, in astrological terms, physically dominate your behavioural attitudes), and you're so obsessed with sexual satisfaction that other women never let their men go anywhere near you. Twaddle. Of course sex holds a prominent position in the way you express your passionate emotions (and they are strong, not flighty passions). 'Sex' usually means 'love' to you and *vice versa*. It doesn't mean you're wanton or predatory. Your sensuality radiates strongly from you, and you find nothing wrong with that, although its intensity sometimes frightens men off — but then again, if they're that wimpy they wouldn't be right for you anyway. Stick to your high standards, and avoid the also-rans (or losers as you call them).

So, who says Scorpios are confrontational and surly? Those who are jealous of your independent stance, dramatic flair, natural seductiveness and your clout. Just because they can't make a grand entrance is not your fault, but just the same, they'd better watch out for that tail of yours. There are times when you can justifiably give it a warning swish. But don't forget that not everyone else can be as perceptive, attractive and magnetic as you are — or as you can be, if your head's not just a little bit too swollen.

Scorpio style

You have scads of it and make sure people around you realise it. You put on a bit of a show, but never a vulgar or trashy one. Your personal expression of style is your insistence on quality rather than quantity — the best for the best (let's be frank — you are not overly modest). And since your abode is so fiercely important to you it will always look neat, tidy, almost austere but unfailingly impressive. The same goes for your personal appearance. You like emphasis and impact — not frills. The intensity of dark red, black, indigo, deep sea-green, ultramarine are your colours — pastels are far too wishy-washy for your dynamic magnetism.

Magnetism is a natural endowment of yours and you should make the most of it. By that I don't mean you have to bat your heavily shadowed eyes and mascara-laden lashes, wet your lascivious lips and growl with a come-hither mating call. Your demeanour will do it for you without the *femme fatale* antics, as will the correct choice of perfumes.

Deciding the best ones for you was not easy. Of course you wear orientals better than anyone else, but not to play the vamp. They suit you because of their sultry passion, insidious tenacity and air of mystery. But to wear them all the time is tiresome and does an injustice to your normal cool poise. This is where florals, sometimes mixed with oriental influences (but mostly tinged with greens), give you the elegant contrast you need. Then there's the hidden side of you (and no other sign has more secrets than you), when the ball-game changes entirely — but more of that later! Suffice to say that your style is a dramatic and sweeping one, never minimalist. It is exact, definite and unforgettable. No one will fail to notice your entrance, your presence or your exit. Your immense panache will leave the losers drooling. You have to be the centre of attention and you can do it without blowing your trumpet. In fact, a Scorpio with poise is a delight to see — and I *don't* mean poised to strike!

Your outer expression is *superiority*. Your inner core is *attachment*.

Here's how to translate all of that into the best perfumes for you.

I have divided them into two categories:

1. *The big guns* — these are the all-important perfumes that should suit you best. They form the core of your personal arsenal.

2. *Your secret weapons* — these augment the basics and are more daring and unusual, but should still suit you.

There is also a choice of perfumes for those of you born on the cusp of Scorpio/Sagittarius, as well as a selection of men's fragrances suitable to give the Scorpio male. (If you were born on the cusp of

Libra/Scorpio see pages 274–278 for your further perfume choices.) I have given each perfume a category as well as a simple and easy guide to its correct pronunciation. At the end of the chapter I have summated all of the perfumes into a table that tells you whether they're best on young or mature women, in warm or cool weather, day or evening, for dark or fair complexions.

The big guns: the indispensable basics

As I said before, orientals seem to be the obvious and correct category of perfumes that best emphasise your strong and passionate personality. Not only are they highly complex in construction, they use many and various exotic ingredients that can be spicy, herby, woody, resinous and heavily floral. They're usually not for the faint-hearted or finicky. They are lushly passionate and operatic — and romantic only in their mystical fantasy. Scorpios love their sense of drama and power as well as their languorous and sultry smoulder. They are, like you, frankly sensual and sexual. So are floral orientals and floral greens, but in an entirely different persuasion. Their approach is softer, more insidious and infiltrating — more mysterious but just as suggestive. It's no use trying to convince yourself you're the sweet young thing next door or a nice old-fashioned granny either in pale, limp-wristed perfumes that will turn cloying and unconvincing on you. Be your undeniably strong self and go for broke (as if you need me telling you)! They are:

- **Shalimar** by Guerlain
  Pronunciation: SHALLY-mar/gair-LARN
  Type: oriental
- **Poison** by Christian Dior
  Pronunciation: pwah-SONN (or POY-zun)/
  KRIST-ee-an dee-OR
  Type: floral/oriental
- **Obsession** by Calvin Klein
  Pronunciation: ob-SESS-shun/KAL-vin KLINE
  Type: oriental/fruity
- **Must de Cartier** by Cartier
  Pronunciation: MOOST (or MUST) duh KART-ee-air
  Type: fruity/oriental
- **Allure** by Chanel
  Pronunciation: arl-LOO-er/shar-NEL
  Type: floral/fruity
- **Narcisse Noir** by Caron
  Pronunciation: nar-seece NWAH/KARR-on
  Type: floral/oriental

SHALIMAR
— because it's the original seductress

It is a legend, though still living. It was inspired by a legend. It was created almost by accident. It is the perfume synonymous with oriental splendour and seduction. Its name is a whispered pleasure of sensual longing. In short, **Shalimar** stands peerlessly alone.

Its creation was a whimsical flourish by Jacques Guerlain in 1925, when a perfume essence manufacturer presented him with a new synthetic version of vanilla, called vanillin. Fascinated by its possibilities, he tipped a bit of it into a bottle of **Jicky**, fiddled around with it, and up came a scent that thrilled the daylights out of him. A little more fiddling and balancing, a dose of the secret house formula of 'Guerlainade', and a great but unnamed beauty was ready to swamp the world of perfume. What to call it? He recalled a 300-year old love story told to him by a Maharajah about Shah Jahan, Mogul Emperor of India who loved only one woman, Mumtaz Mahal, almost to madness. When she died, he built the Taj Mahal as a monument to her eternal memory, but before that he had also created for her alone the secret Gardens of Shalimar (the Abode of Love) in which they shared their unending love.

Guerlain at first wanted to call his miracle of roses, jasmine, vanillin, iris, patchouli, bergamot, musk and sandalwood, 'Taj Mahal', but that seemed too cold, too architectural. Finally he settled on the romantic place where the Emperor and Mumtaz shared their love, and thus **Shalimar** was born.

Little did he know, that once placed in its fabulously extravagant Baccarat crystal bottle it would become the quintessential oriental perfume and remains so to this day. Nothing can match its voluptuous splendour.

Although Scorpios are not usually bowled over by romantic fables, **Shalimar** is the exception. Not only is its legend fascinating, it has been translated into a perfumed masterpiece of balance and beauty, drama and seduction. It envelops its wearer with a determined tenacity — sultry, pervasive, languorous and glamorous. Thank heavens for that accidental dash of vanillin!

POISON — *because it divides and rules*

Stories about the shockwaves of disbelief and derision that met this blockbuster's introduction in 1986 are now *passé*, but **Poison** certainly made its mark and still does with its uncompromising grandeur and power. Looking back, its sheer daring in formulation, presentation and naming paved the way for all sorts of future outrages, but it stands aloof from the riff-raff of imitation and competition with its bold originality.

Its glittering purple bottle should give you a clue that **Poison** is no ordinary perfume with a controversial name. Its formulation is staggeringly unique, beginning with dry acerbic and herbal notes of Russian coriander, anise, pimento (allspice), cinnamon and plum. Different? That's nothing! Now come heavy drifts of Bulgarian rose, wild berries, orange blossom, carnation, jasmine and a huge whack of tuberose. In fact, when a test run of **Poison** was met with almost total success in France, whole hillsides in Grasse had to be specially planted with tuberose to keep up with the imminent mass manufacture of it! Finally, base notes of heliotrope, vanilla, amber, sandalwood, opoponax and musk attempt to pin down and fix this explosive thunderbolt.

Poison still causes schisms, but has never been accused of reticence or even failure to attract masses of attention. Just don't use too much of it — being trapped in a lift with someone who's overdosed on it is literally overwhelming I can tell you! Remember it's a powerhouse perfume — strident, assertive but intoxicatingly mesmerising. Perhaps audacious sums it up best. And Scorpios are very audacious women — even in a lift!

OBSESSION — because it's single-minded

Being single-minded is a typical trait of a Scorpio, male or female, but it can sometimes lead to obsessiveness, which is not always in your best interests. But you usually either grow out of it, talk yourself out of it, or if it looks like getting the better of you, you'll pretend you never wanted whatever the object of it was anyway! But, obsessed or not, **Obsession** won't bring you to ruin. In fact, it might even bring you exactly what you want in terms of to have and to hold.

Obsession certainly sorts out the men from the

boys pretty swiftly. It either turns them off immediately, or turns them on with a vengeance. It is a perfume for the woman who knows exactly what she wants. It was meant to be controversial right from its creation in 1985. In the American tradition, it does nothing by halves. It is straightforward, brash and up-front, and proud of it.

Its single-mindedness is the result of its persistent domination of amber, a golden and glowingly warm resin that is usually used to soften proceedings in other perfumes. In **Obsession** it is used as a detonator, unleashing a flurry of fruity notes of mandarin, peach, bergamot, lemon and greens over a throbbing bouquet of orange blossom, marigold, jasmine and rose, while vanilla, musk, sandalwood, cedarwood and coriander keep the drumbeat rolling as amber makes the final *coup de grâce* and the whole lethal cocktail goes up in flames! And these flames finally smoulder to the come-on of sultry seduction. **Obsession** is the loud and clear clarion call to arms — hopefully yours, if that's what you *really* want!

MUST DE CARTIER
— because it's sumptuous

'Must-have' was the *cri du cœur* of the opulent and self-indulgent '80s when Cartier released their first perfume as a fragrant expression of their pricelessly extravagant jewellery. At saturation point, everything crashed and we were forced to sober up more than a little. Excessive *luxe* was regarded as decadent and irresponsible. But now that sobriety has relaxed a little, what has stood the test of time? Perfumes like **Must de Cartier!**

It was never intended to be more than an extension of Cartier's reputation for the most refined creativity in jewellery, and it remains just that, except that it is a Cartier almost every woman of sophistication can well afford.

Must may not be an absolute must, but a Scorpio woman's life without it would not be quite as desirably elegant.

Must gathers together in great profusion all the ingredients of feminine elegance — from its mesmerising top notes of peach and rosewood interlaced with tangerine to its opulent heart of orchid, jasmine, rose, carnation, ylang ylang, iris, jonquil, orange blossom and musk, all afloat in a gentle sea of amber and vetiver. It is mellifluous and mysterious — like a great bejewelled star caught in the incandescence of limelight.

Fittingly, it was presented to an adoring and fabulously rich clientele at the grand Château de Versailles in 1981, and became the darling of the international glamour set. But **Must** has more than surface glitter and glamour. It has an intensely beautiful nature and a cool individuality that sets it apart from lesser gems, like a rare ruby from a garnet.

To a Scorpio, wearing **Must** is tantamount to stealing the scene without even trying.

ALLURE — *because it's indefinable*

Suggesting such an enigmatic and intensely beautiful perfume like **Allure** might come as a surprise to Scorpios used to more unequivocal and demonstrative perfumes, but **Allure** surprised everyone when it was released as the new classic from Chanel. Who would have expected such a soft and frankly romantic approach from such a highly sophisticated perfume house? After all, **No. 5** and **No. 19** are extremely individual and unsentimental, **Cristalle** is sparkling but outspoken and **Coco** is the last word in super-calculating seduction. **Allure**? Surely too naive and gentle!

But perhaps it harks back to the heady days of pre-depression Paris of 1928 when Chanel herself designed a perfume called **No. 22** — a lush *mélange* of white flowers she called her 'floral symphony'. It was a final fling at the gaiety and abandon of the Roaring '20s. **Allure** is not all that unlike **No. 22**. It is sparkling, constantly changing, mysterious yet finally very independent and free. It's just right for the end of a turbulent century, and perhaps exactly what a Scorpio woman needs as a timely restatement of her cool wisdom and self-respect. It's also a subtle reminder that her sensuality is not to be confused with her freedom to do and go exactly as she pleases.

Allure is a fascinating complexity of Italian citron, honeysuckle, magnolia blossom and waterlily against the zest of mandarin, the sensuality of vanilla, the freshness of vetiver with whispers of rose and jasmine to give it a romantic notion more than a proposal. Altogether impossible to resist. **Allure** glides into a room, not merely enters it. It turns heads, catches eyes, captures hearts. No one could refuse its alluring, murmured invitation.

NARCISSE NOIR
— because it's legendary

Ernest Daltroff was more of an entrepreneur than a perfumer, even though it was he who created the famed House of Caron in the early 1900s and masterminded the great perfumes that came from within its hallowed doors in the fashionable heart of Paris. His first and greatest success was this all-pervading perfume, created specifically for the huge American market. American women, for some reason or other, had a penchant for very strong floral perfumes, mainly rose, but Daltroff gave them not roses but armloads of exotic narcissus which he dramatically named 'black'! Well, they fell for it in droves and his name was made. And **Narcisse Noir** (despite the fact that it's a bit difficult to track down but is certainly available) has never left the ranks of the great, enduring classic florals.

It is one of the strongest and most long-lasting

perfumes I've ever encountered, so a little goes a long long way. It is, of course, dominated by what is described as Persian Black Narcissus, which may or may not be a publicist's fantasy, but be that as it may, **Narcisse Noir** also has notes of rose and jasmine, bergamot and orange blossom, musk, sandalwood and animal civet to stop the narcissus from a complete takeover. And there's more than a dash of oriental spice simmering somewhere in the sultry fireworks.

It all adds up to a completely enveloping and richly smouldering scent that has been known to stop traffic. It is challenging, sensual and very lingering. The good news for Scorpios is that lesser women don't like its strident dash and brashness at all — all the more reason then to make it a very powerful, personal weapon in your arsenal. After all these years, **Narcisse Noir** still knocks 'em dead!

Your secret weapons: the surprises

You make it very difficult for anyone to probe your innermost thoughts. We all know how you value your privacy, and protect your most intimate desires from scrutiny — is this why people call you inscrutable and sometimes too aloof to be bothered with? Too bad if they do. No one gets right inside your head unless you want them to. Okay, you can hide all that, but what you can't conceal is one of your most endearing and enviable characteristics — your devotion and attachment to those who really need help. I don't want to embarrass you, but this is one of your silent strengths, along with fierce protectiveness. Why you choose not to make a fuss about it is your business, but just a little glimpse of this more compassionate and less domineering side of you may give those not so sympathetic toward you a newer, kinder impression — a sort of revelation!

It may also let you relax a little and stop working so hard to be seen as indomitable and efficient all the time. You may even be thought of as surprisingly human and approachable! Of course you don't want to make this a habit in case they get the wrong idea of your basic command of things, but you can express it by softening the way you dress, and the complementary choice of different perfumes. Instead of the gangbusters that fit you perfectly, why not try a couple that are less sensational but just as effective? You don't have to splash on sweetness-and-light florals or romantic enchantments — but a refreshing change from the seductions of the orient or the flash and fire of high-powered florals spiced with daring and danger. I think that by doing this you'll release your enviable trait of sincere attachment without hurting your reputation for no-nonsense tenacity and superiority, or your precious pride either. Scorpios are, after all, extremely nice people. Anyway, try these:

- **White Diamonds** by Elizabeth Taylor
  Type: floral
- **Vendetta** by Valentino
  Pronunciation: ven-DETT-uh/vallen-TEEN-o
  Type: fruity/floral
- **Duende** by J. Del Pozo
  Pronunciation: doo-END-air/YAY dell POZZ-o
  Type: fruity/floral
- **Shocking** by Schiaparelli
  Pronunciation: skappa-RELL-ee
  Type: oriental/floral
- **Vol de Nuit** by Guerlain
  Pronunciation: VO-da NWEE/gair-LARN
  Type: spicy/oriental
- **Ozbek** by Ozbek
  Type: oriental/floral

WHITE DIAMONDS
— because you'll feel rich

Elizabeth Taylor's first foray into perfume was **Passion**, a notoriously exotic and pervasive *mélange*, which might suit you as well as this one, but will not add anything to the softer side of your nature. **White Diamonds** has more glamour and glitz, is far more light-hearted and has the ability to make you feel good when you might be working up to a Scorpion storm and want to cool it a little.

It's very elegantly presented, in the flashy-tasteful

American manner, in a gold *flacon* ringed with look-alike diamonds, so the wealth factor comes immediately into play. Then there's the heady scent that seems to zing and zip all around you in a luxurious aureole of many, many flowers combining for a *whammo* effect. At the top comes Amazon lily, narcissus and jasmine, all using the Living Flower technique of scent extraction, which is then duplicated with amazing fidelity in the laboratory without once smelling artificial! Once they're in unison, tuberose and orange blossom add their considerable powers, along with some Florentine iris to add a woody-violet presence, and some luscious Turkish rose. Swathed in that great quartet of base notes — amber, sandalwood, oakmoss and patchouli and finished with the sparkling veneer of modern aldehydes, **White Diamonds** emerges as a thrilling and exhilarating perfume. It actually makes you feel something wonderful is in the air and about to happen to you. Even if it doesn't, you'll still feel terrifically elated.

White Diamonds is strictly an 'occasion' perfume — you'd never wear it to a polite afternoon tea party, but then again, Scorpios usually avoid such social trivia and go for the big time, all guns blazing. At least you should.

VENDETTA

— *because it's passionately Italian*

I'd love to be able to ask Valentino why he named this beautiful perfume after a ferocious and bloody feud, but there's no knowing with Italian eccentricity, is there? The name aside, if you can track down this elusive perfume, go for it — hoard it if you have to! It's a triumph of elegance and sensuality, which don't often go hand in hand.

Vendetta, in its stunning fluted fan-like bottle designed by the great Serge Mansau for Valentino, is a highly-charged operatic perfume that is vivid, vivacious and voluptuous. It rides high on top notes of hyacinth and orange blossom, then draws you into its depths of rose, jasmine, narcissus and marigold with a tantalising whiff of sweet waterlily before the powerful trio of patchouli, sandalwood and musk fix everything to a barely-contained explosion of fireworks.

Vendetta is very reminiscent of Sicily (which may partly account for its volcanic name). It streams with images of clear blue sky, sapphire sea, blazing sun, breathtaking landscape and volatile charm. But it also is light enough for unbridled laughter, so don't get the impression it's deadly serious or difficult to wear. It's quite the opposite.

In fact, it's a great perfume for Scorpios with its air of candour and dazzle, its innate elegance that's edged with excitement and spirit — just the sort of free-wheeling, exhilarating perfume that can give you a less moody and more gregarious (though still commanding) image. Despite the name, **Vendetta**, like you, has about as much viciousness as a wild and carefree Sicilian *tarantella*!

DUENDE — because it calms you down

Couturiers, even Spanish ones, are notorious for creating perfumes that are often quite at odds with their couture. Don't ask me why, but think of Armani's **Armani**, Dior's **Dune**, Klein's **Obsession**, Gaultier's signature perfume and so on. They seem to go completely against the style and image of their supposedly complementary clothes. The same is true of this very charming perfume from Jesus del Pozo, whose designs are grandly Spanish and dynamic. **Duende** is neither.

Duende is Spanish for 'charm', and this lovely and gentle perfume is certainly loaded with it. It makes no great waves, except gentle ones that wash silently onto the sand and swish out again without any drama. It's not particularly elegant and certainly has no pretensions to opulence or seduction. No great Andalusian passion invades it. It is simply beautiful and at peace with itself. So what's that got to do with a Scorpio woman, you may ask? It has to do with those times when you've just about worked or connived yourself to a standstill and you're exhausted but won't admit it. **Duende** is the perfume that infiltrates through your steely exterior to your soft heart. And isn't that better than going to pieces?

Duende is a delicious mix of melon and citrus oils, jasmine and mimosa bathed in the woody softness of sandalwood and cedarwood, and a good dash of windswept wild thyme. You might almost think it's a recipe for aromatherapy, but it's much more penetrating and satisfying than mere body anointing. It goes straight to your head with a sunny intoxication that steals into your heart and captivates it. And please don't tell me you're immune to such a charming and calming influence!

SHOCKING
— because it deserves a comeback

Between the two World Wars two women dominated Parisian *couture*, the very French Chanel and the Roman-born but Paris-based Elsa Schiaparelli. Far more outrageous than her rival, she turned fashion upside down with crazy hats, rhinestone-studded lingerie, fur bed jackets, zouave skirts, shortie coats, high padded shoulders, all in exceptionally vivid colours, one of which became her trademark. She picked up puce and turned it into shocking pink — a hot, bright pink and the inspiration for her first great perfume, **Shocking**. It created a sensation not just in France, but especially in the U.S.A. where she eventually opened another successful salon. Then, in the 60s it all but vanished.

Now it's made a welcome return, *almost* in its original form. The fabulous bottle is still much the same, thankfully — a glass dressmaker's dummy of a very busty figure — Mae West's no less — with a shocking pink 'S' signature at its navel. Its original formula had, as I recall, a very heavy patchouli content giving it an unmistakable sexy headiness you could smell yards away, Some considered it affronting and offensive!

Now it's more 'perfume-correct'. The patchouli's been toned down to an 'acceptable' level, but it's still there throbbing right through to the fade-out. The top notes are sweet with hyacinth and narcissus but a whack of ylang ylang starts to undermine the pretty proceedings, even through the heart notes of rose, jasmine and lily of the valley. Sensuality reigns supreme in the base with patchouli and musk in alliance with the peristent ylang ylang. The result is not remotely offensive — more of a nostalgia trip in a nice spring garden that's being invaded and infiltrated by oriental seductresses! The initial shock may have gone, but the spirit lives on in **Shocking** — in a far more cultivated though still dynamic way.

VOL DE NUIT

— because it soars ecstatically

First the bad news. You guessed it — **Vol de Nuit** is not readily available. The good news is that it has not been discontinued as some have feared and still appears in good perfume boutiques and some duty-free outlets. Or you can order it through Guerlain stockists or Guerlain itself. Believe me, it's worth every effort.

Vol de Nuit ('Night Flight') is one of Guerlain's

great classics and was a considerable triumph at its release in 1933. It was named in honour of one of France's most daring aviators, Antoine de Saint-Exupery. Does that name sound familiar? It should — he was also the author of the wonderful story *The Little Prince*, which has charmed millions of children. A very accomplished and versatile man, as is the perfume created as homage to his spirit of adventure. (Aren't the French marvellous — naming a woman's perfume in honour of a man?)

Anyway, its inspiration aside, **Vol de Nuit** will take you on a dizzy flight you'll never forget and want to repeat over and over. It's a stunningly elegant light oriental with citrus top notes of orange, mandarin, lemon, bergamot and orange blossom swept away on airy currents of jonquil and vanilla, oakmoss and iris, musk and sandalwood, and a cargo of ethereal spices, plus some elevated aldehydes that give it its soaring, high-flying altitude. Your head will be in more than the clouds — it'll be in seventh heaven!

Go to the ends of the earth if you must to possess this great and joyous adventure in perfume. **Vol de Nuit**'s rapturous elegance and radiance, its independence and liberation will take you on the flight of your life!

OZBEK — *because it has pizzazz*
I'm surprised this fabulous oriental concoction hasn't taken the perfume world by storm, but it remains a

well-kept secret among *aficionados*, which at least protects us from the wrong women wearing it! It's highly individualistic, which makes it perfect for the Scorpio looking for something different to express her own singularity. But **Ozbek** is not a heavy, sloe-eyed vampish oriental number — it's more lush and luxurious, something for the High Sultana, not the harem.

Created by Rifat Ozbek, the English-based Turkish designer of brilliant clothes that effortlessly combine colours and textures in a blend of the ethnic, classic and modern, **Ozbek** is obviously his celebration of the sumptuous wonders of Byzantium in all its legendary splendour. He also designed the tall and tapering glass minaret bottle topped with silver on which perches a tiny Turkish crescent moon — a masterpiece in itself.

The perfume is nothing short of breathtaking. It's something out of Scheherazade's *Thousand and One Nights* — an opulent fantasy, a luscious Turkish delight of sweet temptation and outspoken passion. The initial introduction is a muezzin's call of rosewood, peach and freesia that leads to a sumptuous interior of jasmine, hyacinth, ylang ylang and very heady pittosporum (which smells rather like frangipani, but sweeter), before drifts of wild honey and musk meld the whole exotic potpourri together in a sort of melismatic mantra.

You might gather that **Ozbek** is a pretty lethal weapon to have on hand — it's certainly not for the lavender-and-roses set. It's a perfume so prodigal it bursts and blooms in one ravishingly executed arabesque — so intensely constructed that the first indelible impression you get of it is also the last, until it imperceptibly fades away after a sustained impact of eloquent beauty. If you're a Scorpio searching for your *simpatico* perfume, the delectable and delicious **Ozbek** may just turn out to be your Kismet!

The advantage of the cusp: taking your pick

It's not all confusion — being neither one star nor the other, or feeling you're partly both — if you were born on the cusp of Scorpio/Sagittarius*. You can of course pick and choose from the perfumes suggested from both Scorpio and Sagittarius, but be careful. Depending on your characteristics, they may not all sit easily on you. That's why I've come up with a selection of extras that might solve any perfume problems or indecision you might have. Anyway, the choice is yours, so have fun finding out!

These are four you might like:
• **Maja** by Myrurgia
  Pronunciation: mar-HA/my-RURR-gee-uh
  Type: oriental

If you were born towards the very beginning of Scorpio you might like to check out the choices for those born on the cusp of Libra/Scorpio on pages 274–278.

- **Escada** by Escada
  Pronunciation: ess-KAR-duh
  Type: floral
- **Zinnia** by Floris
  Pronunciation: ZINN-ee-uh/FLORR-iss
  Type: floral/green
- **Yohji** by Yohji Yamamoto
  Pronunciation: YO-jee yamma-MO-toe
  Type: oriental

MAJA — *because it's riveting*

This is Spain in wild and flashing flamenco mood — dazzling, splashy, seductive and slightly dangerous. **Maja** is a volatile and passionate perfume that doesn't cost a fortune but makes its point as emphatically as its more luxurious Oriental–Spanish sisters. It contains the seductions of the East with its wild bouquet of *rose d'orient*, coumarin (which is a heady and sweet combination of caramel/vanilla and lavender), jasmine, oakmoss and tons of sexy, earthy patchouli. The Spanish influence comes from tobacco leaf, Catalonian lavender and geranium, and a hint of Seville orange blossom to send the whole cocktail off into swirls of sunny sensuousness. **Maja** is like a mad fiesta — exotic enough for Scorpios and with enough adventure to intrigue Sagittarians on the loose.

ESCADA — *because it's versatile*

Created by the late Margaretha Ley for the German

fashion empire of Escada, this sparkling and captivating perfume mirrors her wonderfully original way of imposing bright, vibrant colour and prints on classically tailored clothes with outstanding success — just ask any woman who wears the Escada label like a personal uniform! **Escada** the perfume is rich and heady, based on bergamot, peach and hyacinth blazing brightly over elegant roses, jasmine, carnation, orange blossom and iris, with daringly tropical touches of frangipani flower and fresh coconut! All this flamboyance is seamlessly woven into a very beguiling perfume that seems to be able to change its mood to suit yours. Scorpios will love its standout sophistication while happy-go-lucky Sagittarians will hope some of it rubs off on them!

ZINNIA

— because it's a summer beauty

The famed House of Floris seems to be restaging a considerable comeback with a new look and new fragrances, including this charmer. Floris has been around since the beginning of the eighteenth century and has enjoyed royal patronage 'By Appointment' ever since. It may be embedded in English tradition, but Floris was actually started by a Spaniard and it's his exotic influence that appears in many of their beautiful creations — especially in **Zinnia**.

Zinnia is brimful of summery wildflowers joined by the more cultivated charms of rose and violet, warm woody notes and a dash of allspice to give it its outdoors piquancy. It smells like a Van Gogh landscape looks — swirly, dazzling, impetuous and wild. A touch of relaxing sun for businesslike Scorpios, and pure joy for up-and-at-it Sagittarians.

YOHJI — *because it has the killer instinct*
Yamamoto's signature perfume is a challenge even for this formidable cusp. It will test the dramatic ambitions of Scorpios and nettle the optimism of Saggitarians. But if you can wear **Yohji**'s intense brand of *femme fatale* non-conformity, you're a woman to be reckoned with. Yamamoto has always startled, but somehow enchanted, his devotees with clothes that are breathtakingly removed from the conventional, and his perfume follows suit. It does not muck around. Even the top notes of raw green are quickly swamped in amber as the plot takes a plunge into the depths of vanilla, its synthetic cousin vanillin, sandalwood and musk. But the star of the show is yet to emerge, and when it does it eclipses the rest of the cast. It's coumarin, that musky, musty, marzipan-sweet synthesis of tonka beans and lavender that smoulders and flashes with earthy exotica. The unique presence of azalea absolute cools things down a little, but not that you'd notice. **Yohji** reveals itself to be more than an oriental persuasion — it throws down the gauntlet. I love it for its sultry, brooding bravado and its theatrical impact. It'll certainly get you noticed!

The Scorpio male:
gifts to take the sting out of him

When he eventually lets down his fearsome guard, the typical Scorpio reveals a terrific sense of humour that borders on the hysterically funny. He's actually great fun to be with — playful, mischievous and only serious if he thinks another tail is interested in his. The sting will suddenly be ready and a dance of conquest begins, which can either end in passionate and joyous seduction or resentment that he hasn't won — he thinks winning is everything and will put body, heart and soul into being victorious.

And because he does nothing by half measures, he'll either sulk and sneer or be on top of the world. So it follows that most people pander to him, which I think is misguided and only adds to his sense of inflated self-importance. That's why I suggest you give him fragrances (or anything else for that matter) that tend to take the mickey out of him — as long as he doesn't know it. Giving him something he thinks will increase his self-awareness or his ability to seduce anything in sight, might make him unbearable, especially if you have to live with him! So, go for something different, something unusual and individual that isn't loaded with sexual innuendo or bears a name that bolsters his ego to dizzy heights. Steer away from the obvious. Always remember he's basically a very kind and compassionate man (even Scorpios who've strayed somewhat from the path of goodness still remain loyal and caring underneath their naughtiness). Sure, it can be sexy, but not corny. Sure, it can be classy, but not pretentious. Anyway, you'll know if he likes it — he'll splash it on immediately and chances are you'll have to run for cover!

- **Opium pour Homme** by Yves Saint Laurent
  Pronunciation: O-pee-um poor OMM/
  eve sarn lor–ON
  Type: oriental
- **Heaven** by Chopard
  Pronunciation: HEVV-en/SHOW-par
  Type: woody/fruity
- **Havana** by Aramis
  Pronunciation: har-VAR-nuh/ARRA-miss
  Type: spicy/fruity
- **Armani pour Homme** by Armani
  Pronunciation: arr-MAR-nee poor OM
  Type: fruity/oriental

Opium pour Homme

Not quite the sinister seducer you, or he, might imagine, but a sparkling and almost eccentric bag of tricks that is so original just one glance at the principal ingredients will convince you it has definite possibilities of throwing him for a six! Why not, when he first tries it on and innocently asks you 'What's in it?', breathe all this into his ear — '**Opium pour Homme** is *bursting* with blackcurrant bud and star anise, *hot* with fiery Sichaun pepper and Chinese galanga ginger, *mysterious* with precious Oriental woods and caressed with the sweet resin of the Tolu balsam tree from Peru — and they tell me it's *habit-forming*, darling.' It's all perfectly true, and if he doesn't ask for an encore, threaten to use it on yourself. He'll love it immediately. Sometimes with Scorpios, push comes to shove.

Heaven

He might even think he's in it or on his way with this very peaceful and serene piece of absolute deception. On the surface it's all smooth innocence with its bracing citrus top notes, a dash of sweet blackcurrant contrasted with the relaxing and calming effects of soft sandalwood and pungent cedarwood. But at its base lurks the notoriously sexy tonka bean with its clinging, creamy sweetness of caramel and vanilla, and ambrette seeds, which are tiny little powerhouses that release great wafts of something that smells like a cross between brandy and musk. That's enough to stir anyone into action, especially a randy Scorpio. Just remind him it's called **Heaven** and he's supposed to be an angel, not a little devil.

Havana

This would knock the socks off Fidel Castro! It's a wild and wily cocktail that would have been right at home in the heyday of Hemingway when he lived and lived it up hard in Havana. I guess it's a nostalgic throwback to the good times, the gambling and gun-running, the rum-guzzling and cigar-chewing days that are only a faded memory now. But what a homage to that era it is! **Havana** is bursting with the punchy tang of tangerine, the pungent blast of coriander seed, the spicy rip of pimento berry, the sexy, earthy sultriness of patchouli, a heady whiff of no-nicotine tobacco leaf and a cool trail of jasmine to calm down the Caribbean frenzy. It's as colourful as calypso, as frantic as reggae and as seductive as voodoo!

Armani pour Homme

We can't deny a Scorpio his touch of class, and so the ever-urbane Armani provides it — in spades! Super-cool in style, but vibrant and sensuous in reality, **Armani pour Homme** is so sophisticated and civilised he'll need a new wardrobe to go with it. It drips with elitist suaveness from its warmly golden notes of mandarin and bergamot laced with patchouli and sandalwood, to the suggestiveness of musk and the velvet glove treatment of oakmoss. This is not sex — this is almost unbearable foreplay! Naturally it's not for young Scorpios on the lookout — it's for worldly-wise, hungry Scorpios on the prowl. And with his ego and his libido in the firm hands of **Armani pour Homme,** no one is entirely safe!

Who suits what, and when: getting the best out of your perfumes

Because perfumes become not only extensions of your personality but also give emphasis to the way you look and the mood you're in, naturally, to bring out their best, they should be treated with due understanding in regard to their characteristics and qualities. They too have limitations and strengths, just as we all have. So, the following table outlines when best to wear them (Day, Night), the age-group most suited to them (Young, Mature), the general complexion of the wearer (Fair, Dark), and the seasons they bloom best in (Spring/Summer – S/S, or Autumn/Winter – A/W). This table is meant only to be used as an approximate guide or reference point — it is not a hard and fast set of rules by any means.

fume	Day	Night	Young	Mature	Fair	Dark	S/S	A/W
alimar		•		•		•	•	•
son		•		•	•	•		•
session		•		•	•	•		•
ast de Cartier	•	•		•	•	•		•
ure	•	•	•	•	•	•		•
rcisse Noir		•		•		•		•

YOUR SECRET WEAPONS

fume	Day	Night	Young	Mature	Fair	Dark	S/S	A/W
ite Diamonds		•		•	•	•	•	•
adetta	•		•		•	•	•	•
ende	•		•	•	•	•		•
ocking	•		•		•	•		•
de Nuit	•		•	•	•	•		•
bek		•		•		•		•

SCORPIO/SAGITTARIUS CUSPS

fume	Day	Night	Young	Mature	Fair	Dark	S/S	A/W
ja	•	•	•		•	•	•	•
ada	•	•		•		•	•	•
ania	•		•		•	•	•	•
ji		•		•		•		•

LIBRA/SCORPIO CUSPS

fume	Day	Night	Young	Mature	Fair	Dark	S/S	A/W
lou		•	•			•		•
u		•		•		•		•
ite Jeans	•	•		•	•	•		•
assardi Light	•	•		•	•	•	•	•

MEN'S FRAGRANCES

fume	Day	Night	Young	Mature	Fair	Dark	S/S	A/W
ium pour Homme	•	•	•		•		•	
aven	•	•	•		•		•	•
vana	•	•	•		•	•		•
nani pour Homme	•	•		•	•		•	•

Sagittarius

The archer

November 22–December 21

You and the goalpost

I t's not a goalpost it's a target of some sort. It's what you aim your arrow at as you rush by on your way to something else. It isn't that you have to win anything, it's just that you can't resist having a shot at anything that takes your fancy. In fact, you probably don't even look back to see if you've scored — it doesn't really matter! (This, especially in the case of Sagittarian women, includes people who have probably been smitten by your arrow thinking it's been fired off by Cupid, and can't understand why you haven't stopped to collect your prize!) It isn't heartlessness, it's your carelessness and your recklessness — your quiver of arrows is never empty! In fact, when all's said and done, goalposts don't interest you all that much — you just pretend they do. They are merely the space where you almost casually kick your way to success in the great game of life, more to impress admirers of your skill and accuracy rather than winning anything.

You're such a happy soul — unfailingly enthusiastic, disarmingly frank, expansive, generous and stimulating. People even forgive you for your unconscious thoughtlessness and your habit of unintentional seduction when you had nothing of the sort in your mind! How surprised and embarrassed you are when you realise you've left a trail of broken hearts in the headlong expression of your freedom. Don't they understand you are not one to take on commitment unless *you* give the green light? It never ceases to amaze you that people who ought to know better want to pin you down to promises. Promises! They're the bane of your restless life, aren't they? You are sincere about relationships, but never deadly serious!

Have you ever seen the pastoral symphony scene in Walt Disney's *Fantasia*? It's an idyllic episode set in Arcadia, and could well have been called 'A day in the life of a Sagittarian'. It's full of the joys of life with baby Pans and cupids, flying horses, unicorns,

Bacchus, and a tribe of very fetching male and female centaurs (your half-human, half-animal astrological symbol) being playfully romantic. The females swim and splash, luxuriate by the pool, have their hair and faces done, meet their mates and go off for rollicking good times with Bacchus, before a storm arrives and they run for cover (which is typical — Sagittarians don't care for storms or stormy scenes that put out their fires!) until all's well that ends well, and love and kisses win the day. A good time was had by all.

In an updated way, that's how you prefer to live your life, and usually do. Not much gets in the way of your insatiable appetite for adventure. At least it stops you from being on your own — a fate worse than Chinese water torture in your book! Unfortunately, you shouldn't always give into self-indulgence thinking it's true happiness — one day you may find it's all a daydream, and you can't face the harshness of reality. That's when Sagittarians give in to disillusionment, gambling, shiftiness and hot-headedness. Fortunately you're a pretty lucky lot, but you must realise that if your luck runs out, there should be something more substantial you can fall back on. Often there isn't and you become bad-tempered, preachy and even fanatical about things. However, if you have the true innovative creativity of your sign, like your fellow-archer Beethoven, you might go through the horrors of hell, but eventually you'll come up trumps with a more profound and aspirational outlook on your life. I hope so, because sad Sagittarians make other people feel sad, but well-adjusted (or re-adjusted) ones are absolute joys and the world would be drearier without their smiling kindness and optimism. Just be careful where you fire those innocent arrows of yours. Try looking backwards now and then — you might be shocked at the devastation you've caused. Then it might be high time to stop and gently draw out an arrow from an ailing heart. Think of someone else for a change, seriously. You can do it — you know you can.

Sagittarian style

Because at heart you dislike conformity and love to break rules, your sense of personal style is a curious one — Sagittarians express themselves in an erratic, sometimes eccentric way. They can be distressingly untidy and think that just flinging random things together makes an individual statement. They can be outrageously flamboyant and flashy, or so classically kempt they look almost severe. A lot will depend on your career requirements, but even here your individualism and versatility within those bounds will be strikingly evident.

The same is mirrored in your home-life. It will either be wildly untidy, or colourful and slightly vulgar (although *you* won't think so) or so pared-down to bare essentials it looks monastic! But it reflects what you are, so what the heck. At least people will always be welcome. Although you'd really rather entertain outside your home where everything's done for you, people are always welcome into where you live. But they'll have to take what comes. You are not married to domesticity, and figure there are better things to do with your life than making lampshades out of dried banana leaves and raffia bows. Still, if the door bell suddenly rings, you'll throw the odd cushion on the couch, flick a duster over the flowers, fling on a caftan, spray yourself with whatever perfume comes to hand and put on your widest smile, and hope it's more than just the postman!

The good thing about this though is your adaptability. In fact, since you're always restless and want to be on the move, anywhere you happen to be at the time you happily call home, although you're a bit scared of getting too attached to it. You don't *mind* being attached, but nor do you like the suffocating idea of putting down permanent roots. A good deal of your life is spent mooning through travel magazines and brochures, and most of you will never lose the itch to fly off to distant and exotic destinations. The lure of excitement, adventure, new places and new faces is critical to your happiness, even if it does nothing for your stability.

Stability is almost a dirty word to you, and I guess that's why you're depicted as a centaur. They're regarded mythologically as being wild hunters — laws unto themselves — and slaves to their animal passions. Well, you don't tend to take too much notice of others and have a pretty healthy sexual appetite, so no wonder stability takes a back seat!

When it comes to presenting yourself for public exposure (which takes up a lot of your time), the object really is to express the more vivid and individual facets of yourself. You will never be one of the mob, so why look it? Instead you'll always strive to be striking but not dolled-up, with an almost casual air of outdoorsy freshness. This is why I think people don't suspect the innovative and often fiery side of your nature, so maybe it's high time to show it — you've always secretly wanted to shock, so why not? Your style is so erratic you'll probably get way with it.

Your outer expression is *freedom*. Your inner core is *fearlessness*.

Here's how to translate all of that into the best perfumes for you.

I have divided them into two categories:

1. *The big guns* — these are the all-important perfumes that should suit you best. They form the core of your personal arsenal.

2. *Your secret weapons* — these augment the basics and are more daring and unusual, but should still suit you.

There is also a choice of perfumes for those of you

born on the cusp of Sagittarius/Capricorn, as well as a selection of men's fragrances suitable to give the Sagittarian male. (If you were born on the cusp of Scorpio/Sagittarius see pages 310–314 for your further perfume choices.) I have given each perfume a category as well as a simple and easy guide to its correct pronunciation. At the end of the chapter I have summated all of the perfumes into a table that tells you whether they're best on young or mature women, in warm or cool weather, day or evening, for dark or fair complexions.

The big guns: the indispensable basics

There's no doubt that no matter how sophisticated an image you might like to give yourself, most people see you as almost the opposite — unaffected, natural, energetic and vivacious. Of course they respect your individualism, but no matter how refined and defined you really are it's your basic attraction to fresh, uncomplicated and dynamic perfumes that gives you away. Perfumes that are heavily seductive, over-flowery or too fussy are not your best weapons. They simply go against your grain, and either fight or dull your good-natured and outgoing personality. I'm not suggesting that you have to smell as pure and simple as a newborn baby, or that you've just emerged from a cold shower, but using perfumes with freshness, lightness and clarity will underline your infectious and gregarious personality. You love being with other people so much you don't want to risk offence with something that smells too startling. If this sounds a bit predictable to more temperamental and risk-taking Sagittarians, you get your chance to bust out in your back-up perfumes. But stick to these basics and be confident they'll add to your attraction rather than upstage it.

- **Jicky** by Guerlain
  Pronunciation: ZHJEE-kee (or JICK-ee)/
  gair-LARN
  Type: woody/herbal
- **Quelques Fleurs** by Houbigant
  Pronunciation: KELKA fler/OOBEE-gon
  Type: floral bouquet
- **Madame Rochas** by Rochas
  Pronunciation: mar-DARM ro-SHAR
  Type: floral
- **Evelyn** by Crabtree & Evelyn
  Pronunciation: EEVA-lin
  Type: floral
- **Pleasures** by Estée Lauder
  Type: floral
- **Coriandre** by Jean Couturier
  Pronunciation: corry-ARND-ruh/
  zjharn coo-TOOR-ee-ay
  Type: green/oriental

JICKY — because it's defiant

Women not partial to the energy of the great outdoors loathe this perfume, which is why it's right up your alley. Since you're not one for fussing around at home or getting all prettied up to look ultra-feminine, this highly individual and surprising perfume should become not just an ally but a favourite. **Jicky** broke new ground when it was first introduced in the Naughty Nineties way back in 1889 (truly!) and is still breaking it with its sheer audacity and originality of composition. After over a century, Guerlain still count it as their lovable and forever-young rebel!

Jicky dared to revolutionise the way women — and men — thought about perfume. It broke the mould of sickly floral perfumes with its use of synthetic essences (in fact its creator, Aimé Guerlain invented the scientific process of perfume synthesis) mixed with natural ones. It begins with a rush of bergamot, lemon, mandarin and lavender, then adds the pungency of rosemary, basil and jasmine, a whack of marzipan-like tonka bean and a dash of spice before the entrance of vanilla, rosewood, leather and the very first use of oriental benzoin. I'll bet even Aimé was amazed at what he'd come up with. So will you if you've never smelt it before!

At first, women scorned its daring, unfloral smell but the chaps took to it with such a vengeance that by the turn of the century it had well and truly made its mark. By then, women had changed as well — it was the time of the suffrage movement — and **Jicky** was no longer considered slightly scandalous but very appropriate to the new mood. In fact, you could probably say it was the very first feminist fragrance! It never looked back after that, and still excites women with a strong sense of spiritedness.

Jicky is a very powerful perfume. I don't mean it hangs around when you wish it would go away — indeed, it's quite subtle in approach. But it has the power to make a point about you, clearly and cleanly. It makes you feel at once exhilarated and removed from the conventional and contrived. It also evokes an enormous sense of nostalgia — perhaps for those first heady days of kicking over the traces and making your presence felt. That's why it's an ideal perfume to get young Sagittarians on their perfumed and positive way to womanhood.

Why is it called **Jicky**? Officially after the nickname of Aimé's favourite young nephew. Unofficially (and more romantically) it was the name he called his secret English girlfriend whose hand in marriage was sternly denied by his own father who demanded he return to France and head up the Guerlain business. So where his English rose dipped out, millions of future women won. After all, without this *petite tragedie*, this ageless and timeless perfume would never have been created.

QUELQUES FLEURS
— because it's a beautiful survivor

Being a survivor is not the only reason this perfume still remains one of the most bewitchingly beautiful floral bouquets ever created, although heaven knows it's been through a lot in its illustrious career. Almost as old as Guerlain's perennial **Jicky**, Houbigant's miniature masterpiece of floral harmony created a sensation at its launch way back in 1912, when fashionable Edwardian women on both sides of the Channel and the Atlantic fell totally in love with its charms, and little wonder. It was the first perfume of the century to offer them something more complex and fascinating than the single-flower or single-essence perfumes they were used to — it was the very first contemporary floral bouquet scent!

It enjoyed its success right through to the Second World War, and then seemed to disappear for lack of the precious hand-picked natural ingredients that went into its making. Even after the war it languished and was thought to be old-hat and out-of-date — the aldehydic moderns had really taken over by then — and it looked like curtains for **Quelques Fleurs**. But it's always had a fanatically-faithful following, and by sheer feminine demand it eventually made its quiet but welcome return.

It's been modernised a little, of course, and has lost some of the cloying sweetness the Edwardians doted on but today's Sagittarians would find a little sickly.

But it's still bursting with flowers, especially in its middle notes after an exhilarating opening fanfare of citrusy bergamot. Lilac, rose and jasmine are the principal beauties, with flashes of exotic orchid appearing as it settles down to a golden glow of amber and sandalwood.

For a floral bouquet, **Quelques Fleurs** is full of vivacity, as if a green summer breeze had wafted through its garden of flowers. It's neither heavy nor elaborate, but full of light-hearted *élan*, just like you on a good day! It's a perfume you'll find you can wear easily anytime and anywhere and be complimented on. And because it's managed to survive fads and fashions it will no doubt appeal even more to fair-minded Sagittarians.

MADAME ROCHAS
— because it's pure elegance

This beautiful and poised composition of flowers and spices is a great going-out perfume. It, like you, revels in meeting and impressing new people with its elegant attitude that never becomes haughty or aloof. Despite being tagged a classic, **Madame Rochas** is ingratiating and fascinating. Put simply, it turns heads — the right ones!

Only long-standing devotees might notice a little change in emphasis of its approach. It has undergone slight corrective surgery — not so much a drastic face-lift, but a gentle peeling back of its heavier flowers and musk to reveal a new youthful radiance with a more transparent accent on its fresh green and spicy notes. It's a minor re-orchestration, which, when you consider it's well over thirty-something, is not such a bad thing. Anyway, it's still unmistakably the one and only **Madame Rochas**, so don't expect a French revolution.

Orange blossom, hyacinth, green leaves and spicy aldehydes introduce it with an eloquent freshness before the smooth and sweet beauty of rose, jasmine, lily of the valley, honeysuckle and iris give it a refined feminine persuasion before sandalwood, cedarwood, oakmoss, vetiver and a hint of tonka bean usher in a very understated sensuousness of musk. All very beguiling but not in the least heavy or high-powered. **Madame Rochas** is always the lady — and asks the same of you, so get out of the jeans and into the little black killer for the occasion.

I know a lot of Sagittarian women are loath to go for elegance in favour of a more casual look, but there are times when it's nice (or necessary) to remind yourself there are more sophisticated games than netball to play, and even though you like to flout or bend the rules a bit, hitting the target accurately is your real aim in life. There's no more captivating and civilised way to achieve that than to dip your arrow in **Madame Rochas**.

EVELYN — because you'll bloom in it

Sagittarians are suckers for the scent of a single beautiful flower. They have been known to rely on pure lily of the valley, freesia, boronia or lavender as their source of perfumed pleasure. And they are not immune to the scent of a rose in all its piercingly poignant beauty.

That's why I strongly suggest **Evelyn** — a gloriously true English rose fragrance available as an *eau de parfum*, as well as a range of bath and toiletry products, so you can layer yourself head to foot in its rosy rapture.

Crabtree & Evelyn commissioned the famous David Austin Roses of Wolverhampton in the West Midlands of England to breed a rose especially to develop into a perfume to add to their already popular single-flower range. It took eight years before a rose of unique distinction was to become the basis of **Evelyn**. Only then was it given to a highly-reputable French perfumer in Grasse to capture its essence in a new perfume. The Living Flower technique (here called Head Space Analysis) was used to scientifically produce the precise profile of the still-living bloom in all its subtle shifts of floral emphasis during the day — even nuances of jasmine, violet and lily of the valley were detected and reproduced in its composition — and with the addition of a velvet-soft peach accent **Evelyn** was at last given to the rose-doting world.

Becomingly packaged in a pink rose printed

design, the peachy-pink liquid is contained in a charmingly straightforward bottle with an antique-style top and looks quite irresistible. It's a fragrance I think Sagittarians in need of something definite but light, romantic but playful and just plain adorable will fall for. It is so faithful to its highly bred and haunting source, that a rose by any other name would naturally be called **Evelyn**.

PLEASURES — *because it's full of them*

I'm surprised a perfumer as astute to the market hadn't thought of such a light and lovely floral bouquet before the eventual release of **Pleasures**, but no doubt Lauder had its reasons. Women needed this kind of option when the fruit-salad avalanche of new perfumes threatened to bury them alive under the assumption that flowers were out and perfumes now catered to taste-buds almost as much as noses! What about Lauder's **Beautiful**? Well, it's an avalanche in its own way too — extremely floral and tenaciously lovely, but too strong for some. **Pleasures** solves it all. The flowers used are much brighter and lighter and there's not a slice of watermelon or a raspberry in sight! What we have instead is an unpretentious but endearing charmer that will appeal to the Sagittarian love of freshness and vivacity.

Pleasures offers a piquant top note of young white lilies and tender violet leaves singing merrily over a basic melody line of delicately spicy white peonies, sweet pink roses, drifts of jasmine and lilac (Mrs Lauder's favourite essence). Underneath this is the peppery counterpoint of baie rose and accompanied by soft creamy sandalwood and a dash of earthy patchouli.

Pleasures is as exhilarating and as redolent of earth and air as a garden after a summer shower. It never becomes cloyingly sweet or even overly persistent, but allows you to react to its transparent exquisiteness with your own means of free-wheeling charm. It is not a perfume that ties you to it by any means. It wants you to be comfortable wearing it, and I'm sure you will be.

Don't be deceived by its apparent lightness when you first try it — **Pleasures** has the ability to linger quite a while without overstaying its pretty welcome. Nor be misled into thinking it's exclusively for the young — it's not only comfortable but quite flattering on more mature Sagittarians who still have a gleam in their wandering eye! I think **Pleasures** is a very welcome addition to Lauder's stable of formidable thoroughbreds.

CORIANDRE — *because it's a spicy knockout*

There's no doubt of hitting the target fair and square with this ground-to-air perfumed missile. It's an explosive little number full of surprises. The first one is that it does *not* smell like a freshly picked bunch of the piquant herb it's named after. **Coriandre** has never even seen a herb garden let alone an oriental kitchen!

It's far above the commonplace. In fact, **Coriandre** dislikes daylight and the outdoors quite definitely and is very much a night stalker. It loves parties, promises and assignations of a non-committal nature. In other words it's a bit of a good-time girl. Some may call it tarty, but tarty or not, it will sweep everyone else aside when you make your entrance in it.

I must warn you that you'll have to make a little effort finding it, but good perfume boutiques and duty-free outlets usually have it in stock. For those in the know, **Coriandre** is a very popular commodity! Anyway, you won't fail to notice it in its tall green packaging and its bottle with a gleaming dark green top. And what lurks inside is even more magnetic.

Coriandre is a torrid and tropical mix of heady orange blossom, geranium leaf, rose, lily and jasmine with large overlays of oakmoss, green angelica, dark sappy tree resins, almost an overdose of patchouli and musk, and to top it all off — what else but acerbic, tangy coriander? There is definitely no mistaking its intoxicating smell.

There are some over-sophisticated women who once swore by **Coriandre** but now consider it a bit *passé*, which only makes it more exclusive — so if you fall for its dynamic non-conformity, it could well be exclusively yours!

Your secret weapons: the surprises

Sagittarians like surprises and surprising people — it's their innate sense of playfulness and good fun coming out (not that you need much encouragement in that respect!). Being out and about, being gregarious, charming and witty is necessary for you to keep your fires burning merrily away. But being taken for granted, being thought of as 'a good old reliable never-changing Sagittarian ratbag' is just not on! You don't like presumption, or over-familiarity for that matter. And that's when your temperament warns that you need a damned good change! So what do you do? Hopefully you don't let loose that notorious firebrand temper of yours, nor become tactless and sarcastic (which you do with deadly and stinging accuracy). No, you turn to your not-often exposed side of fearless and uninhibited unpredictability.

Suddenly you put on a different face — a little more controlled and aloof, a little more cool and calculating. This is your brave front, and you can keep it up for as long as you like — no one is going to question it or tell you you're above yourself, are they? You almost become another person — dignified, suave and not to be crossed. You're actually taking your inner courage in both hands and using it to make your presence felt and your stance noticed. It's not a perverse transformation, it's merely a new emphasis, a new way of presenting yourself and being taken a little more seriously than usual. Naturally you need all the ammunition to carry it off — including perfumes like these that speak volumes for your individuality, your daring and your wit (which can be very pointed).

- **Giorgio Beverly Hills** by Giorgio Beverly Hills
  Type: floral/oriental
- **Havana pour Elle** by Aramis
  Pronunciation: har-VARN-uh poor ELL/
  ARRA- miss
  Type: floral/fruity
- **Aliage** by Estée Lauder
  Pronunciation: allie-ARZJHE/ESS-tay LOR-duh
  Type: green
- **Gianni Versace** by Gianni Versace
  Pronunciation: gee-ARN-ee vair-SAR-chee
  Type: floral
- **Red Door** by Elizabeth Arden
  Type: floral/oriental
- **Diva** by Ungaro
  Pronunciation: DEE-vuh/oon-GARR-o
  Type: floral/oriental

GIORGIO BEVERLY HILLS
— because it's still divisive

Years after its controversial release to an unsuspecting world in 1982, this high-powered blockbuster still creates schisms, although it no longer seems to have the dubious ability to clear restaurants! Nevertheless, it has barely diminished in popularity and has a large and faithful following, to the point where it has recently spawned a somewhat lighter version of its formidable self called Giorgio Aire, which is quite different.

The smell of **Giorgio Beverly Hills** still comes as a bit of a shock, mostly because too many women have not learned it should be used very sparingly, otherwise it quickly becomes the subject of nasal aversion, especially in confined spaces (business offices in particular). It is an extremely potent cocktail where nothing is spared in the cause of maximum impact and minimal subtlety. The ingredients tell you why.

Its top notes explode in a tumult of mandarin, bergamot, orange flowers and green galbanum, then are given a second detonation of powerhouse gardenia and tuberose. You'd think all this action might settle down a bit, but no — aldehydes see to it that the top notes keep on repeating themselves as a volley of jasmine, rose, jonquil, carnation, ylang ylang, lily of the valley and hyacinth add floral fireworks, fixed (if that is the appropriate word) with sandalwood, cedarwood, vetiver, musk, amber and oakmoss. Where's the patchouli to give the *coup de grâce* you might ask? Perhaps they thought it might be overdoing things a bit to include it!

But **Giorgio** obviously appeals to women who love its brash and bright outspokenness, and to men who don't find it hard to get away from. For the odd

Sagittarian lacking self-confidence, **Giorgio** will soon fix matters, and for those with scads of it, **Giorgio** will reaffirm it with a flourish. It's simply a matter of whether it appeals to you or not. If it does, then go for **Giorgio** and go for broke. One thing is certain — you'll soon know who your friends and allies are. But please don't wear it like there's no tomorrow — there will be, and **Giorgio Beverly Hills** will no doubt still be with us. It may even be declared an American national treasure, heaven help us!

HAVANA POUR ELLE — because it's torrid
If you always wanted to experience Havana in its wild and wonderful heyday, this is about as close as you'll get in a perfume. It's a vivid and exotic adventure that knows no boundaries, no restraints.

In an unusual role reversal, **Havana for Men** was created first and often secretly swiped from the bathroom shaving cabinet when he wasn't looking. So, being wise in these marketing matters, Aramis created **Havana pour Elle** to put a stop to any accusations of invading male territory, as well as providing both sexes with almost matching fragrances sharing the same evocative and picturesque name — and the same impact!

Havana pour Elle is of course much more feminine than its male counterpart, but it's certainly not a sweet and sentimental little concoction. It's far more reminiscent of the glamour-puss heydays of

Rita Hayworth in *Gilda* or Lauren Bacall in her Bogart movies. It conjures up smoky nightclubs and dazzling diamonds, the dizzy spin of a roulette wheel and starlit kisses under swaying palms. It's sensual, sexy and seductive — with tons of swank!

Its ingredients are awash with vivid Caribbean colour — a sultry and volatile cocktail of flowers, fruits and spices. There's the voluptuous allure of the Queen of the Night orchid with its rare vanilla-like scent, night-blooming cereus, the Caribbean raintree flower, magnolia blossom and heliotrope, mango, melon and even pineapple with a dash of sweet daphne and lily of the valley to lower the temperature somewhat. **Havana pour Elle** is sensational — just don't confuse his with yours. His is like a happy calypso — yours throbs like voodoo drums in the sultry tropical night. Wow!

ALIAGE — *because it's such a good sport*
Anyone for tennis? Believe it or not, Estée Lauder, herself once a tennis fanatic, wanted something fragrantly different to feature on the court. It's said she was inspired by the smell of palm leaves swaying in the noonday breeze, and up came **Aliage**.* Well, despite Mrs Lauder's fervent endorsement, it didn't exactly swamp the popularity stakes, but has carved out a unique niche of a dry green ground-breaker that highly

---

* If you see this spelt 'Alliage', don't worry. It's just the Australian spelling — everything else is exactly the same!

individualistic women (sporty or not) match to their own sense of the unconventional. And unconventional it certainly is, to the point where it is now a highly-valued cult perfume with a silent but devoted following.

Aliage is based on green leaves and green galbanum with lots of oakmoss and vetiver to intensify its extraordinary pungency. It's softened a little with hints of gardenia (but not enough to make it remotely flowery), a blush of just-ripe peach, wild thyme, citrus oils, while pine oil and rosewood keep the mixture strictly in the forest. It's a bit like the first whiff of a very dry martini with a twist of lime (hold the olive). **Aliage** is the driest perfume I know and quite uncompromisingly commanding.

It won't be every Sagittarian's favourite by any means, but those of you who dote on rushing around sporting fields or launching into nautical adventures will find it a natural and exhilarating adjunct to such energetic exertions. To less frantic Sagittarians who still like to veer away from the conventional, **Aliage** is a fiercely zesty and daring statement of your individuality. Just don't try wearing it with a glitzy ballgown, or you'll come a cropper.

GIANNI VERSACE
— because it reveals your desires
This was Versace's first big perfume, and typically, it's

his version of a Venus Flytrap. Of course it is far more attractive, and not quite so obvious in its intent. But it does use the same method, more or less. It uses allure to achieve the desired effect of sure-fire but subtle feminine seduction.

Does that sound too heavy for you? Well, it isn't really. Feminine seduction comes in many devious forms — Sagittarians usually achieve it through a good sense of humour that is also suggestive (or failing that, drinking the male under the table!). But remember, **Gianni Versace** is one of your surprise perfumes, and there's no more successful seduction than taking your prey by complete surprise! And this exquisite perfume will do just that.

It's an elegant arrangement of beautiful flowers — narcissus, jasmine, honeysuckle, tuberose, ylang ylang, orange blossom and Italian lavender with subtle hints of cinnamon, cardamom and patchouli. But it's the warm resin of olibanum (otherwise known as frankincense) and sensuous musk that hold the key to this smoothly persuasive and deceptive composition. They underline the floral motif to give **Gianni Versace** its mesmerising magnetism. Deceptive, you ask? Well, its strategy is one of disarming beauty that's so gradual he's so busy thinking how lovely you smell before he realises you've closed in for the kill. That's how **Gianni Versace** works — softly, softly. It's just the ammunition you need to remind yourself that you're more than a damned good sport — and him that you can be a highly desirable woman if he plays his cards right — right into your hands.

RED DOOR — *because it's inviting*

Named after the famous pillarbox red doors that lead into the beauty secrets and rituals of Elizabeth Arden salons around the world, **Red Door** is an open invitation to brush up your act.

Let's face it, Sagittarians can sometimes forget they're not the only runners in the race and scratch their heads in disbelief when some pushy competitor overtakes them and gets to the goal before they can break the ribbon and the record! Well, this is the time when you take good honest stock of yourself and change a few things to get you back in the running again. And **Red Door** is a pretty good way to begin.

It's a confident perfume with a certain briskness about it that comes from flowers with high top notes — such as red roses, lily of the valley, jasmine, orange blossom, wild violets, freesia and tuberose mixed joyously with the deliciousness of cherry-pie heliotrope, peach and plum, the sharpness of vetiver, then softened (sort of!) with sandalwood, honey, amber and musk. But there's a lovely surprise in store that sets **Red Door** firmly apart from its mid-price range competitors. It's the unique inclusion of the haunting scent of a rare Chinese orchid called cymbidium karan, which is grown under strict conditions for Arden and flowers only in winter. It adds a sweet vanilla/musk beauty that combines perfectly with the piercing elegance of the red roses that appear in both the head and heart notes of **Red** Door. Without it, the perfume would be lovely but unremarkable.

Red Door, despite its floral clout, is for go-ahead women. It's assertive and uplifting — just what you need when you feel a bit like an also-ran, and don't want to!

DIVA — because it gets applause

Sagittarians who feel they haven't got quite what it takes to be super-cool and sophisticated often give up and settle for what they know they do best — and that's dealing with the world in an honest, frank, straightforward and happy-go-lucky way. And although they often envy other Sagittarian women who are elegant and sophisticated, it doesn't occur to them they can be just the same, with a little effort. They may be hiding their own star quality simply through lack of changing their act!

Of course I'm not saying a single perfume will do the trick, but it helps when you're out there polishing up your routine and getting auditions. Perhaps this shamelessly extroverted but elegant perfume from the shamelessly extroverted but elegant Ungaro, can help heaps.

Diva is a big showy splash of Egyptian jasmine,

Moroccan and Turkish roses, Florentine iris, Sicilian mandarin, Sumatran ylang ylang, Mysore sandalwood and Indian coriander and cardamom. It does not muck around. It's full-throated and fearless, indulgent and sensual, but never very serious. **Diva's** there for applause, not for the Nobel Prize. It easily soars above opposition, cuts swathes through crowds, turns handsome heads, and expects not only wild encores but buckets of long-stemmed roses thrown at it.

The great diva Maria Callas (also a Sagittarian) had already sung her last note when **Diva** was created in 1988, but I'll bet she would have loved it. So will you, and you don't even have to raise your voice to bring the house down. *Bravissima!*

The advantage of the cusp: taking your pick

It's not all confusion — being neither one star nor the other, or feeling you're partly both — if you were born on the cusp of Sagittarius/Capricorn*. You can of course pick and choose from the perfumes suggested from both Sagittarius and Capricorn, but be careful. Depending on your characteristics, they

---

* *If you were born towards the very beginning of Sagittarius you might like to check out the choices for those born on the cusp of Scorpio/Sagittarius on pages 310-314.*

may not all sit easily on you. That's why I've come up with a selection of extras that might solve any perfume problems or indecision you might have. Anyway, the choice is yours, so have fun finding out! They are:

- **Versus Donna** by Gianni Versace
  Pronunciation: VERR-suzz DONN-uh/
  gee-ARN-eevair-SAR-chee
  Type: floral/fruity
- **Gardenia** by Crabtree & Evelyn
  Type: floral
- **Jolie Madame** by Pierre Balmain
  Pronunciation: zjho-LEE mard-ARM/
  pee-AIRbal- MARN
  Type: floral
- **Green Tea** by Elizabeth Arden
  Type: fruity/oriental

VERSUS DONNA
— because it's full of surprises

Since you're probably one of those poor unfortunates whose birthday collides with Christmas, you often get palmed off with one gift to celebrate both events or you're simply forgotten in the yuletide rush. I suggest you either put your order in for a nice big bottle of this very merry perfume, or give it to yourself so you can get into the swing of things. **Versus Donna** is versatile, and both fun-loving Sagittarians and label-driven Capricorns will adore its ravishing mix of raspberry, blackcurrant, plum and sandalwood lavishly laced with the heady delights of tuberose and sweet Australian boronia with a touch of iris, amber and musk for a little (though not much) sophistication. It's a devilish and flirtatious number, so you have to be young enough to keep up with it. Anyway, you'll have a very happy birthday to remember, and easily upstage Santa Claus!

GARDENIA — *because it's hypnotic*

The lush creamy scent of gardenia is one of the most difficult and expensive to distil, and no perfumer has yet really succeeded in totally capturing its voluptuous depth and richness in a bottle — not even Chanel in her fearfully expensive **Gardenia** perfume in 1925. But Crabtree & Evelyn's charming **Gardenia** is very near the mark. It's not an assault on the nose, but a refined and soft beauty that settles well on the skin where it blooms with a luminosity that never shouts for attention but quietly infiltrates the air around you. It may not smell *exactly* like the gardenias in your garden, but it's as close as you'll get in a perfume, and you can always wear a gardenia flower to complement the perfume. Best of all, **Gardenia** also comes in a range of toiletries, so you can permeate yourself in its luscious smell. You'll smell like Christmas in all its gardenia glory.

JOLIE MADAME — *because it's elitist*

Translated as 'pretty lady', this exquisite but elusive (try boutiques, again!) perfume is a tribute to the good taste of sophisticated Sagittarians (and those who are trying) and super-cool Capricorns. It's dazzling, disturbing yet discreet, with a magical mix of gardenia, rose, iris, jasmine, tuberose, narcissus and artemisia (an intriguingly aniseed smell once used in the now-forbidden liqueur *absinthe*). It also has more than a hint of the loveliness of lilac, a little patchouli and a wonderful leather finish that gives it a sensual smoulder. It is certainly not your usual roses-and-jasmine flummery, but extremely feminine in a refined but provocative way. In fact, the term *très chic* could have been coined to describe its magnetic charm. Believe me, **Jolie Madame** is worth every effort to track down and find. It is a truly elegant and endearing classic!

GREEN TEA —
because it's refreshingly different

I suppose **Bvlgari** set the fashionable trend by adding green jasmine tea to their signature perfume, but it was only a tantalising whiff. Others followed, adding a cautious pinch to their brews, but it's taken Elizabeth Arden to go the whole hog, so to speak, and actually name a perfume after one of its principal ingredients. I say one, because **Green Tea** is chock-a-block with other delicious goodies that make up the most exhilarating cuppa you're ever likely to find in a perfume. To mention a few — lemon, rhubarb, caraway, celery and fennel seeds, peppermint, jasmine, oakmoss, carnation — and, naturally, green tea leaves. It all mixes and simmers merrily away until just one spray of it will set your nose twitching and your taste-buds salivating with delight — it's a terrifically refreshing pick-me-up in a perfume and just the cuppa for Sagittarians to revive flagging spirits, and Capricorns to calm down with when they get a bit flustered.

The Sagittarian male: grooming on the run

Not necessarily from the law (although he's such a reckless gambler you never know!) but on the run from himself. The Sagittarian man hates being pinned down and if anyone looks as if they're ready to nail him, he'll be off like a roadrunner. This applies even to when he's finally submitted himself to a little domestication — if you want him to smell his best out there in the workaday world, you'll probably have to stand at the front door and give him a good squirt of manly fragrance before he hits the road! No kidding — Sagittarians, although they insist on scrupulous personal cleanliness, often forget the finishing touch. A good way to teach him to remember is to whisper in his ear 'Haven't you forgotten something important, darling?' and slam the bottle you gave him, at considerable expense, down in front of him. Eventually he'll learn.

But you have to give him the right ammunition first. Don't bother with anything suave and sophisticated, or anything deeply seductive. He'll turn his nose up at them. Always remember, he thinks he's the original Peter Pan and wants to smell as fresh and free as his youth — every day, even if he's pushing eighty! So go for the exhilarating and outdoorsy men's stuff. There's plenty to choose from, but if it's uncomplicated and smells like a brand new day coming up, he might even get around to wearing it. If he's a bit more sophisticated than the average Sagittarian sports-crazed fanatic, then you can give him something more unconventional and even a bit kinky (see **Jean Paul Gaultier** below). It will appeal to his wicked sense of humour, even if he chooses the company in which he'll feature it very carefully. Sagittarians are terrified of being found out they're soppy romantics underneath all that lightning speed and those little-boy grins!

- **Tommy** by Tommy Hilfiger
  Type: fruity/herbal
- **Michael Jordan Cologne** by Michael Jordan
  Type: citrus/herbal
- **Kouros** by Yves Saint Laurent
  Pronunciation: KOOR-ross/eve sarn lor-ON

Type: spicy/oriental
• **Jean Paul Gaultier pour Homme**
  Pronunciation: zjharn pole GOAT-ee-ay poor HOMM
  Type: woody/spicy

Tommy

This dynamic young American designer knew what he wanted in his first try at a distinctively different men's fragrance. He wanted a fresh new outlook that gets the American male (young, of course!) prepared to see in the twenty-first century with wide-eyed wonder and optimism. That's what he got. **Tommy** almost leaps out of the user-friendly stars and stripes bottle with a rush of Florida grapefruit, tangy wild herbs spiked with cinnamon, Cape Cod cranberry, a night-blooming sweet cactus flower called Saguaro, a dash of the yellow rose of Texas, and some New England sycamore and maplewood. **Tommy** is as American as apple pie, as bright as the Star-Spangled Banner, but fits in quite amiably with the great Australian outdoors. Only the smell of gum leaves and billy tea is missing.

Michael Jordan Cologne

He doesn't have to be a fanatical Jordanairre to give this very zesty and feisty cologne the Sagittarian tick of approval. The dramatic black box, with a centre cutout revealing a glass basketball, the black rubber autographed cap and sneaker tread base will assure him it's A-OK and remind him of his own superstar aspirations. And the smell? Clean, brisk, energetic and simply terrific! No wonder, with the wham of citrus and green grass, cypress and cedar leaf, lavender and clary sage, juniper berry and even a shot of cognac, would you believe! — rimmed with the magnetic special effects of musk, patchouli and sandalwood. **Michael Jordan Cologne** has it all there for him to identify with — the image of the super-powerful, super-hunk superstar in action. Just watch him go! He'll be slam-dunking all over the place — showing-off in other words.

Kouros

Despite its Greek name, **Kouros** smells slightly east of the Mediterranean. It's loaded with aromatic and pungent spices from somewhere like Zanzibar, wild grasses that might grow in Madagascar, patchouli and incense from India, moss from Java, and jasmine from Sri Lanka. In other words, it's a typical Saint Laurent oriental fantasy that avoids being cloying by balancing the sultry with the snappy, resulting in a terrific attitude of sunny warmth underlined by a devious seduction. But, back to its Greek inspiration. A kouros is actually a classically sculptured figure of a sporting Hellenic youth in the prime of his handsomeness, so if you explain this to your Sagittarian, he might identify with **Kouros** and actually get to use it!

Jean Paul Gaultier pour Homme

Almost as outrageously different as its female counterpart (even down to the corseted female torso, except this time it's blue not pink), **Jean Paul Gaultier pour Homme** will appeal to, or at least mightily amuse, the male Sagittarian who likes a little kinkiness and craziness in his reckless life.

It sounds innocent enough — green herbs and citrusy bergamot as an opening gambit before wading into the wilder shores of Spanish lavender and some very aphrodisiacal and unnamed spices, then almost swamping itself in the lusciously creamy sexiness of double vanilla — but naturally it's far from naive! Well, what else did you expect from Gaultier — a lemon-fresh lotion that wouldn't offend his granny? Not likely.

Who suits what, and when: getting the best out of your perfumes

Because perfumes become not only extensions of your personality but also give emphasis to the way you look and the mood you're in, naturally, to bring out their best, they must be treated with due understanding in regard to their characteristics and qualities. They too have limitations and strengths, just as we all have. So, the following table outlines when best to wear them (Day, Night), the age-group most suited to them (Young, Mature), the general complexion of the wearer (Fair, Dark), and the seasons they bloom best in (Spring/Summer – S/S, or Autumn/Winter – A/W). This table is meant only to be used as an approximate guide or reference point — it is not a hard and fast set of rules by any means.

Perfume	Day	Night	Young	Mature	Fair	Dark	S/S	A/
Jicky	•		•	•	•		•	
Quelques Fleurs	•	•		•		•	•	
Madame Rochas	•	•		•		•	•	
Evelyn	•		•	•	•		•	
Pleasures	•		•	•		•	•	
Coriandre		•		•		•		•

YOUR SECRET WEAPONS

Perfume	Day	Night	Young	Mature	Fair	Dark	S/S	A/
Giorgio Beverly Hills		•		•	•	•		
Havana pour Elle		•	•	•	•	•	•	
Aliage	•		•	•	•		•	
Gianni Versace		•	•	•	•	•	•	
Red Door	•		•	•	•	•	•	
Diva		•		•	•	•		

SAGITTARIUS/CAPRICORN CUSPS

Perfume	Day	Night	Young	Mature	Fair	Dark	S/S	A/
Versus Donna	•	•	•		•	•	•	
Gardenia	•	•	•	•		•	•	
Jolie Madame	•	•		•		•	•	
Green Tea	•			•	•		•	

SCORPIO/SAGITTARIUS CUSPS

Perfume	Day	Night	Young	Mature	Fair	Dark	S/S	A/
Maja	•	•	•	•		•		
Escada	•	•			•	•	•	
Zinnia	•		•		•	•	•	
Yohji		•		•		•		

MEN'S FRAGRANCES

Perfume	Day	Night	Young	Mature	Fair	Dark	S/S	A/
Tommy	•		•		•	•	•	
Michael Jordan Cologne	•		•	•	•			
Kouros	•	•	•	•	•		•	
Jean Paul Gaultier pour homme	•	•	•	•	•	•	•	

Capricorn

The goat

December 22–January 19

You and Mount Everest

Mountain goats are clever, sure-footed and dexterous, but they instinctively never go beyond their natural capabilities — they never exceed the limit. Capricorns unfortunately do. Which is why they often don't make it, or come a cropper and don't know why. It's usually because they think they know best and go right on ahead, while their friends look on helplessly, and their enemies wait gloatingly for the disaster to come. The best thing, however, is that you learn from your mistakes and you'll give it another go — again and again if necessary — until you've succeeded (mind you, you may have secretly shortened your sights a little for the next attempt, but you're not letting on, are you? You're nobody's fool!).

Capricorns are admirable people, especially the women, who have to put up with many more obstacles than their male counterparts. This makes you all the more determined to achieve your goal, which you've set out and planned meticulously before you even take the first step. Failure is not on your agenda, even if it does become a momentary reality. It's not a mountain you want to conquer, it's Mount Everest, and you have the self-discipline and blind faith in yourself to do it. You have a very vivid imagination — you can see yourself planting your own personal flag on the summit to the cheering crowds below. But what's next?

That's your dilemma. When can you rest on your laurels? You can't. And that's when anxiety sets in. Beneath your indomitable exterior you are usually a bundle of insecurity, which makes you moody and prone to be temperamental, which nobody understands. The best thing to do then is have a good rest and gather your resources around you afresh. There's nothing like a new challenge, and it doesn't always have to be to crash through the glass ceiling, which is a male-made myth to deter you, anyway. Forget it. You love being busy, so choose something else to excel at. Like looking after your friends and family — getting them interested in new projects. You're a born organiser and it's nice to see someone else succeed, especially if you've had a guiding hand in it. It's also a damned good way to quash your often ill-deserved reputation for being calculating and cold. You're not. You're an Earth sign remember, so you are naturally warm, generous and protective. Just bend a little — and don't forget that dazzling natural smile of yours. You can win over anyone with it.

When it comes to family life, you're a winner. Capricorns will move heaven and earth to see their loved ones have what they need and deserve. You'll work your well-manicured fingers to the bone to get it. And when it comes to seeing your children achieve, you are almost terrifying! Other women have come to learn never to get in the way of a Capricorn mum loudly championing her brilliant brood (and you'll want to know why if they're not brilliant!).

In love, you are so surprising it's almost shocking. You'd never exhibit your considerable passion in front of anyone except its recipient, and a new partner will often get the fright of his sexual life when you let loose! The amazing thing is the ferocity of your desires — demanding but all-giving as well, but when your passion's spent it's back to practicalities with barely the flicker of a lascivious eyelid. And to think not even your best friend suspects! Still, it keeps your lover on his toes (if he recovers) and you figure that's how things ought to be — realistic — a time and place for everything. But if things aren't up to scratch in the love department, then it's you who makes the abrupt and final decision to terminate it. And you never regret it. You're too preoccupied filling the vacant position! Your bed rarely gets cold.

In business, you're super-efficient but sometimes officious if things are not being handled properly and accurately. This makes you testing to work with, and even more demanding if you're the boss. But when a job is well done you'll be unstinting with praise and admiration (as long as you're still on top of the heap, that is!). People are in awe of you, but it's the ones who aren't intimidated by you who will always stand by you. And it's this that warms the cockles of your sometimes cool heart, because you fear loneliness and insecurity so much, making enemies out of allies is not on in your book. You need people — more than you care to admit. Thank heavens you have a big enough heart and the intelligence to know that climbing Mount Everest is one thing but getting a helping hand on the way down is just as important. The mountain will always be there, but helping hands mightn't — so take them firmly and thank them. Humility costs nothing but means everything.

Capricorn style

You are one of the most adept signs in the entire zodiac. Once you've put your mind to one particular thing — whether it's running a business or running a house, creating a garden, learning how to cook something others shy away from — no task fazes you. You have such a clear and analytical mind, you'll grasp the rules and follow them perfectly. You may be adept, but you are not terribly adventurous. Having learned how to excel in something you're inclined to put it in your book of practical achievements and leave it there until it's needed again. You're a little scared to deviate from it, so you tend to appear adventurous by relying on clever variations on a well-tried theme. No one notices or cares, but this tendency makes you more conventional than you ought to be. But on the other hand, it makes everything around you look absolutely perfect. Your house and garden will be a picture, your children well-dressed, even your pets will look as if they've just been shampooed and conditioned — or should be. Your hectic schedule sometimes gets in the way, but you're sensible enough to delegate so that things are spick and span because you organised it. So don't worry about occasional untidiness — at least your mind is tidy! You want everything in your life to be 'just so', and when it comes to your personal appearance, it's all stops out until you look absolutely — well, fabulous!

You are fastidious to a fault. You would never dream of appearing anywhere unless you looked better than anyone else, even if it takes hours to achieve the effect. Your taste in clothes is simple but dramatic, you keep accessories to a minimum so their quality will be noticed, and you are so relentlessly worried about adding the right perfume you get into a tizz and usually fall back on the one that has worked successfully for you before. There's nothing wrong with that, but it accentuates that lack of audacity of yours, but we'll fix that up soon. In the meantime, you'll be your cool and charming self (no one can see the butterflies that often turn your tummy into a whirlpool), dressed immaculately in the ambers, golds, greys, deep blues and your beloved black that underline your acquired but convincing elegance. You dress to impress, to consolidate and to achieve whatever has to be achieved, and you do it with style. Style to you is status. And status is paramount.

Your outer expression is *success*. Your inner core is *ardour*.

Here's how to translate all of that into the best perfumes for you.

I have divided them into two categories:

1. *The big guns* — these are the all-important perfumes that should suit you best. They form the core of your personal perfume arsenal.

2. *Your secret weapons* — these augment the basics and are more daring and unusual, but should still suit you.

There is also a choice of perfumes for those of you born on the cusp of Capricorn/Aquarius, as well as a selection of men's fragrances suitable to give the

Capricorn male. (If you were born on the cusp of Sagittarius/Capricorn see pages 346–350 for your further perfume choices.) I have given each perfume a category as well as a simple and easy guide to its correct pronunciation. At the end of the chapter I have summated all of the perfumes into a table that tells you whether they're best on young or mature women, in warm or cool weather, day or evening, for dark or fair complexions.

The big guns: the indispensable basics

A Capricorn woman will always be hard to please when choosing a new perfume. Indeed the choice of her very first perfume when growing into womanhood probably caused her mother to come close to a nervous breakdown. But, like all Capricorns, she finally found exactly what she wanted, and stuck to it. Sticking to one perfume is not always a wise thing. Firstly, all perfumes do not suit all occasions or the outfits they have to accompany and give subtle emphasis to. Worst of all, they tend to over-identify you and could even start unpleasant rumours about how unaudacious and unadventurous you are — 'Not that same perfume again!' they shriek. You get to rely on this perfume so much the rest of them pass you by — and Capricorn women don't care to be left behind.

So explore, open your mind, experience new perfumes (by that I mean perfumes new to you). I think you'll be surprised that while you've been falling back on old faithful, a whole new world of scent has opened up. Maybe it's time you did too. Of course, the ones that will tend to attract you will be highly individual and have about them a definite aura of success to match your own, but you can't be indomitable all the time, so I've also suggested one or two that might help you expose the gentler, more amusing side of your nature. Here they are:

- **First** by Van Cleef & Arpels
  Pronunciation: van KLEEF and ar-PELL
  Type: floral/oriental

- **Bal à Versailles** by Jean Desprez
  Pronunciation: barl ar vair-SIGH/zjharn day-PRAY
  Type: floral/woody

- **Youth Dew** by Estée Lauder
  Pronunciation: ESS-tay LOR-duh
  Type: oriental

- **Ungaro d'Ungaro** by Ungaro
  Pronunciation: oon-GARR-o doon-GARR-o
  Type: floral/oriental

- **J'adore** by Christian Dior
  Pronunciation: zjhar-DOR
  Type: fruity/floral

- **Private Collection** by Estée Lauder
  Type: green/floral

FIRST

— because it epitomises success

Many smart Capricorns I know switched to this knockout beauty when it came on the scene bearing the weighty credentials of one of the world's great jewellers. Why? Because **First** actually smells like a leader — a perfume among perfumes, a standout. It is highly sophisticated, very self-assured and doesn't smell remotely like anything else on the *chic* perfume circuit. Small wonder when you look at its amazing composition.

First may not have been the actual first perfume to feature the essence of blackcurrant bud, but it was the first to put it up front and make it the dominant and dynamic note that catapults the whole attitude of the composition into the front line. Backed with the sweetly piercing power of *rose de mai*, then adding the emphasis of fruity elements such as peach, raspberry and mandarin, it then brings in jasmine, hyacinth, lily of the valley, carnation and a hint of tuberose to form a fusillade of fabulous intensity. The big-time line-up of amber, oakmoss, tonka bean, honey, sandalwood, musk and a drop of animalic civet consolidates the harmony before aldehydes add their gloss to give **First** its long-lasting presence and brilliance.

You'll be glad to know not every woman feels comfortable in it. You have to match its uncompromising and up-front stance, which should be a pushover for the more status-seeking of

Capricorns. But don't be scared of it. Underneath its elevated elegance, **First** is unusually beautiful, as well as rich and powerful. And that's a scenario that should appeal to you!

BAL À VERSAILLES
— because it's aristocratic

You might resist such a demanding invitation at first, but delve deeper into it and you'll discover the greatness and gloriousness of this expensive and elegant classic and hopefully identify strongly with its superiority.

Bal à Versailles doesn't try to win you over with sweet floral overtures. It couldn't care less if you like it or not. But with its air of *noblesse oblige* and haughtiness, it's almost mandatory to have in your arsenal if you want to be apart and above the *hoi polloi*. Mind you, it isn't a snob, but it will test your mettle in the rarefied ambience of the privileged upper social strata.

An incredibly complex and luxurious composition based on amber, sandalwood and vanilla, **Bal à Versailles** is drenched in roses from Bulgaria and Anatolia, heaps of Grasse jasmine, Morrocan orange flowers, and a spicy floral essence called *cassie* (not to be confused with cassis or blackcurrant bud). In the richly throbbing base notes are vetiver, musk, civet and olibanum. But the trio of amber, vanilla and sandalwood is really the catalyst for this astonishingly unique harmony.

Bal à Versailles is not a perfume to be taken as lightly as a waltz around the ballroom. It has more of the formal grace and subtle seduction of a minuet — being named after the great seventeenth century palace built by Louis XIV and saturated in its opulent atmosphere. It should only be used when the occasion demands a certain grandeur — art gallery openings, first nights at the opera, a spectacular dinner — and, of course, at elegant balls (if there are such things these days!). It is not comfortable in casual surroundings or casual clothes — **Bal à Versailles** is extremely elitist!

YOUTH DEW — *because it's a survivor*

Inadvertently, **Youth Dew** has lived up to its name. Here we are at the end of a century and it was born in the middle of it — 1953 to be precise! It has stayed the distance (although it went seriously missing for a few shadowy years) and not shown so much as a wrinkle on its indomitable face. But why should a hard-nosed Capricorn care about that? Because **Youth Dew** has the peculiar ability to make you feel not only successful and important, but desirable as well! Of course you don't *have* to smell as if you want to be the object of sexual attention, but it's comforting to know you can at least radiate sexuality without actually delivering the goods!

It's the stance of **Youth Dew** — its potency and potential as a weapon — that should persuade you to use it now and then for a strategic purpose. It's not the sort of perfume you can wander about the supermarket in, and even a slight overdose of it will alienate everyone within its range, so do be careful with it.

Mrs Lauder hinted an uncle of hers first created it for a Russian princess, so you know immediately it's got opulence going for it. It is in fact a very strong oriental based on bergamot, carnation, clove, cinnamon, ylang ylang, rose geranium and jasmine. It's backed up with the clout of musk, patchouli, amber and vetiver, all in hefty doses. Not to be trifled with!

It has been described by Lauder herself as 'sex in a bottle', so you know where you stand, although I don't think **Youth Dew** is quite as blatant as that. It is incredibly infiltrating, but at least it has presence and bravado.

UNGARO — *because it's memorable*

This is a seriously under-rated perfume, but one you encounter so rarely it could well become one you get to be known by (and if that's the case, don't ever tell anyone what it is you're wearing, even if imitation is the sincerest form of flattery). **Ungaro** should be kept a close personal secret if it suits you.

It's not by any means either an elusive or a strident

perfume. Like its innovative and daring creator, it has great dash and sophistication and a unique ambience of smouldering seduction under its rich and resonant exterior. It's like one of his fabulous dresses — a dramatic and conflicting juxtaposition of colours, prints, textures and drapes that would be absurdly gauche in the hands of a lesser genius.

Ungaro is basically a brilliant, splashy harmony of Florentine iris and sandalwood garlanded with total abandon by jasmine, orange blossom and rich Turkish roses. But not for long! Big emphatic sweeps of sweetly clinging tonka bean, glowing amber, and the tantalising spiciness of cardamom invade the floral/woody top notes with a lushness that gives the proceedings a dark and brooding brilliance and sets **Ungaro** on a more passionate and thrilling path — one that could lead to all sorts of fairly sophisticated but unbridled shenanigans!

That's why I think it's underestimated, and why **Ungaro** is a singular perfume, which while pretending to conform to all the principles of poise and refinement, is actually a very foxy number indeed. One look at its poison blue bottle, emerald top and fuchsia ribbons gives the game away!

J'ADORE — because it's aspirational

Apart from Guerlain, there's no more inspired and varied collection of perfumes than there is in the hallowed pantheon of Dior. All the way from the original (and some think still the most beautiful) **Miss Dior** which was once synonymous with the New Look but has become a classic, right through to the daring of **Poison**, the originality of **Dune** and the brio of **Dolce Vita**, women from all walks of life have responded to and identified with these glorious creations, and I think the reason is because they always give something aspirational as well as inspirational to look up to. They become more than mere perfumes — they are temples of elegance, refinement and security. And the latest, **J'adore**, is certainly no exception.

It's an incredibly beautiful perfume presented with great reverence to the woman who'll wear it. Its seductive presentation is almost impossible to resist — you feel you just *have* to have that sensually curved amphora-like bottle with its long slender neck ringed in a Masai-like gold collar and topped with a clear crystal orb, even without smelling what's inside. And somehow you know, you feel, it will be ravishingly lovely. And it is.

When Dior asked perfumer Calice Becker to create a modern blockbuster for them, her mind went straight to a huge bouquet of opulent flowers embellished with fruit. But the flowers aren't the traditional choices, and nor is the fruit. With Dior everything has to be different, which is why the top notes are mandarin mixed with ivy leaves, leading into the unique use of champaca flower, a velvety-scented relative of magnolia and considered sacred in India, bolstered with vanilla orchid, rose and violet. All of this is laid on a smouldering bed of rich Damascus plum, precious amaranth wood and blackberry-infused musk.

No wonder Dior turned to Baudelaire to wax lyrical on their exquisite achievement. He said that Woman must astonish and charm because she is an idol who must be adorned to be adored. Now, we all know that most Capricorns will agree with those sentiments, which is a perfectly justified reason for you to bedeck both body and soul with the exquisitely charismatic benedictions of **J'adore**.

PRIVATE COLLECTION
— because it's privileged

There are plenty of stories behind the Lauder perfumes, but this one is probably the most elite. Estée Lauder was always privy to new perfume developments in her laboratories and often borrowed an unreleased or unrealised one to try out on herself socially. This one really twitched the noses of her immediate circle and when asked about it, she loftily replied it was one from her 'private collection'. Naturally, she made it her own from thereon in, knowing only she had access to it. Eventually, to impress a couple of chums, the Duchess of Windsor and Princess Grace of Monaco, she made gifts of it to them. But in business, a million bucks is a million bucks, and she was smart enough to see its enormous potential, so with grace and favour released it to the world at large. She was right — **Private Collection** is still making millions!

As you'd expect it's a very sophisticated and opulent perfume in the grand American manner, full of rich Bulgarian rose, jasmine, orange blossom, hyacinth, heliotrope and chrysanthemum, which form a heady backdrop to the intensity of green leaves, Indian sandalwood, woody/green linden blossom and velvety green oakmoss. Hence its *chypre* freshness and *élan*.

Private Collection is a perfect extension of the Capricorn coolness and clarity of style. It certainly makes its presence felt, but never shouts above the crowd. Instead it has the rare quality of being able to swan into a room and weave its sure-footed trail leaving a perfumed wake that is both inviting and infectious. If you're not given to sophisticated gatherings it won't do much for you, but if you're trying to better your options or simply impress the hell out of the social set, **Private Collection** is a must.

Your secret weapons: the surprises

To many people who think they know you well, Capricorns seem to have no surprises up their sleeves. You are seen (often erroneously) as quite transparent, well-organised and accomplished all the time. Since nearly everything you attempt turns into a success, they think you're all hard work and not much play. If only they knew! But you're not going to tell them how ardent and passionately adventurous you can be — none of their business, so you hint at it in other ways. Or at least you should. It's quite easy and you don't have to drop your guard or step alarmingly out of character. When you feel like it (and it has to be like that since you're not normally a spontaneous or erratic person) let them know you're *very* human — full of wit, sly sarcasm, a good sport, subtly suggestive, and even capable of making a play and stealing someone else's man! If you doubt this, always remember Ava Gardner and Marlene Dietrich were both your star sisters! So, the message is, change your perfume now and then from the powerhouse dynamos that help you get ahead, and go for these slightly wilder ones. Not one of them is outrageously unconventional, but all of them exude either a distinct predilection for overt sensuality, or are able to soften your ambitious edge to something more feminine but definitely not prissy.

- **5th Avenue** by Elizabeth Arden
  Type: floral
- **Nina** by Nina Ricci
  Pronunciation: NEE-nuh REE-chee
  Type: floral
- **Tiffany** by Tiffany

Type: floral/fruity
- **Red Jeans** by Gianni Versace
  Pronunciation: gee-ARN-ee vair-SAR-chee
  Type: floral
- **SpellBound** by Estée Lauder
  Type: floral oriental
- **Seringa** by Floris
  Pronunciation: ser-ING-ug (hard 'g')/FLOOR-iss
  Type: green/floral

5TH AVENUE
— because it's snazzy!

It's not pretentious enough to be ritzy, not glamorous enough to be glitzy, but this charmer in its glass skyscraper bottle exudes so much self-assured *panache* you'll not only feel well-dressed wearing it, but also exude an aura of total femininity without the slightest hint of being vulnerable.

5th Avenue is an avalanche of flowers tumbling down from a great height — a Manhattan floral pageant rather than a ticker-tape parade. No expense is spared. Wonderful springtime top notes of lilac, linden blossom, magnolia and lily of the valley are backed up by voluptuous tumbles of Bulgarian rose, jasmine, violet, tuberose and ylang ylang followed by a rush of spices and fruit — bergamot, mandarin, peach, cloves, nutmeg, vanilla. It's quite a spectacle — rich and ravishing, but surprisingly far from being over-the-top.

So if you have the usual Capricorn aversion to overly-floral onslaughts, **5th Avenue** may take you by surprise with its eloquent elegance. It will underscore your sporadic bouts of romanticism but never make you feel full-blown. In fact, it is such a magnetic perfume you may find **5th Avenue** your perfumed passport to seventh heaven — a destination not often achieved even by the most perservering of Capricorns!

NINA — *because it illumines you*

Look for this elegant beauty at duty-free outlets and better boutiques because it's becoming a rarity. It is Ricci's most sophisticated perfume, created in 1988 by Robert Ricci in homage to and remembrance of his mother, the great couturier Nina Ricci who held sway over Paris fashion in the '30s before closing down when World War Two broke out. **Nina** mirrors her wonderfully feminine but daring ways of expressing true *chic*.

It's a mellifluous and luxurious mix of many flowers — mainly rose, jasmine, violet, orange blossom and mimosa with intriguing touches of marigold, basil and cassia buds. Bergamot and peach add fruity lustre, while patchouli, ylang ylang, musk and moss purr beneath the brilliant sparkle of its surface.

Nina Ricci once said that any perfume of hers must be a work of art, and **Nina** is the quintessential example of that, with its *frisson* of feminine deliciousness, its headiness that turns other heads, its calm self-assurance and poise, and the flattering way it envelops a woman in a scented air that's bursting with expectation. Couldn't you do with a bit of that scintillation?

TIFFANY — *because you'll smell rich*

If you've never entered the hushed and glittering portals of Tiffany & Co. even to gawp at some of the most exquisite jewellery, gold and silver in the world, you can do it by proxy with a bottle of this mega-rich perfume which was created especially to commemorate the company's 150 years in business. At least the brilliant Art Deco bottle, inspired by the facade of their New York flagship store, will look almost like a shining jewel with its pared-down but chunky crystal bottle designed by Pierre Dinaud, with thick silver shoulders and top and gold inlays to boot. It even makes you feel more secure just looking at it.

You may very well expect not to like the perfume itself, and if you don't you can still stare lovingly and avariciously at the bottle without touching a drop of what's inside, but your Capricorn curiosity will get the better of you eventually, so you might as well know it's a jolly good perfume and not as stridently American as you might have feared. **Tiffany** is what you might call loaded with class.

No expense is spared in the formulation of this very warm and glowing scent. From its rich (sorry) opening notes of mandarin and blackcurrant cassis to the invitation into its pulsating heart of jasmine, rose, ylang ylang, iris, orange blossom, lily of the valley and violet leaves, and even further into the comforting depths of vetiver, sandalwood, vanilla and amber, **Tiffany** is as smooth as silk and as caressing as a velvet glove wearing a discreetly expensive diamond bracelet. You won't feel a thing except total contentment and happiness — as if you've made a wise investment that's paid off handsomely.

Tiffany positively oozes the sort of elitism that Capricorns secretly like — not snooty or pretentious, but maybe just a little bit self-satisfied. And there's nothing sinful in that when you know you've made the right choice, even if it's played havoc with the budget. Just think of it as blue-chip stock, but don't forget to go easy with it — American perfumes are made to last, so don't overdo it or you'll let the side down. Always remember, it's elegant and refined, even if it makes you smell filthy rich!

RED JEANS — because it unwinds you
Versace's big three perfumes are all in the major league, all with varying degrees of sophistication and baroque elegance. **Red Jeans** (along with its new companions **Yellow Jeans** and **White Jeans**) was designed specifically to let the Versace woman relax in a perfume that is far less demanding — for when she climbs into her Versace jeans and top and lets her hair down. In other words, you'll still look terrific and

smell it, but with less effort.

There is absolutely nothing complicated about **Red Jeans**. It's an almost frivolous highball of springtime freesia, delicate waterlily, just-open jasmine with a hint of green still in it, a dash of violet and violet leaf, a drift of sandalwood and tonka bean to settle down the high notes, and a secret ingredient that alludes to the soft warmth of cashmere. Whatever this is gives **Red Jeans** an underlying earthy note so the whole thing doesn't evaporate in its own splashy giddiness.

Red Jeans is a light and bright little tease you put on just as you would something casual but with lots of chic. It certainly isn't a 'cheapie' and demands the proper respect its label deserves. Definitely not for bigtime glitz, but perfectly willing to party. Best of all, it's especially good at making you smile when you don't really want to. It also takes the mickey out of you when you're taking yourself too seriously and nobody's game enough to tell you.

SPELLBOUND — *because it means business*

A lot of women have an aversion to this potent and persistent seducer, probably because they don't have the pizzazz to carry off its high drama.

SpellBound can be a bit intimidating, and the secret of course is not to overdo it — just a quick squirt or dab on pulse points will do the trick for hours. Any more is an overload, and will break the spell.

It's a sweeping perfume, brave and brooding with its insistent throb of spicy flowers like carnation and heliotrope urged on by tuberose, orange blossom, narcissus, black rose and jasmine, and heavily wooded with cedar and rosewood before the real heavies of peppery pimento, coriander, clove, opoponax, blackcurrant and musk suffuse the smouldering potion with an orientalism that's breathtakingly emphatic. **SpellBound** does nothing by halves!

The spell it weaves is entirely dependent on the discretion with which you use it — a fascinating aura of it will be absolutely magnetic, too much and it almost hurls out a challenge that may or may not be taken up. But the gauntlet **SpellBound** throws down is a velvet, not steel, one. It may be a bit too anxious to joust, but only if you are. I must say, though, it'll be a pretty unequal contest, and you'll probably win again — and that's the real reason Lauder created this vamp that never takes no for an answer.

SERINGA
— because it wraps you in summer

Does the name of this intoxicating perfume come from the botanical name for mock orange or is it a spelling variation of the genus for lilac bushes? Possibly either, since its formulation contains lots of orangey notes as well as a good dash of sweet lilac blossom. But the mysterious word was apparently found in a dusty old Floris catalogue dated 1870. So, it's anyone's guess. Personally, I'd go for the mock orange option, and I think you might when you smell its heady delights.

Seringa is a summer beauty, green with crushed orange leaves, tangy with mandarin, bergamot and delicate lemony petitgrain. Once this theme is established the flowers tumble in, all of them opulently vivid. There's rose, orchid, cyclamen, ylang ylang and a definite breezy rush of lilac. And as if to consolidate the point, flowers also appear in the base notes — violet, jasmine and tuberose — most unusual, but it works. Musk, oakmoss and amber do their usual charming and warming tricks to deepen and fix the perfume so it doesn't evaporate in its own exultant euphoria.

Now, you might have a sneaking suspicion I'm leading you too far up the romantic garden path, which is one you don't usually follow, but there are times in the well-planned and organised life of a Capricorn when this is precisely the direction she should take. It seems to meander a little, but not too far — **Seringa** takes a very definite standpoint. It may be a country girl but it can take on the city slickers and teach them a few canny tricks. And I think it's just the sort of ammunition smart Capricorns should have to throw up a smokescreen when necessary. Anyway, **Seringa** is so dazzlingly lovely it might search out and find that well-hidden vulnerable streak of yours. Sometimes it's nice to give in and go with the flow for a change.

The advantage of the cusp: taking your pick

It's not all confusion — being neither one star nor the other, or feeling you're partly both — if you were born toward the beginning of Aquarius*. You can of course pick and choose from the perfumes suggested for both Capricorn and Aquarius, but be careful. Depending on your characteristics, they may not all sit easily on you. That's why I've come up with a selection of extras that might solve any perfume problems or indecision you might have.

- **Trésor** by Lancôme
  Pronunciation: tray-ZOR/LARN-kom
  Type: floral/fruity
- **Donna Trussardi** by Trussardi
  Pronunciation: DONN-uh troo-SAR-dee
  Type: floral
- **Tommy Girl** by Tommy Hilfiger
  Pronunciation: HIL-fig-uh
  Type: floral/fruity
- **Elizabeth Taylor's Passion** by Elizabeth Taylor

If you were born towards the very beginning of Capricorn, you might like to check out the choices for those born on the cusp of Sagittarius/Capricorn on pages 346–350.

Type: floral/oriental

TRÉSOR — *because it's nostalgic*

Capricorn and Aquarius are signs not generally noted for sentimentality, but nostalgia of the gentle and haunting kind is a gentility both signs could do with a little more of now and then — in Capricorn's case to ease tension, and in Aquarius' to be less detached. **Trésor** is a perfect balm for both — a lovely rose-saturated charmer of elegant grace and poise. You may find it a little too sweet to begin with, but gradually its heady opening note of white rose gives way to gentle persuasions of apricot, peach and lilac, shimmering with vibrations of violet, jasmine, lily of the valley and rich heliotrope, all underlined with musk and vanilla. It's a mesmerising and warm confection, very self-assured but not aggressive in the least. **Trésor** means 'treasure' and it will become one to those who realise that an occasional little admission of softness might add to, and not detract from, their individuality.

DONNA TRUSSARDI
— because it enjoys being young

This is the new girl on the block, and a very pretty one too. For young Capricorns it has enough presence to make an impression on the boy next door, and for Aquarians it has enough friendliness to win over the whole street! **Donna Trussardi** is not very serious, but certainly not naive either. It's an infectious bouquet of jasmine, hyacinth and lily of the valley, given a twist of mandarin and a dash of cardamom, coriander and ginger. So it's a perky little number right off, but adds a grown-up facet to its nature with rose, ylang ylang and violet tinged with blackcurrant bud and patchouli. It's totally disarming with its happy attitude and winning ways. Doors will open in welcome when **Donna Trussardi** pays a call!

TOMMY GIRL — because it's good fun

Sorry, but only young goats and water-carriers are being addressed here. **Tommy Girl** was created for that delicious half-giggly, half-serious time of life when a girl is out there to declare her independence, and anyone getting in the way will be called 'old and obstructionist'. Get the message? They don't come much more energetic, exuberant, charming or open than this slap in the face to adulthood. It's as brash and as sassy as it sounds — think back to Doris Day's tomboy period and that's **Tommy Girl** territory. It's tangy with grapefruit, mandarin and green leaves spiked with spearmint, before some rather pubescent flowers sashay in — apple blossom, camellia bud, blackcurrant bud and pretty American wildflowers that have just popped up after rain. It's as homely as apple pie (hold the cloves), as innocent as Bambi, and about as seductive as wearing tooth-braces. But

Tommy Girl honestly defines the market it's intended for, and you can't knock that — not even if you're past it!

ELIZABETH TAYLOR'S PASSION
— because it's unbridled

It's purple hearts and flowers all the way in her very first and most (excuse me) passionate perfume. Almost over-the-top opulence and throbbing emotions are the message from this unapologetic seductress. It's beaten out by insistent jungle drums, commanding you to fall under the hypnotic spell of highly-perfumed white flowers — gardenia, lily of the valley, jasmine and rose, intertwined with ylang ylang, spices, musk, patchouli and some very intoxicating incense. **Passion** unleashes an eloquent desire to be noticed and needed. Its seduction is not blatant but insinuating and highly suggestive. Like its creator, it loves the hunt for the fulfillment of luxury and the excitement of grand passions, and never loses sight of its target. **Passion** is far from subtle, but certainly not vulgar either. It will unsettle the coolest of Capricorns and reveal their liking for a little outright lust now and then, and challenge the seriousness of Aquarians who may just succumb to its siren call and feel all the better for it.

The Capricorn male: the sweet smells of success

They think of themselves as the quiet achievers — dogged, strategy-driven and relentless until they get to the top of whatever they have to conquer.

They get an 'A' for effort if nothing else, and a gift that symbolises their sure-footed climb to success and reflects their serious commitment will put you in the good books of the typical Capricorn. And it's always better to be in favour with them — they can be very unforgiving if people don't do the right thing by them. Of course it all boils down to the massive ego of the male goat (think of Muhammed Ali's humble Capricornian claim of 'I am the greatest!'). Oh, your Capricorn might bleat long and hard that he's a modest and self-effacing chap, but don't you believe it — he craves recognition for his accomplishment. And don't forget either that he's a born status-seeker and will go to great lengths to impress his superiors.

Don't be too hard on him. At least he's honest, faithful, hard-working and a good provider. And he means well. So look after him — he's a precious, if sometimes conventional and dull commodity — and although he'd never admit it, he loves receiving gifts. He sees them as admiration more than flattery. Don't give him anything flashy or over-the-top. That would wreck his responsible image. Something that smacks (or smells) of first-class, prestige and success will send secret shivers through him. Capricorn men are like little boys inside — they always know they were born to be School Captain, and eventually The Boss.

- **Habit Rouge** by Guerlain
  Pronunciation: abby HROO-zjhe/gair-LARN
  Type: green/woody
- **Tiffany for Men** by Tiffany
  Type: citrus/herbal
- **Pasha** by Cartier
  Pronunciation: PAR-shah/KARR-tee-air
  Type: oriental/spicy
- **Eternity for Men** by Calvin Klein
  Type: woody/green

Habit Rouge

In English it means 'red hunting jacket', but has nothing dreadful to do with foxhunts. Instead, it's a very distinguished but bracing fragrance that exudes masses of self-confidence and bonhomie. Its up-front notes are very fresh lemon zest and bitter orange that give way to a more masculine earthiness of patchouli and amber, with dashes of spice giving a final flourish of derring-do. Since it's been a top-seller among very discerning and sophisticated males since 1965, **Habit Rouge** has earned its classic rating in the Guerlain hierarchy — and so it should. It is neither strident nor pushy, but asserts its own presence with a clean-cut, tally-ho briskness that has made it a favourite of princes and playboys alike. Your Capricorn may not admit it, but he'd give his eye teeth to be in that sort of elite club!

Tiffany for Men

Can't you just hear that plaintive Capricorn call of 'If you can have Tiffany perfume, why can't I have something as rich and classy?' You're probably tired of that cloying spicy number he's been wearing for months (or is it years) anyway, so give the guy a break and give him a big, handsome flask of **Tiffany for Men**. It looks solidly impressive in its tall glass bottle with a massive silver top, so he'll think he's come up a notch or two in the world even without opening it. But when he does, you'll both be knocked sideways! **Tiffany for Men** exudes success with a powerful shock-wave of prohibitively expensive oils of bergamot (for a citrus blast), coriander (for sexiness) and juniper berry (as addictive as a martini). It's certainly different, but impeccably suave and dangerously virile. So if he wants to be a millionaire, and what Capricorn doesn't, at least he can smell like one!

Pasha

This should impress him mightily with its Cartier pedigree, its splendid packaging that's understated enough to announce its superiority, and its dignified but sensual fragrance. **Pasha** has the sort of unspoken authority that tends to make anything stupid enough to challenge it look like a rank upstart! Named after the all-powerful Turkish commanders who put the fear of Allah into their enemies, **Pasha** is a huge conglomeration of very expensive spices and herbs, lit with amber and sandalwood and generously invigorated with citrus oils. But once **Pasha** settles rather grandly on the skin, mischievous oriental notes of pepper and mint appear, giving it a piquancy that takes some of the high dignity out of it and makes it quite approachable — but still to be respected for its elevated excellence. That ought to appeal to the aspirational aspects of Capricorn.

Eternity for Men

To bring him down to earth again after all that mountain-climbing, try the emotional blackmail of **Eternity for Men** — a gift with a name like that is something his ego couldn't possibly resist, and he'll use it even if he doesn't like it, simply because of its connotations of commitment. It's a very smooth affair of lavender and mandarin, greened with basil and vetiver, a touch of romantic jasmine and the soft sexuality of sandalwood. Not perhaps what you'd call a perfumed hint from the lusty pages of the *Kama Sutra*, but sensual enough to give him ideas of eternal happiness that might even include you! I wouldn't count on it, but it's worth a try!

Who suits what, and when: getting the best out of your perfumes

Because perfumes become not only extensions of your personality but also give emphasis to the way you look and the mood you're in, naturally, to bring out their best, they should be treated with due understanding in regard to their characteristics and qualities. They too have limitations and strengths, just as we all have. So, the following table outlines when best to wear them (Day, Night), the age-group most suited to them (Young, Mature), the general complexion of the wearer (Fair, Dark), and the seasons they bloom best in (Spring/Summer – S/S, or Autumn/Winter – A/W). This table is meant only to be used as an approximate guide or reference point — it is not a hard and fast set of rules by any means.

THE BIG GUNS

Perfume	Day	Night	Young	Mature	Fair	Dark	S/S
First		•		•	•	•	•
Bal à Versailles		•		•	•	•	
Youth Dew		•		•		•	
Ungaro d'Ungaro	•	•		•	•	•	•
J'adore	•	•	•	•	•	•	•
Private Collection	•	•		•	•	•	•

YOUR SECRET WEAPONS

Perfume	Day	Night	Young	Mature	Fair	Dark	S/S
5th Avenue	•	•	•	•	•	•	•
Nina	•	•	•		•	•	•
Tiffany	•	•		•	•	•	•
Red Jeans	•		•	•	•	•	•
SpellBound		•		•		•	
Seringa	•		•	•	•	•	•

CAPRICORN/AQUARIUS CUSPS

Perfume	Day	Night	Young	Mature	Fair	Dark	S/S
Trésor	•	•	•	•	•	•	•
Donna Trussardi	•	•			•	•	
Tommy Girl	•	•	•		•		
Elizabeth Taylor's Passion		•				•	•

SAGITTARIUS/CAPRICORN CUSPS

Perfume	Day	Night	Young	Mature	Fair	Dark	S/S
Versus Donna	•	•	•		•	•	•
Gardenia	•	•		•	•	•	•
Jolie Madame	•	•		•		•	•
Green Tea	•				•		•

MEN'S FRAGRANCES

Perfume	Day	Night	Young	Mature	Fair	Dark	S/S
Habit Rouge	•	•				•	•
Tiffany for Men	•	•		•	•	•	•
Pasha	•	•		•		•	•
Eternity for Men	•	•		•		•	•

Aquarius

The water carrier

January 20–February 18

You and Shangri-la

People often categorise you as a zodiacal water
sign, which of course you're not. You are an air
sign, and typical of air's elemental but invisible
presence. You are symbolised by a person (usually a
woman) carrying a jar of water, which just about
summates your principal personality characteristic.
You are the one who collects the sustaining necessities
of life and brings them to others, to help and to heal.

This makes you sound a bit of a ministering angel, which is often, but not always the case. Sometimes, instead of simply offering another person a few life-saving drops of water or even a steady trickle, you go too far and practically drown them in your generosity and good-will.

This generosity, I hasten to add, is *not* material. It is, like everything else about you, abstract. It is practical to a point, but the thinking behind it is more charitable than tangible. This is why you are perceived as 'a good person' and can always be called on to help with advice and care. You are always there, always reliable, but once you've done your task, you seem to evaporate into thin air (obviously, someone else has called for help, so you're off to solve that new crisis). This admirable quality tends to make you aloof from more lasting and serious self-commitment, which is just as well, since getting involved with just one other person is, to an Aquarian, getting into deep water — a situation that can easily deluge *you*. Your head is really in the clouds, and these quick trips down to earth and reality can take too much out of your ethereal and free-floating spirit — the one that seeks eternally for betterment, revelation and peace. You are, in fact, your own Shangri-la, your own remote and beautiful but imaginary palace of perfection. This is where your heart lives and your mind soars, and is precisely why you rarely allow anyone to get too close to you. (Well, there may be one or two, but certainly not a crowd!)

Everyone else envies Aquarians for their apparent cool-headedness, their acumen and inventiveness in an extraordinarily diverse range of subjects, and their unflappability in the most serious situations. They are not aware (and you're rather glad they're not) of your innate lack of confidence when it comes to your own personal insecurities. Nor are they aware of your inability to translate a lot of your dreams into realities.

The reason is simple. You can't bear people knowing too much about you and your innermost desires. Somehow you find that demeaning and invasive. Your privacy and independence are your most valued and protected possessions, and if there are internal battles to be fought you'll do all the fighting. You are an army of one, which accounts for your strange egocentricity, your aloofness and your very fixed ideas about everything. You are certainly not vague or reticent when it comes to giving your considered opinion, which you expect to be taken as absolute self-evident fact. Fortunately, because of your niceness and common-sensical attitude, people believe you, so there's very little argument in your life. You don't like argument — you like acceptance.

Communication is your strongest ally — you are genuinely interested in the human condition, in reforms that will make things better for humanity, for seeing right triumph over wrong, and for the oppressed to be liberated. Which is why you make the very best champions of causes, especially women's rights. A man who questions your idea on that score is asking to be trounced. You won't be insulting, but determined to convert him to your (and other women's) way of thinking. This can lead to your being accused of prejudice against men, that you don't give them a chance, that you're a bit of a crusher. Not quite true, but it is an indication of your putting principles ahead of compromise — a word that you barely ever think of, since you don't care for its ambivalent connotations.

Aquarians are not changeable people — they can be turbulent when taken by surprise, and eccentric if they get too far from reality — but their reliability and compassion, their ever-ready kindness and co-operation and their exemplary civility and courtesy, are traits to be respected and admired. If only, you dear sweet angels, you could be a little less austere and unsentimental — if only you could learn to be less thin-skinned and more pliant, you would be some of the loveliest souls of the zodiac. But not even you are perfect, so stick to your guns and keep on ministering. Perhaps, though, that Shangri-la of yours is getting to be a bit too like a monastery. Perhaps you should throw caution to your own winds and invite more people into your private paradise — you can anoint them with that preciously drawn, life-sustaining water as they cross the sacred threshold! Just remember, though, that giving sometimes needs to be more than well-meaning and intangible. Sometimes you might actually have to show your generosity in purely material and emotional terms. Aquarians have a reputation for being kind but a bit stingy. Perhaps welcome them with a little fine wine instead of free water?

Aquarian style

Aquarians are naturally meticulous when it comes to personal appearance — even ministering angels are not expected to look scruffy. You're usually found in exacting professional positions — from airline attendants to public relations and administration, librarians and teachers — that require either uniforms (which you like) or in the arts and related creative areas which allow you to have highly individual ways of dressing to express your dedicated outlook on life. You can either carry this over into your domestic life with a style that is best described as clean-cut and ordered, or if you're not required to be rigid, in a rather haphazard fashion that can border on eccentricity (or outright untidiness). But, since you have a very principled conscience, you never feel comfortable until things are in order — especially your public image!

You gravitate to the unusual — furniture with a difference, decor that is understated but original, colours that reflect your serene self-control. That's why you don't need the bombast of excessive flamboyance, and prefer the clarity of blues, the calmness of neutrals and creamy colours, the subtlety of pastels. You rarely feel comfortable in black or red — maybe it's something to do with the fiery depths that go against your airy ambience. You do, however, like vibrancy and vividness, as long as it's not vulgar.

There's a finely judged paring-down to essentials in your style. Some would call it austere and spartan, but it's actually your careful selection of things that matter, that mean something to you — a harmony of balance and refinement with nothing extraneous or jarring. But you also like to make the occasional clean sweep of things, mostly to specifically remind people you can often be quite unpredictable and even non-conformist. You like the odd surprise, and surprising people so their ideas about you don't get too fixed (or too close to the bone). You see to it that nobody could ever call you boring. This reminds them that calm air can easily become a breeze, a wind, or a tornado — even in your usually placid and implacable life in those castles in the air!

Your outer expression is *altruism*. Your inner core is *imagination*.

Here's how to translate all of that into the best perfumes for you.

I have divided them into two categories:

1. *The big guns* — these are the all-important perfumes that should suit you best. They form the core of your personal perfume arsenal.

2. *Your secret weapons* — these augment the basics and are more daring and unusual, but should still suit you.

There is a choice of perfumes for those of you born on the cusp of Aquarius/Pisces, as well as a selection of men's fragrances suitable to give the Aquarian male. (If you were born on the cusp of Capricorn/Aquarius see pages 381–385 for your further perfume choices.) I have given each perfume a category as well as a simple and easy guide to its correct pronunciation. At the end of the chapter I have summated all of the perfumes into a table that tells you whether they're best on young or mature women, in warm or cool weather, day or evening, for dark or fair complexions.

The big guns:
the indispensable basics

An Aquarian does not like fussiness around her, so fussy perfumes are not in her book — and it's a pretty slim volume. You probably won't ever be an avid scent collector but will single out three or four that appeal to your no-nonsense attitude to life and your assured place in it. They won't be (I hope) the heavy sensualities of meaningful orientals, but nor (I also hope) will they be pretty or giddy and romantic. Romance to you smacks of the sentimental. In the meantime, you'll choose what smells right to you — clean, clear, scintillating and, above all, original. Stick to those to make the quiet impact you consider is more appropriate to your nature than making a grand and sweeping entrance in a grand and sweeping perfume you'll feel uncomfortable wearing. You don't really see perfume as a means of getting you what you want. Vampish seduction is too far-fetched for your rational thinking (in fact, you think it's hilarious!). You simply want your perfume to subtly project what you are and what you stand for — gentility, simplicity and independence. That's why you're attracted to soft-spoken but eloquent perfumes, airy and uncomplicated — with a little touch of quirkiness that sets them, and you, apart from the usual run of things.

You don't take personal adornment all that seriously and would be quite content to splash on a little basic cologne if it weren't for your conscientious need to be contemporary, assertively original and free-thinking. These ought to fill the bill quite successfully:

•**Eau d'Eden** by Cacharel
  Pronunciation: o DEE–dun/kash-ar-ELL
  Type: floral/fruity
•**Anaïs Anaïs** by Cacharel
  Pronunciation: an–ASE an–ASE/kash-ar-ELL

Type: floral
- **L'Eau d'Issey** by Issey Miyake
  Pronunciation: lo-DISS-ee/ISS-ee mee-AR-kee
  Type: fruity/floral
- **Diorella** by Christian Dior
  Pronunciation: dee-or-ELL-uh/
  KRIST-ee-an dee-OR
  Type: floral/fruity
- **Jaïpur** by Boucheron
  Pronunciation: jy-POOR/BOO-sher-on
  Type: fruity/oriental
- **Feminité du Bois** by Shisheido
  Pronunciation: fem-INN-it-ay doo BWAH/
  shish-AY-doe
  Type: woody

EAU D'EDEN
— because it isn't all about Eve

This is the newer, younger, lighter version of Eden —
the nymphet that no doubt will sink its older
namesake with its splashier, racier and more
capricious ways. Well, like it or not, that's the trend
nowadays, so although Eden may have had its day, this
elfin upstart at least carries on the torch of an
ingeniously-formulated aquatic and succulent scent.

Eau d'Eden is more about the Garden of Eden
than its naughty inhabitants so you don't have to
worry about tackling a sexy, serpentine sizzler. This is

a much more pastoral approach to the Elysian Fields of peace and harmony that Aquarians love to wander through with seraphic smiles on their faces. You do have to be a young Aquarian though — **Eau d'Eden** is not designed for anyone over twenty-five, and even that's pushing it. But it does smell deliciously inviting with its playful gathering of peppery nasturtium leaves, yellow iris, peach, honeysuckle, jasmine, sandalwood and white musk — and that engaging couple, sweet william and wild rose, who good-naturedly join in the innocent festivities. It's a happy little frolic — splashy and sparkling, shot through with shafts of heavenly light, and not a nasty old serpent in sight to seduce the unwary.

Its biggest challenge is to grab your attention in the tidal wave of rather similar 'keep-it-light, keep-it-bright' fragrances that are so obsessed with attracting the youthful they almost forget to be proper perfumes. But in the experienced hands of Cacharel, who have already charmed us with **Anaïs Anaïs** and seduced us with **Loulou**, this youngster is wonderfully thought through from its engaging and evocative scent to its brilliant bottle of aquatic coloured glass, its frosted silvery blue cap that could be a river pebble, and the luscious raspberry pink lining of its box. You know you're safe with **Eau d'Eden** — there's not an apple to be seen anywhere!

ANAÏS ANAÏS — *because it's angelic*

This was made for airborne Aquarians and their aura of eternal innocence — even those who have long since lost it! It's a symphonic rhapsody named after a Persian love goddess, but don't let that fool you. **Anaïs Anaïs** is far from being erotic, and approaches seduction in a much more beguiling way — through its languorous sense of submissive innocence mixed with a nostalgic yearning for the tranquillity of pure love. Who could resist such an invitation?

How does **Anaïs Anaïs** achieve this feat without being cloyingly romantic? Mainly through Madonna lilies. Each bloom of these heavenly perfumed white beauties releases but a few drops of lily oil essence, which makes it all the more precious. Their lilied loveliness is then gilded a little with hyacinth, jasmine, rose and ylang ylang, lily of the valley, all sweetly haloed in orange blossom, vetiver and oakmoss before a powdery softening with Californian cedarwood. It's a gently hypnotic persistence that gives forthright Aquarians just enough heavenly ammunition to entice attractive earthly bodies to float up, up and away with them all the way to Shangri-la!

L'EAU D'ISSEY — *because it's idealistic*

Issey Miyake is something of an oriental mystical miracle let loose in the civilised jungles of Parisian couture. He continues to amaze and mystify with his fabulous phantasms of fluid design. So it was no surprise that when designing the ambience and style for his signature perfume, his brief to his chosen perfumers was to come up with a fragrance that had the innocent purity of water! Water, of course, is not known for its perfumed persuasion, but he persisted that the impossible could be achieved, and it was with the spectacular release of his now legendary **L'Eau d'Issey**.

The extraordinary bottle shaped like a clear cone with a simple marble-shaped stopper reminiscent of a drop of water, is enough to bowl over Aquarians with its artful sense of balance and precarious symmetry, but what's inside is just as astounding. The feeling, the transparency, the purity of water has been interpreted in an aquatic and ozonic perfumed masterpiece of freesia, apricot, cucumber, lily, rosewater, peony and cyclamen in a delicately textured but surprisingly tenacious harmony that defies description except on its own unique terms. It is, simply, visionary!

L'Eau d'Issey stands out like a sentinel, both physically in its dazzling design, and in its uncompromising synergy of highly fragrant elements refined to a degree of anonymity — the quintessence of clarity itself, but clarity that invites you into another world of a sensuality measured by intangibles rather than by recognisable sensations. It's Issey Miyake's inscrutable world of pleasures that seems to be suspended in air to hover mystically just above earthly reach. Rather like Aquarians, really!

DIORELLA — because it has spontaneity

I hope the pundits at Dior never delete this enchanting scintilla from their dazzling line-up of more sophisticated and serious perfumes. I also hope that its good-natured simplicity of style and spontaneity are not totally replaced by the ever-increasing quirkiness that so many new perfumes seem to think is necessary to keep up with a market that (supposedly) insists on change for the sake of change.

Diorella has escaped all that nonsense so far because it is a true classic — a perfect marriage between green chypre harmonies and the zest and zing of citrus notes in full regalia. Its sharp and fresh green notes come from galbanum, oakmoss, vetiver and leaves, awash with the sunny goldenness of lemon, orange, mandarin, bergamot and the springtime headiness of jasmine, honeysuckle and carnation tinged with peach and melon. It's a joyous and lilting aria that sings of orchards, meadows and a sunlit sea — entirely lovable and extroverted without being the least bit pushy.

Diorella was actually inspired by Dior's spirited men's fragrance, **Eau Sauvage**, which kept being raided by women for their own use. Dior simply took the recipe and feminised it with touches of floral sweetness and mossy subtlety. It smells vaguely akin to **Eau Sauvage** but far more refined and immeasurably more elegant. Aquarian women who insist on smelling light, bright and vivacious without a hint of heaviness love **Diorella** — long may it scintillate in the Dior galaxy. A lot of upset women will want to know why if it doesn't!

JAÏPUR — because it's majestic

Aquarian ladies, no matter how assiduous and austere in outlook, know true beauty when they see it, or in this exceptional case, smell it! **Jaïpur** is so poised, so civilised and serene, even they may be tempted to enter the world of regal luxury (less straight-laced Aquarians will probably not hesitate to investigate). **Jaïpur**'s luxury is not of the lavish and extravagantly opulent kind — it is mysterious, languorous and tantalising. It has none of the *prima donna* theatricality of its sister perfume **Boucheron**, but wears instead a misted veil that's meant to fascinate rather than state the obvious.

Its fabulous bottle looks for all the world like an exotic amulet, and no wonder, since it was inspired by a bejewelled Indian nauturan bracelet once worn by wealthy brides of Jaipur when they married their fabled princes or men of appropriately high caste and wealth. The perfume it contains is a soft oriental whisper — as gentle as a kiss blown on air from expectant lips. There are delicious whiffs of peach, plum and apricot that slide sinuously into a garland of acacia, freesia, black rose, purple heliotrope and violet, and the elusive spicy sweetness of peony. Musk, sandalwood and amber breathe underneath this mesmerising spell. Nothing shrieks, nothing sizzles, nothing smoulders. **Jaïpur** is not a slinky siren in a sari, but a slyly seductive but exquisitely innocent princess. Cool, quietly sensuous **Jaïpur** is as subtle as the long-drawn sigh of a suggestive alliance. It is for those times when your heart-felt yearnings need a little amplification to take you a perfumed step further to an Aquarian nirvana.

FEMINITÉ DU BOIS — *because it's mystical*

When you've ministered or administered enough for one day and feel the need to contemplate or even meditate, this wondrous and startlingly different perfume will waft you away on its scented wings to inner calm.

Feminité du Bois is the brainchild of that iconoclastic and immensely imaginative designer of anything to do with feminine beauty, Serge Lutens. It is he who has reintroduced a rejuvenated Shiseido to sophisticated women with his bold design strokes and even bolder beauty ideas and creations. This enigmatic perfume, he declared, was to epitomise the new and daring innovation of Shiseido.

It is not a perfume that pleases a lot of women who expect prettiness and find only mystery and unconventionality. To some it smells medicinal, but to others on a slightly elevated perfume plane, **Feminité du Bois** is more of a fabulous and fearless tonic. It is certainly fascinating with its utterly unique formula that emphasises the hypnotic scent of cedarwood from Morocco's Atlas Mountains beyond Lutens' house in Marrakesh. **Feminité du Bois** begins and ends with cedarwood with an underscoring of orange blossom, honey, clove, cardamom, cinnamon and beeswax, and the caress of musk to fix its haunting Moroccan melisma. It is worlds away from romantic roses and jasmine. Contained in a sinuously curved purple bottle, **Feminité du Bois** is like no other perfume. It is austere yet sensual, pervasive yet soothing, adventurous yet relaxed. It is a panacea for Aquarians who may have been flying too high or want to fly higher into more rarefied climes.

Your secret weapons: the surprises

By saying I think your inner core is imagination I also include your propensity for fantasy — a wish to be something more than you are in the most ideal environment you can picture. This part of you is often either hidden or ignored but it is always there as a private refuge. It's your way of coping with the all-too-unpleasant realities of life as well as those parts of yourself you find annoyingly inadequate. This refuge could be seen as the gardens of your Shangri-la — a place where you can wander among the most beautiful things you can think of, free from care and free to see yourself the way you would like to be — even if it's only for a while before you have to come down to earth. And it's precisely because you have the ability to know what true beauty is that you can always cope with whatever has to be faced, no matter how commonplace or dull. You can, through this imaginative part of you, light up your own life as well as others'. You don't have to make radical personal changes, you don't even have to pretend to be someone more beautiful or glamorous. You merely have to be you, only softer. (You must admit that sometimes you criticise yourself for being a bit too serious and stern!) Bring out this softer side — it doesn't have to be frivolous — just charmingly feminine and relaxed. The perfumes I'm suggesting you try will help enormously because they're all beautiful and dreamy — a couple are even witty and vivacious — exquisite but unusual florals, or floral and fruit blends. They could well be composed of the fantasies that grow in your Gardens of Shangri-la. They are:

•**Jardins de Bagatelle** by Guerlain
  Pronunciation: zjhar-DARN duh bag-ar-TELL/
  gair-LARN
  Type: floral
•**Giorgio Aire** by Giorgio Beverly Hills
  Pronunciation: JAW-jo AIR
  Type: floral/green
•**Bouvardia** by Floris
  Pronunciation: boo-VAR-dee-uh/FLORR-iss

Type: floral
- **Fleur de Rocaille** by Caron
  Pronunciation: fler duh rok-AY/KARR-on
  Type: floral/spicy
- **Summer Hill** by Crabtree & Evelyn
  Type: floral
- **Laura** by Laura Biagiotti
  Pronunciation: LOW (as in WOW)-ruh bee-adj-ee-OTTIE
  Type: floral/fruity

JARDINS DE BAGATELLE
— because it's utterly entrancing

The breathtakingly beautiful Bagatelle gardens in Paris were inspired by and planted for Queen Marie Antoinette in 1777 and to this day astound spring and summer visitors with thousands upon thousands of roses and flowering bulbs sending their intoxicating perfumes in a gloriously muddled *mélange* through the scented air. It's this mesmerising fantasy that Jean-Paul Guerlain gathered as inspiration for **Jardins de Bagatelle** in 1983. And what a heavenly inspiration it is.

Its enormously opulent bouquet is so artfully composed that not even the dominant note of tuberose is allowed to over-rule the sweet-scented yearnings of white rose, jasmine, magnolia, lily of the valley and narcissus. Together with an aureole of orange blossom, violet leaf, bergamot and vetiver, it all becomes an exultant shout of joy and light-headedness even the most determinedly of unromantic and pragmatic Aquarians will find hard to resist.

Jardins de Bagatelle is a typically Parisian enchantment. It is not, however, a languorous laze-about that expects to be admired and adored. It's too exuberant for that, and is, in fact, a very energetic perfume — full of vivacity and naturally aware of its elegant and classical heritage. It's the sort of perfume that doesn't wait for things to happen — it gets in amongst the action and becomes an impetuous and irrepressible part of it. So, if you imagined yourself taking on the uncharacteristic part of the capricious coquette, or the laid-back lady waiting for something lovely to happen, forget it! This fabulously floral fanfare will more than match your liveliness — and take the spotlight off your sober reputation. And not before time either!

GIORGIO AIRE — *because it's a breeze*

Many Aquarians are devoted to the pleasures of fresh air, sunshine and even sport! Others claim to be too busy for such airy-fairy indulgences, but in either case a shot of **Giorgio Aire** will hoist your spirits, recharge your energy levels and perk up your good humour when you need it. It is also a fragrance that can easily transport you to secret regions of wishful thinking — a trait not found on the surface of too many Aquarians.

Before we get deeper into this, if you have an aversion to the controversial **Giorgio Beverly Hills**, you have no need to worry with this quite distant relative. If, on the other hand, you quite like the power of **Giorgio**, you'll find this a perfect adjunct when you want a lighter perfumed approach. They do not really resemble each other very much except in their exuberance and their packaging (**Giorgio Aire** has aqua stripes instead of yellow).

Coming from sunny California, **Giorgio Aire** mostly confines its complex composition to the many fragrant wildflowers grown all over that State. So it's not surprising to learn its main notes are rather esoteric and not to be found in other perfumes. There are wild pink camellias, which have a narcotic but bright scent, Red Californian Poppy (the State Flower), which is said to have a high and heady fragrance, yellow linden blossoms with a therapeutic scent reminiscent of lime, the purple American Windflower, which has the sensuous smell of wild passionfruit, white Tuberanthia, which is reminiscent of tuberose, and green bamboo leaf, which has a succulent, sappy and fresh green tang. All of these untamed desert blooms are gathered together and fixed with a strong base of natural sandalwood, marigold, amber and a dash of vanilla.

Fresh as the prairies, **Giorgio Aire** is not nearly as ferociously tenacious as its dowager aunt, but nevertheless stands out in a crowd — without shouting, I'm glad to say.

Aquarians will like its straight-from-the-hip honest approach, and rely on its casual clout, its sunny innocence, and its exuberant imagination to give a bit of a shove to an exhausted spirit that needs a bit of automatic lift-off.

BOUVARDIA
— because of its old world charm

Not to be confused with sentimental nostalgia, **Bouvardia** is both delicate and unpretentiously elegant. Once a great favourite with Floris fans for its evocation of the beautiful and uncommon flower it's named for, **Bouvardia** now makes a welcome reappearance with a slightly more modern formulation that makes it more lasting and gently persistent than was previously possible.

Bouvardia comes from Mexico and was a fashionable delight in North American and English wedding bouquets, buttonholes and table decorations in the Edwardian era. After World War One, fashion in everything, including scents, changed drastically and it has taken all this time for this sweet-scented old-world flower to come back in vogue again.

Floris — old hands at this type of thing — have now given the fragrance of the white bouvardia flower a subtle, slightly oriental boost with gardenia, carnation blended with Zanzibar clove, bay leaf, vanilla and sandalwood with hints of rose and jasmine in the background. Thus the perfume has a more sophisticated and immediate appeal than in its heyday of single flower scents. Without sacrificing any of its old world charm and grace, **Bouvardia** has now simply been amplified and given a fresh new sheen.

Bouvardia is not meant to be taken as anything but an endearing and uncomplicated perfume. It makes no great statement and will offend no one. It will, however, give an Aquarian, young or old, a sense of calm confidence in knowing that sometimes all's right with this crazy planet — especially when she allows her fantasies to lead her into a world of simple enchantment — even if it's only for a fragrant dalliance.

Fleur de Rocaille
— because it's haunting

The revered House of Caron created this heavenly little masterpiece as long ago as 1933 when as '**Fleurs de Rocaille**' (Rockflowers) it became a surprising success with fashionable young women wanting to break free from their mothers' overpowering oriental perfumes. Nothing as light and as lovely had ever been tried before, and the post-flapper generation made it their own innovative statement. This might seem a bit fanciful now when its breakthrough formulation has since been imitated and adulterated by hundreds of would-be similar perfumes, so it might be seen as not terribly original at all.

But Caron have reintroduced it (although you'll still only find it in boutiques and some duty-free outlets) with a slight reorchestration to its notes — a subtle modernisation that remains basically true to the essential pepperiness of its floral uniqueness. Roses, jasmine and violet still give **Fleur de Rocaille** its light-headed delicacy, but now there's more emphasis on a sub-theme of clove-scented carnation, lilac and lily of the valley gently underlined with sandalwood and musk. Now **Fleur de Rocaille** is just a little more sophisticated under its innocent sweetness, and definitely more worldly.

Strictly for the young Aquarian, **Fleur de Rocaille** is an ideal starter perfume with an approach that is all charm and coquettishness, but ready with a sly smile in the right direction. It always reminds me of alpine flowers in spring — fresh-faced and seemingly delicate, but not really shy at all — just playing hard-to-get. Aquarians of all ages can identify with that!

SUMMER HILL — *because it's peaceful*

This perennial favourite from Crabtree & Evelyn won't set the house on fire with excitement, but it will give you a warm welcome every time you use it to soothe and smooth out life's little trials and tribulations. It's one of those fragrances that simply says 'How nice to meet you' and means it.

Its formulation is no world-shaker but is a pleasant change from over-stuffed floral arrangements bursting to impress Aquarians who aren't all that prone to either pushiness or flattery. In its quietly assured way, **Summer Hill** creates an informal, rambling garden of spring flowers that will bloom through a shaded summer and on into early autumn. At its heady top are freesia, new jasmine and fresh peach blossom, with a lingering of lily and a whisper of tuberose. Orange blossom adds its inimitable intoxication, and sweet roses chime in with a midsummer melody accompanied by a counterpoint of carnation and an earthy base note of sun-warmed woods. Nothing could be more melodic and mellifluous. You almost expect a bee to buzz and a bluebird to skim past!

It's all happiness on **Summer Hill** — no dark clouds, no heatwaves, not even a mosquito sting! It's a rapturous, lilting perfume that makes no demands, and promises nothing but halcyon days and starry, starry nights. Get the pretty picture? A welcome change from the hard edges and petty annoyances that get in the way of the Aquarian highway to heaven.

LAURA — *because it's dreamy*

Laura could not be more different from Biagiotti's firecrackers **Roma** and **Venezia** if it tried! But apparently the queen of Italian ready-to-wear decided it was high time to cool off the tempestuous Italian temperament with a perfume that reflected the looser and more casual approach to street elegance, and thus **Laura** was born. It's a very languid and lissom perfume, inspired by the placid and pellucid waters of the Northern Italian Lake District, and this is reflected in its calm, unruffled serenity of scent as well as its tall clear bottle and sky blue stopper. If your idea of Italy is hustle, bustle and flamboyance, then **Laura** is the direct and delicious antithesis. It's definitely northern Italian — breathlessly alpine rather than spectacularly Mediterranean.

Lusciously ripe fruits begin the ascent with white peach, lychee and watermelon, to which are gathered a light-headed bouquet of freesia, waterlily, rose petals and violet (both petals and leaves). Completing the journey are green ferns, vetiver, sandalwood, a sprinkling of vanilla and a scattering of juniper berries. It's head-in-the-clouds territory, crystalline and limpid, but not at all wimpish. **Laura**, in fact, is gregarious and bubbly without going over the top into frivolousness, so the Aquarian stance of discretion and demeanour will not be affronted at all. On the contrary, I think you'll find **Laura** quietly aspirational but haunting enough to unleash some of those hidden desires lurking under the cultivated Aquarian formality you innocently think is fooling us all.

The advantage of the cusp: taking your pick

It's not all confusion — being neither one star nor the other, or feeling you're partly both — if you were born toward the beginning of Pisces*. You can of course pick and choose from the perfumes suggested for both Aquarius and Pisces, but be careful. Depending on your characteristics, they may not all sit easily on you. That's why I've come up with a selection of extras that might solve any perfume problems or indecision you might have. Anyway, the choice is yours, so have fun finding out.

- **Les Belles de Ricci** by Nina Ricci
  Pronunciation: lay bell duh REACH-ee/
  NEE-na REACH-ee
  Type: fruity/floral
- **Folie douce** by Grès
  Pronunciation: folly DOOSE / GREH
  Type: fruity/floral
- **Eau de Camille** by Annick Goutal
  Pronunciation: o duh kam-EE/
  ANN-ick goo-TARL
  Type: green

---

* *If you were born towards the very beginning of Aquarius you might like to check out the choices for those born on the cusp of Capricorn/Aquarius on pages 381–385.*

LES BELLES DE RICCI
— *because it's a delicious outrage*

Fresh and refreshing from Paris comes Ricci's totally unexpected little rebel, **Les Belles de Ricci**. I predict it will go like a rocket, especially among teenagers and young twenty-somethings who have been starved of a perfume designed specifically with their life-styles in mind. I also predict more mature women will either wish they had enough bravery to sport it, or will throw caution to the winds and wear it anyway! And why not? It's a dazzler!

It's no hearts-and-flowers nosegay. Right from the outset it merrily kicks over the traces with a formulation based on tomato — yes, tomato!

Not just the flowers, but the leaves and the luscious fruit as well (remembering that the tomato is not a vegetable anyway). The head notes, which in this case are *très euphorique* indeed, are the acerbic green leaves (which give off a fabulous zingy scent when watered), bitter orange, mint and basil. As if that's not daring enough, the heart notes suddenly whoosh in with bright tomato flowers, freesia, magnolia, wisteria, and the wonderful honeyed pepperiness of nasturtium. While all this is quivering, the base notes bring in a lush sensuality of tomato fruit all ripe and luscious and summery, mouth-watering raspberry and pungent figwood. It's as vibrant and as cheeky as nymphettes running around the garden stark naked in broad daylight. (This may go against the grain of some sober Aquarians, but Pisceans wouldn't think twice about it!)

Les Belles de Ricci is so candid and impish, so stunningly original and downright audacious, it will persuade you to try it anyway on the basis of a dare. And who could resist its fabulous aniseed green and metallic pink packaging and its cute frosted spiral bottle? Certainly not uninhibited Pisceans or young Aquarians given to eccentricity. **Les Belles de Ricci** is all in good fun, anyway, so what the heck — go bananas (or tomatoes) in it!

FOLIE DOUCE — *because it's a flirt*

One whiff of this delicious charmer and you'll curse the day you turned thirty. If, however, you haven't (or haven't admitted it) then you'll more than likely fall head over heels in puppy love with **Folie douce**. And it's a love affair that's likely to last until you feel gulity about wearing it when you know you run the danger of smelling like mutton dressed as lamb!

Fortunately, both Aquarians and Pisceans have a sort of Peter Pan youthfulness, so you might get away it anyway, and there's always those other two great Grès beauties, **Cabotine** and **Cabochard** if you're a bit past the flibbertigibbet teenage stage. But **Folie**

douce is hard to resist with its frou-frou of fruity citrus, blackcurrant, lemon and bay leaf notes sparkling merrily away among mimosa blossom, ylang ylang, heliotrope and iris with vanilla, cedar, musk and sandalwood trying to keep the lid on such a bubbling *bonne femme* concoction! **Folie douce**, in its pretty red-bowed bottle is made for unpredictable, upbeat fun. Even its publicity promises 'to turn your world upside down', which sober Aquarians could do with and try-anything-once Pisceans can't wait to happen.

EAU DE CAMILLE
— *because it's a green fantasy*

Annick Goutal creates inspired scents that inhabit an exquisite world of their own. They are very light and fresh, elegant and original, and **Eau de Camille** is probably her artistic triumph. Its composition is frankly green, sharp and acerbic but so refined its intense greenness seems misty and mysterious. Inspired by the scent of midsummer flowers wafting through trails of ivy in her garden, she set about capturing the mesmerising drifts of sweet lilac and wild honeysuckle filtered through the sappy tang of ivy and the freshness of new-mown grass. Then she named this little captivation after her young daughter Camille — so there's no association whatever with Dumas' infamous Lady of the Camellias. **Eau de**

Camille is too fresh, young and innocent for such high drama — which is why it should appeal to both serene Aquarians and daydreaming Pisceans. A word of warning — it will be found only in very good boutiques and duty-free outlets.

PARFUM DE JOUR
— because it' makes your day nicer

Casablancan-born Joseph Ettedgui probably needs no introduction after he took the London fashion knitwear scene by storm and was touted as 'the man who made the decade', was declared top knit designer of the year four times, and opened up an empire of successful shops across Europe and the U.S.A. etc. — all this from a kick-start from his *avant-garde* hairdressing salon in the King's Road in the '70s. A signature perfume was inevitable and it arrived at last in a small but *chic* black bottle in the mid-'80s, and was at that stage called **Parfum du Jour**.

Its immediate success from the limited outlets of his shops prompted a retailing rethink and now Joseph's **Parfum de Jour** has spread its wings to be widely available in a new clear glass, silver-topped bottle with a fascinating image of a female nose and lips printed invitingly on the surface but looking as if it's suspended in the perfume itself. And the scent itself? Well, as a French friend of mine and a devotee of **Parfum de Jour** sighs wistfully 'it reminds me of those lovely English bluebells!' And well it might with its highly-complex formulation created for Joseph by none other than the master perfumers at Penhaligon. There are apparently over 100 ingredients in play, with the principal notes being jasmine, rose, hyacinth, lily of the valley and ylang ylang topped with mandarin and blackberry cassis and underlined with sandalwood and amber.

My very discerning friend never has it out of her travel bag. She says it's the ideal *eau de parfum* to take on long trips, and lasts for hours on end without ever once becoming intrusive or boring. Now, if a Frenchwoman gives an English scent that sort of accolade, you know Joseph, as usual, has got it right! Aquarians will like **Parfum de Jour** for its bright lightness, and Pisceans because they're pushovers for anything like English bluebells.

The Aquarian male: easy to love, hard to get

And that's putting it mildly. How many women have thrown themselves at an Aquarian male only to find his hallowed feet simply step over them and take flight where no mere prostrating mortal can follow — quite often not even an Aquarian woman! It's a crying shame because they are often what a maiden (or otherwise) pines for — the answer to her prayers — a man of deep intelligence (not all that deep, mind you!), gentle compassionate nature (when things go his way), and that soulful look as if he carries the silent and secret scars of some woman's evil-doing unto him in the past (and which he will use to get sympathy until his dying day). They're smart cookies, Aquarian men. They don't like being pinned down to anything — especially an admiring female. They have to do the choosing and make the approach, which is no guarantee it will become anything more than a close encounter of the passing kind. While you're planning the wedding, they'll have given you the slip if you betray even a trace of your ambush. Sorry, but those are the facts. Unfortunately that never seems to stop women determined to bring them down to earth, and you will no doubt rush out and buy all sorts of expensive tokens of your undying affection. Forget it. Aquarians loathe extravagance and being made a show of in front of their friends, of which they seem to have thousands — safety in numbers, my dear! So if it's fragrance (which they quite relish and actually use) make sure it smells uncomplicated, discreet but slightly off-beat — just like they are — and it has a designer label they can identify with. You probably still won't hook him, but he might give you a passing peck on or near the cheek as he disappears into thin air. They can be a thankless lot, Aquarian males!

•**Eau Sauvage** by Christian Dior
  Pronunciation: o sor-VAHZJHE/

KRIST-ee-an dee-OR
Type: citrus
•**Jungle Pour Homme** by Kenzo
Type: green/fruity/spicy
•**Versace L'Homme** by Gianni Versace
Pronunciation: vair-SAR-chee LOMM/
gee-ARN-ee vair-SAR-chee
Type: woody/oriental
•**Cerruti 1881**
Pronunciation: chur-OOTY
Type: citrus/oriental

Eau Sauvage

You simply can't go wrong with this one. If he says he doesn't like it, what he really means is he doesn't really like you. It's been around for ages but smells as fresh as tomorrow. It's light but not limp-wristed, sharp but not dangerous, cool but not remote. In fact **Eau Sauvage** is one of the most ingratiating and uncomplicated men's fragrances ever created and still teaches its over-wrought competitors a thing or two about simplicity of style. Its tang comes from petitgrain (which is like oranges and lemons), softened with a touch with lavender and rosemary, and greened with vetiver and oakmoss. Just perfect — and if he doesn't like it, you will, so snitch it!

Jungle Pour Homme

Aquarian men are not prone to prowling through unmapped, dangerous jungles of any kind, preferring to stick to the straight and narrow and conservative. But since they're always going on about how deeply unconservative and eccentric they really are underneath the cool façade, why not throw down the gauntlet with something as wildly quirky and offbeat as Kenzo's lush tropical monsoon **Jungle Pour Homme** and see if he's telling the truth? He'd never dare admit he finds its extravagant and torrid mix of sweet lime, tea, blue cedar, leathery Atlas cedar, nutmeg and chocolate-vanilla Thai benzoin a bit too over-the-top for his delicate tastes — and he might even suddenly surprise you with an uncharacteristic roar of the primal kind! **Jungle Pour Homme** is well-known for bringing out the wild beast in even the most timid couch potatoes.

Versace L'Homme

Aquarian men are inclined to be snobs but pretend it's their shyness and reticence. Reticence? Have you ever watched open-mouthed as one of them works a room, charming everyone in sight? It's almost an art form! And **Versace L'Homme** is just the thing for impressing Very Important People. (You'll notice your Aquarian friend will elbow out his peers with a deftness that's nothing short of jaw-dropping!) This was Versace's original statement for blokes, and it's still a knockout — one of the smoothest charmers in the business. Full of tangy citrus smells first off, it deepens with elegant swathes of lavender, jasmine, ylang ylang and nutmeg, before clinching the deal with vetiver, oakmoss, patchouli, musk and tea-smelling Paraguayan guaic wood. It's the very quintessence of the peacock in full dazzling display — and very, very Versace. Get out the social ladder and watch him climb!

Cerruti 1881

Cerruti's clothes for men have a distinctive cut, style and dashing modernity that sets them apart from the merely expensive conventional. So does his elegant but unstuffy **Cerruti 1881** for men. It's neither heavy nor lightweight, but a real social sparkler with plenty of punch and verve. Its sunny top notes of aromatic herbs are liberally laced with citrus and a twist of lemon before the exotic sensuality of patchouli, musk and ylang ylang blows in from the Orient to stir things up a notch — very seductive but in a teasing way. That's the way Aquarian males usually operate — ruffling the surface with promises of things to come and then gliding away, leaving you panting for more. They can be cruel!

Who suits what, and when: getting the best out of your perfumes

Because perfumes become not only extensions of your personality but also give emphasis to the way you look and the mood you're in, naturally, to bring out their best, they should be treated with due understanding in regard to their characteristics and qualities. They too have limitations and strengths, just as we all have. So, the following table outlines when best to wear them (Day, Night), the age-group most suited to them (Young, Mature), the general complexion of the wearer (Fair, Dark), and the seasons they bloom best in (Spring/Summer – S/S, or Autumn/Winter – A/W). This table is meant only to be used as an approximate guide or reference point — it is not a hard and fast set of rules by any means.

me	Day	Night	Young	Mature	Fair	Dark	S/S	A/W
l'Eden	•		•		•			
s Anaïs		•		•		•		
à d'Issey	•	•		•	•		•	
ella	•	•		•		•		•
r		•	•		•	•		•
nité du Bois	•	•		•		•	•	•

YOUR SECRET WEAPONS

me	Day	Night	Young	Mature	Fair	Dark	S/S	A/W
ns de Bagatelle	•	•	•		•	•	•	•
gio Aire	•		•		•	•	•	
ardia	•	•		•	•			•
de Rocaille	•	•	•		•		•	
ner Hill	•		•	•		•	•	
a	•	•		•	•	•		•

AQUARIUS/PISCES CUSPS

me	Day	Night	Young	Mature	Fair	Dark	S/S	A/W
elles de Ricci	•	•		•	•	•	•	
douce	•	•	•		•		•	
e Camille	•		•	•		•	•	
m de Jour		•	•		•	•		•

CAPRICORN/AQUARIUS CUSPS

me	Day	Night	Young	Mature	Fair	Dark	S/S	A/W
r	•	•	•	•	•	•	•	•
a Trussardi	•	•	•		•	•		
ny Girl	•	•	•		•		•	
beth Taylor's sion		•		•		•		

MEN'S FRAGRANCES

me	Day	Night	Young	Mature	Fair	Dark	S/S	A/W
Sauvage	•		•	•			•	
e Pour omme	•	•		•	•	•		•
ce L'Homme		•	•		•	•	•	
ti 1881	•	•	•		•	•	•	•

Pisces

The fishes
February 19–March 20

You and the rainbow

If those happy little bluebirds fly over the rainbow,
Pisces will not only be flying with them but
asking what happens next! You're ready for
anything, especially if it involves fantasy or the
supernatural. You're not so much psychic as intuitive,
weirdly mystical and sometimes even startlingly right!

But very few will ever be lucky (or unlucky, as the case may be) to fly with you, as much as they'll rarely catch you on their fishing line either, unless the bait is absolutely irresistible. Which is a clue to your whole personality.

Just about everything is irresistible to a true Pisces, and the more exotic and expensive the better. You know the value of an emerald over a run of the mill diamond, but if the emerald's out of reach the diamond will do. The trouble is you want everything — and now! Saving up like normal people is unthinkable, and if you can't afford it you expect someone to give it to you — in fact you'll back them into a corner so they can't say no!

Material possessions rule you, but because you rarely have any money of your own, you'll get what you want in other, sometimes underhanded ways. But you won't be shame-faced about it. Conniving? Manipulative? Never. You're too clever for that. In fact, in terms of sheer cleverness and invention (including whopping fibs and outright lies!) you are unequalled in the zodiac. You simply get what you think you can't be without.

You have very admirable qualities — ones that can make people so envious they get to dislike you for no good reason at all — not that it would worry you. Other people's opinions are interesting, but hardly to be taken seriously. You listen to advice, nod your head a lot, then do exactly what you planned to do in the first place. Is this because your intuition and far-seeing wisdom is superior to theirs? I hate to say it, but it probably is.

But getting back to those admirable qualities. You are kindness itself and will go out of your way, or even walk over anyone else, to help someone in distress, mentally or otherwise. You are absurdly compassionate and far too generous (wilfully extravagant is really what I mean). You are bright, even fearsomely intelligent, and have an inbuilt sense of theatricality — you can light up a room just with your entrance. You have a brilliant but often bitchy sense of humour, and don't really mean to be bitingly sarcastic (well, not all the time). After all, it's not your fault that you can see through people with an unnerving accuracy, which sometimes gets right up some sensitive noses. But you are never, never boring —although you'll be the first to tell someone else if they are. Your frankness is sometimes quite blood-curdling!

You have the potential to be by far the most creative people of all, but if you fall prey to self-indulgence, which is far too often the case, your artistic expression becomes sporadic and obscure. This leads to your reputation for procrastination and leaving brilliant beginnings to wilt, instead of being carried out and finished in triumph. An excess of the good life is usually responsible, or a dreadful blow to your super-sensitive ego that throws you into a maudlin and self-pitying depression — not a pretty sight in usually optimistic Pisces. It's then you (or someone close to you) who has to pull you up and give you a good slap on the backside, a thorough talking-to, or a physical fright by a member of the medical or psychiatric profession. Only them and God himself will get your attention.

But you have the extraordinary ability to wake up to yourself and bounce back, redress your mistakes, and re-invent yourself! Your resilience is miraculous, and you'll never look back after such a chastening. So, you see, it is necessary to listen to others now and then, and get a clear perspective on yourself and not the rose-coloured self-portrait you've flatteringly painted. And it's also then you can demonstrate your incredible versatility. You can adapt to anything in any situation and look as if you've been doing it all your life! You won't stick to it of course — there's that rainbow again and those pretty bluebirds twittering in your ear. But the weird thing is, it isn't all pie in the sky — clever Pisces can actually move effortlessly between fantasy and reality without the annoyance of a horizon in the way. Other lesser mortals can only stand and sigh — or criticise you as being hopeless dreamers. It's only jealousy, so slip on the glittering ruby shoes, the dazzling emerald earrings and fly over that irresistible, life-giving rainbow of yours.

Nobody can keep you grounded anyway, which is a shame in a way, because they'd love to, even knowing what a slippery fish you are.

Pisces style

Pisces (male and female) have a sneaking suspicion that they actually *invented* style, since they're sure they're the only ones who either possess it or can fully appreciate it. Style to you is not just fashion or taste, it is a way of living your life. If every single thing around you doesn't have some sort of connecting relevance to what you think and how you live, then it has no place, and is promptly removed. This is not to say that you are artful arrangers of rooms or make dazzling interior decorators — your style is too haphazard for that sort of discipline — but what you have is an innate eye for beauty that others may not see at all, or look at without seeing its potential. Thus, you usually surround yourself with a homogenous collection of this and that, not necessarily themed to death with a colour scheme or a particular period or style of design. But it all seems to connect, to live together and harmonise, because it all reflects your eclectic but choosy taste in things like colours that are happily allowed to clash, comfortable furniture that won't make people uncomfortable, far-sighted paintings, spectacular floral arrangements that can be startlingly opulent or stunningly simple (you get very morose without flowers or plants around you), and lots of music — usually showbiz soundtracks or esoteric classics. It all has to be there. And when you want it!

You are not a real collector of one particular thing

and look oddly at someone who might have a stamp collection or a roomful of drag, but you gather things around you with an eye to being beautiful in an offbeat way. When it comes to entertaining you are extravagant but thoughtful. Most Pisces (male and female) are wonderfully imaginative cooks, and will go to no end to set a table as if royalty was about to descend. Every detail will be in place without the slightest formality — Pisces loathe formality. But a night with a Pisces, either at dinner or elsewhere, will be one to remember, since you thrive on anything nocturnal. Daylight is not your favourite time, except for gathering flowers, smelling new scents, buying clothes and having a good afternoon nap. It has to be admitted that sort of life is pretty stylish — if a little indolent. But you tend to think you not only invented true style but are the only star sign laid-back enough to enjoy it! And by immersing yourself in books and music, gardens and perfumes, dressing simply but emphatically, you make sure you live a charmed life. Heaven knows you moved heaven and earth to achieve it. Which is a clue to your determination — anyone foolish enough to label you a wishy-washy, directionless and gullible fish will soon learn that Pisces can be as dazzling as a rainbow trout but, if need be, as deadly as a piranha!

Your outer expression is *creativity*. Your inner core is *instinct*.

Here's how you translate all of that into the best perfumes for you.

I have divided them into two categories:

1. *The big guns* — these are the all-important perfumes that should suit you best. They form the core of your personal perfume arsenal.

2. *Your secret weapons* — these augment the basics and are more daring and unusual, but should still suit you.

There is a choice of perfumes for those of you born on the cusp of Pisces/Aries, as well as a selection of men's fragrances suitable to give the Pisces male. (If you were born on the cusp of Aquarius/Pisces, see pages 416–421 for your further perfume choices.) I have given each perfume a category as well as a simple and easy guide to its correct pronunciation. At the end of the chapter I have summated all of the perfumes into a table that tells you whether they're best on young or mature women, in warm or cool weather, day or evening, for dark or fair complexions.

The big guns:
the indispensable basics

A life, even a day, without perfume to you is practically unthinkable. The sensuality of scent, even if it's not in a bottle, mesmerises and excites you as much as music does. You seem to have a more cultivated and questioning sense of smell than most other signs, and would never give a flower a passing, polite sniff — you come to a virtual standstill to breathe in its secrets and its pleasures. You dislike very few perfumes, and will try anything once. This is because you can always see everything from a different point of view — why a particular perfume is so offbeat, to the point where you'll end up falling in love with it because nobody else appreciates it! Its your famous ability to understand what's inside as well as what's obvious. But the ones that become favourites are favourites for life, and you will never forsake them for something new and fascinating. You'll simply add the new one to your collection as a welcome friend. Since you have an unerring instinct to match the perfume to the mood or the occasion or to what you're wearing, it follows you need quite a few perfumes at hand to choose from. This makes you a very valued customer — a treasure in fact — at perfume counters, but the despair of your bank manager. You are not only impulsive but totally compulsive, and will never deny yourself something new and usually fearfully expensive (you justify it as personal investment!). But that is your nature and nothing short of losing your sense of smell will ever alter it. Your taste in these matters is awesomely eclectic, but usually deadly accurate. It's sheer instinct matched with experience and an astonishing ability to be forever daring. That's why you never smell the same — nor, for that matter, do you ever look the same, relying on shock tactics to be noticed. But it works, so why try to alter it? Nobody has ever succeeded in altering you for very long anyway, least of all yourself. So, it follows that your up-front perfumes range from the ultra-dramatic to the ultra-romantic. But no matter what they are, they'll be the quintessence of their category — you'll make sure of that! They are:

- **Samsara** by Guerlain
  Pronunciation: (correctly) sam-surr-AR
  (acceptably) sam-SAR-ruh/gair-LARN
  Type: floral/oriental
- **1000** by Jean Patou
  Pronunciation: (either) one THOW-sand or (in
  French) MEAL/zjharn par-TOO
  Type: floral
- **Vent Vert** by Pierre Balmain
  Pronunciation: varn VAIR/pee-AIR bal-MARN
  Type: green
- **L'Heure Bleue** by Guerlain
  Pronunciation: ler BLER/gair-LARN
  Type: floral/oriental
- **Paloma Picasso** by Paloma Picasso
  Pronunciation: pal-O-muh peek-AR-so
  Type: green/floral
- **Dune** by Christian Dior
  Pronunciation: duh-YOON/KRIST-ee-an dee-OR

Type: floral/oceanic

SAMSARA — because it's charismatic

The word itself is Sanskrit for 'eternal return' and it is one of those rare perfumes to which its many devotees do return like homing pigeons after dallying with lesser beauties. It's because **Samsara** radiates a calm and calming assurance, a peace within itself, that a woman once drawn into its orbit, is content to be caught and held in it. It is one of the most persuasive perfumes you can ever discover and keep on discovering as it unfurls its endless magic.

The idea for **Samsara** was born when the great perfumer Jean-Paul Guerlain asked an intimate friend what she would like most to smell in a new perfume — a perfume for the New Age woman — and she replied one that smelled equally of jasmine and sandalwood. He travelled to India for his inspiration and, finally, eleven years later in 1989, **Samsara** was unveiled to the world. As he said after its immediate and rapturous acceptance, he was but 'the stonemason' while his dear friend was 'the architect'. Rather self-effacing, but romantic nevertheless.

Just what is **Samsara**'s magnetism? It's far from being an oriental and is more than a mere floral bouquet, but combines both with a seamless artistry that's sheer perfumery genius. Perhaps it's the intense 22% content of the world's finest sandalwood married to the rarest jasmine grown in India. Perhaps it's the subtle intertwinings of ylang ylang with peach, plum and bergamot, or the infiltration of roses, tuberose, violet and narcissus, the throb of geranium, bay rose, cinnamon, vetiver, vanilla and tonka bean. But it definitely is the fact that almost all of the ingredients used in **Samsara** are entirely natural and therefore have a bloom, a radiance and an immediacy no synthetics could hope to sustain. But whatever is **Samsara**'s secret, it has effortlessly become a classic that will endure.

On the skin it spreads its serene silkiness and envelops the wearer in a veil of intangible allure as it sends out its mesmerising message. That message is both provoking and beguiling. It is a whispering of eternal pleasures but present fulfilment. And that, as you well know, is the essential message, the intimate wish of Pisces women.

1000

— because it's one in a thousand

In his heyday of the early 1930s, Jean Patou was regarded as the most innovative and elegant of all *couturiers*, even more so than Gabrielle Chanel who had as many detractors as she did devotees. Although he was long gone from this earth when **1000** (or **Mille** as it is known in France) was created in his name, he would surely have loved this most opulent of all perfumes. **1000** was launched in 1972 in limited editions of numbered bottles — very elitist indeed, and of course, prohibitively expensive.

It has never reached the dizzy heights of success of its much older sister **Joy**, but has slowly gathered a devoted but silent following — no devotee really wants to reveal precisely what perfume she is wearing if it is a rare one, and **1000** is becoming rarer by the day, but it is still available on order, or in boutiques and duty-free outlets.

1000 is devastatingly elegant and deliberately haughty with its extremely precious and mostly natural essences dominated by rose and jasmine, lily of the valley, osmanthus and iris. But this extravagant accord, plus underpinnings of bergamot, angelica, coriander, tarragon, patchouli and oakmoss, is entirely eclipsed by the haunting and persistent presence of violets — those big sumptuous Parma beauties that were all the rage in the '20s and '30s. Here they make a triumphant comeback that is spectacularly beautiful — even ravishing! Without their exultant shout, **1000** would not be the same overwhelming olfactory experience it is.

Pisces are not generally known for gentility or for elitism, but somehow this great and grand perfume will make you wish you were. But then again, you also have the incomparable knack of carrying off even the most unlikely challenges to your basically gentle nature, so **1000** in all its fabulous glory — its luxurious aura — its magnificent impact — will not only make you feel literally one in a thousand, but one in a million! And since something as trivial as unaffordable expense has never stopped you from adorning yourself in the best that money can buy, **1000** is not merely an indulgence but an absolute Pisces necessity.

VENT VERT
— because it's utterly stunning

They don't come any greener than this phenomenal perfume — the seminal and quintessential triumph of green perfumes. **Vent Vert** (which incidentally was created by a female 'nose') changed the entire course of perfume by upending the romantic tradition when it burst on an unsuspecting world in 1947. It was not just the reintroduction of the long-forgotten green category that reached its zenith in the '20s and then faded in face of the orientals, it reintroduced it with an entirely unique and brave standpoint. It was sharper, younger, franker and more exuberant than any other perfume then on the market, and it captivated everyone (except the fuddy-duddies, of course). And although it seemed to fade away in the '70s and '80s, it came back in the early '90s to thrill an entirely new generation.

Here, I must point out that its original formula has been somewhat revised and is not quite as ruthlessly acerbic or individual, but to those to whom it is a new experience, that will be no matter. It's still a boutique and duty-free exclusive — you won't find it readily, more's the pity!

But even the new **Vent Vert** is a miracle of construction. It begins with the sharp leafiness of green galbanum, leaves, buds and grasses, with basil, lemon and lime to make its piquant point. Orange blossom, lily of the valley, hyacinth and green rose are called in to soften and sweeten the emerald shock, but are cunningly edged with nutmeg, sage, fern, oakmoss and vetiver with a dash of musk and a whisper of sandalwood. The result is exactly like the ecstatic smell of freshly mown grass — piercing, reassuring and nostalgic.

I can't begin to tell you how much I love and pine for the original **Vent Vert**, but I think any Pisces woman with Nature in her veins will adore the new version just as it stands. It isn't all *that* dissimilar. It has the same magical evocation of summer, the same intoxicating spell that will captivate you forever in its luscious green fantasy.

L'HEURE BLEUE
— because it's achingly beautiful

Most Pisces women I know are pushovers for the romantic stillness and breathless nostalgia of dusk and twilight, and it is this magical time when apricot sunsets glide by gradual osmosis into starry velvet nights that inspired the creation of this rapturously lovely perfume.

Jacques Guerlain himself was so entranced by what he called the Blue Hour of his beloved Paris of 1912, he set about to interpret it in a perfume of comparable mystery and magic. **L'Heure Bleue**, coming as it did at the end of an era of majestic tranquillity and immense sophistication, was to become the perfumed quintessence of its time before the horrors of war overtook the world. Somehow, through many other such upheavals, **L'Heure Bleue** still breathes its message of serene calm and languid beauty.

Composed with great artistry and complexity, **L'Heure Bleue** is a soft evocation of Bulgarian rose, jasmine, iris and heliotrope poised delicately over a deliciousness of bergamot, peach, lemon, orange blossom and the orientalism of ylang ylang and coriander. Wisps of musk, vetiver and sandalwood float in with the Guerlain trademark sensuality of vanilla.

You'll be glad to know that not all women fall willy-nilly under the spell of **L'Heure Bleue** and find it too remote or difficult to wear. Which leaves the way wide open for Pisces who revel in anything other people find insurmountable or unfriendly. To you, **L'Heure Bleue** will be a yearning expression of your innate wistfulness, your love of peace, and your total surrender to even the most improbable romances — lucky you.

PALOMA PICASSO
— because it exudes passion

When this fabulous innovation hit the perfume counters midway through the extravagant '80s, those of us still lamenting the passing of so many great green perfumes gave out a jubilant shout. It seemed in one fell swoop from Picasso's daughter, the green movement had been reinstigated — and grandly at that! (**Vent Vert** had mysteriously disappeared with its new formulation yet to come.)

For her first foray into perfume, Paloma Picasso said she wanted something *she* could wear with pride and pleasure — something warm and earthy, sophisticated but flamboyant, something to awaken the senses with a shock! **Paloma Picasso** is the magnificent result — a brave, passionate, pulsating perfumed upheaval of great honesty and beauty. It is an immensely proud perfume, haughty and imperious and yet tremendously easy to wear. It does not shout for attention, it merely expects (and gets) it. Nor will it compete with you. Instead it adds another, more open dimension to you — one of sheer *panache*. That's why it's so exciting and ingratiating.

Paloma Picasso is an opulent composition of *chypre* (that green, mossy, leafy, woody harmony) infused with the richness of Bulgarian rose, Mysore jasmine, hyacinth, mimosa and ylang ylang vibrating sensuously over a powerbase of patchouli, musk, angelica and citrus oils. It is vivacious, vibrant and voluptuous, and as its creator warns, for *real* women and not novices! It is, quite simply, a knockout — and we all know how Pisces women who've gladly lost their innocence, love to be something of a knockout themselves. It's all too easy in **Paloma Picasso**!

DUNE — *because it's haunting*

This is one of the most fearless and audacious perfumes created for many a decade. It resembles nothing before it, and nothing else since has presumed to imitate it. The best they can do is pay homage to its daring departure into a new world of perfumed oceanic ingredients that elevates it to new heights of sheer originality.

The brainchild of Maurice Roger (the mastermind behind **Poison** and **Fahrenheit**), **Dune** was created specifically for the woman of the '90s — a much more environmentally aware creature with straightforward standards and no-nonsense attitudes. He threw out all the time-worn ideas of flowery romance and the sultry smoulder of orientalism, and gathered together the hauntingly nostalgic childhood scents of deserted beaches under cloudless skies reflected in pure clean seas. These are the inspirational elements of **Dune**, all intimately connected with the Pisces adoration of the sea in all its beautiful and mysterious majesty.

The composition of **Dune** is breathtakingly unique. The wild smells of broom flowers, wallflowers, lilies and peonies combine with mossy lichen and warming amber in a windswept sweetness that merges into secret oceanic notes that add a seaweedy freshness and a brisk tang to give **Dune** its remarkably effective dryness and warmth. It really *is* like sitting amid white sand dunes whispering with sea grasses in a salt-laden ocean breeze smelling of exotic flowers from invisible shores. But I must warn you that **Dune** is also highly tenacious, so don't overdo it, in which case it will be more like a *tsunami* than the gentle heaving swell that's love music to Pisces ears.

Your secret weapons:
the surprises

Pisces are known for springing surprises and get great delight out of shocking people with theatrical entrances in clothes and colours others might shrink at the thought of wearing, so it comes as no great surprise to Pisces themselves that they're unshockable. But what you do rely on to carry off these flights of fancy is an acute sense of instinct and intuition — and those enviable qualities you have scads of, don't you? So when it comes to your second-string of perfumes, the only surprise is that you won't find them challenging at all but will add them to your arsenal and use them when the time, place and mood are appropriate — which in your case could be anytime, any place, anyhow! Fortunately for you, I've chosen a very contrasting selection, so there's bound to be at least one or two you either haven't heard of or at least have yet to try. A couple are a bit difficult to track down, but your magnetic intuition acts like a geiger-counter in these matters and you probably won't have any trouble at all making a direct beeline to their exact locations. Nothing you want ever seems to evade you for long, does it? — least of all an esoteric perfume!

•**Asja** by Fendi
Pronunciation: AZJHE-yah/FEN-dee
Type: oriental

•**Passion Flower** by Crabtree & Evelyn
Type: floral/oriental

•**Acqua di Gio** by Giorgio Armani
Pronunciation: ARK-wuh duh JO/JAW-gee-o ar-MAR-nee
Type: floral/green

•**Ô de Lancôme** by Lancôme
Pronunciation: oh duh larn-KOM
Type: citrus/green

•**Gianfranco Ferre** by Gianfranco Ferre
Pronunciation: jarn-FRUNK-o fair-AIR
Type: floral

•**Jean-Louis Scherrer** by Jean-Louis Scherrer
Pronunciation: zjharn-loo-EE shair-AIR
Type: green/floral

ASJA — *because it's your kismet*

I know you can't resist the odd temptation to smell smoulderingly sultry and mysterious, so if you really have to, it might as well be in this oriental sizzler. **Asja** is far more elegant and sophisticated than a lot of its sloe-eyed partners in crime, and at least has the Roman pedigree of Fendi going for it.

One look at **Asja** in its gold-and-black striped bottle inspired by a seventeenth-century Japanese porcelain bowl will be enough to convince most impressionable Pisces they simply *must* possess this perfume, and the deal will be clinched with one heady sniff of its exotic splendour! Asja draws on the Turkish heritage of the Fendi family, which is evident in its great smoky whiffs of Bulgarian rose, Egyptian jasmine, Persian mimosa and Turkish carnation. From further east come the spice notes of cinnamon and clove, nutmeg and cardamom, lots of ylang ylang, musk, sandalwood and vanilla, with edges of blackcurrant bud and orange. It's rather like meandering through a bazaar at high noon, and just as potent.

Asja is strongly disliked by discreet and refined women, which naturally makes it open season for rebellious Pisces who like to pick up outcasts and flaunt them (usually with terrific success) at the very people who turned up their noses at it! In any case, **Asja** is a wonderfully opulent and sultry seductress which, if not used with too great an abandon (it's strong stuff!), will have you twirling about in gold bracelets and seven veils that may or may not stay intact through your uninhibited performance.

PASSION FLOWER
— because it's mouth-watering

The lure of the tropics! The lushness of passionfruit, mango, papaya and ripe banana! An equatorial fruit salad? No, it's Crabtree & Evelyn's exotic little beauty that wafts around you like a nostalgic memory of Bali and other dusky and desirable destinations.

Based, naturally, on the scent of *Passiflora* in full bloom and made even more delicious with the essences of other luscious tropical fruits, **Passion Flower** is meant to be used without too much discretion to cool off in the heat of the day or add to the languor of midsummer nights.

Its sweet message wafts through the air conjuring up distant images of moist rainforests, crystal clear waterfalls, dazzling sunlight and swaying palms — almost tangible impressions of tropical paradises you'd rather be swanning around in, instead of more mundane locations. **Passion Flower** will transport you there — without making you smell too much like an over-garnished pavlova.

It's a natural for pleasure-seeking Pisces who tend to love kicking off their shoes and slipping on a sarong. If there's not a passion flower on your vine, forget the usual hibiscus behind the ear and anoint yourself with the pleasures of **Passion Flower**. Someone will probably try to eat you, but passion in any form has never unduly worried a Pisces woman, has it? What's more, this is a very affordable passion to possess!

ACQUA DI GIO
— because it's like skinny-dipping

Pisces love the sea, even if they never set foot in it. But if they do, they're like mermaids, splashing around and having a lovely time of it. You can get much the same exhilarating — thrilling! — effect from splashes and sprays of Armani's inspired version of his big sister perfume, the wonderful **Gio**, called appropriately **Acqua di Gio**.

The relationship is there between both fragrances, but only just. Whereas **Gio** is tenacious and terrifically sophisticated, **Acqua di Gio** has flashes of its tuberose and citrus power, but not in such heavy concentration. In fact you may as well treat **Acqua di Gio** as a different perfume altogether, since its formulation is composed of much lighter ingredients. For a start it has dazzlingly fresh 'sea' notes (synthetic essences that smell strongly of the ocean and its environs) with loads of springtime white flowers (mainly freesia and hyacinth with a hint of rose), a salivating dash of white grape, and the spicy delicacy of sweet pea. Underneath this playful innocence are deeper hints of musk and soft woods, but nothing much to ripple the sparkling surface.

I think you'll fall for its scintillating freshness, its seaside frivolity and its effervescent sense of freedom. It's a bit like a water ballet really, and you can easily picture yourself as a water sprite gambolling under crystalline waterfalls. **Acqua di Gio** is not meant for Loreleis though, so don't go to all the bother of slinking around the poolside just because you're in an Armani — it doesn't quite work like that, and someone might push you in anyway!

Ô DE LANCÔME
— because nothing smells fresher

Thank heavens advertising pulled this one out of its near-extinction. Ô has been around for quite some time but was treated like a trade secret for some obscure reason. Those of us in the know swore we'd never get through a long hot summer without it (yes, men used it almost as much as women), and when it looked like disappearing altogether, a hue and cry went up, and, repackaged and given a modest blaze of publicity, Ô not only swept back into our lives but picked up a brand new following as well! So, if you haven't smelt its unique pleasures, now's the time to indulge!

Ô is no ordinary citrus *eau de toilette*. It has the usual ingredients but with greater sparkle and impact.

It always reminds me immediately of the fabulously fresh and raw smell of lemon leaves crushed in the hand — sharp, intense and salivating! Its formulation has a few surprises up its summery sleeve — apart from the zing and zest of lemon and lime, there's a whiff of jasmine bud, a whisper of prunewood, and dashes of oakmoss and vetiver. It's so deliciously heady you want to drink it — but don't! Just splash it around with total abandonment.

GIANFRANCO FERRE
— because it's meltingly lovely

Perhaps the Age of Innocence is just a wistful memory (if it ever existed at all) and the Age of Elegance is teetering into extinction in the face of rampant vulgarity and crassness, which is why it's all the more wonderful to know a perfume like **Gianfranco Ferre** (the one in the virginal white box, not the flashy gold one) is still with us — if only in rare quantities. But search and find, because it's probably The Beautiful One you Pisces have been yearning for. It is not only mesmerising, but hypnotically irresistible.

Gianfranco Ferre is nothing like its explosive sister **Ferre** by Ferre. It is tender, ardent and blissfully, meltingly feminine. But it is neither passive nor wimpish. It is simply angelic. Its composition is an overwhelmingly glorious gathering of pure white flowers — orange blossom, tuberose, honeysuckle, rose, gardenia, narcissus and lily of the valley, blessed with the poignant liaison of hyacinth and jasmine — lots of jasmine. There are gentle murmurs of shimmering green leaves, herbs and spices, moss and musk, but the floral bouquet is so mesmerising it effortlessly steals the scene with its sheer exquisiteness.

Gianfranco Ferre is reminiscent of many things — each time you smell it, different images will flood you — nostalgia for a bygone age, velvety summer nights, gardens at twilight, the remembrance of someone very dear. It is redolent not just of sweetly surrendered innocence but of the intimate enchantment of falling in love. I'm well aware that Pisces are hardly in need of romantic hypnosis, but **Gianfranco Ferre** may begin a fantastic osmosis that could well beguile not just you, but another as well.

JEAN-LOUIS SCHERRER
— because it's like wearing emeralds

Get down on your knees and beg your boutique to find this for you (they can, and will!). Its elusiveness not only makes it more desirable, but exclusive to she who possesses it. It is, quite simply, one of the great perfumes of the century. Like its warmer, ambery sister, **Scherrer II**, this is so Parisian its chic is almost tangible! A brilliant dark emerald green in its tall hexagonal bottle, **Jean-Louis Scherrer** has an incandescent glow that wraps itself around you in a blaze of verdant glory. The dark richness of Bulgarian rose allied with Grasse jasmine gathers up the high-sung notes of Dutch hyacinth, green leaves and ferns, the wood violet smokiness of Florentine iris, plunges into a wild jungle of moss, vetiver, pungent herbs, explosive spices, then cools off the volatility with warmly glowing amber, softly enticing musk and heady sandalwood. When the flashpoint simmers down to a brooding synergy, **Jean-Louis Scherrer** is ready to radiate its intensely deep dazzle.

This is a perfume that somehow unleashes its seductive power with a scintillation that is neither light nor dark. It is a multi-faceted jewel of flashing splendour and luminescent elegance. It may seem a bit daunting at first whiff, but **Jean-Louis Scherrer** does not suspend itself in the air to wait for considered opinions — like a whirling dervish it whips around you and sweeps you off your feet. Its sheer velocity and impact is not just seductive — it's outright possession! How highly vulnerable Pisces control its power — or themselves — is another one of life's little challenges. But if I were you, I'd give in and go wherever it takes you.

The advantage of the cusp: taking your pick

It's not all confusion — being neither one star nor the other, or feeling you're partly both — if you were born toward the beginning of Aries*. You can of course pick and choose from the perfumes suggested for both Pisces and Aries, but be careful. Depending on your characteristics, they may not all sit easily on you. That's why I've come up with a selection of extras that might solve any perfume problems or indecision you might have. Anyway, the choice is yours, so have fun. Here are four:

- **Montana Parfum de Peau** by Montana
  Pronunciation: mon-TAR-nuh par-FOOM duh PO
  Type: woody/oriental
- **Fracas** by Robert Piguet
  Pronunciation: frack-AR/hrobb-AIR pee-GWAY
  Type: floral
- **Blue Grass** by Elizabeth Arden
  Type: floral
- **Sonia Rykiel** by Sonia Rykiel
  Pronunciation: SONN-yuh rik-YELL
  Type: fruity/floral

If you were born towards the very beginning of Pisces you might like to check out the choices for those born on the cusp of Aquarius/Pisces on pages 416–421.

Montana Parfum de Peau
— *because it's a powerhouse*

Not the easiest perfume to find, but one bottle will last you a long, long time. So will one or two sprays. **Montana** (which is what it's actually called on its brilliant cobalt blue box) is one of the most potent perfumes you'll ever have to train yourself to be discreet with. It's such a devastatingly fabulous scent, you'll want to go bananas with it, but don't. Discretion is definitely the better part of valour with this dynamo. It's a highly complex and almost combustible fusion of fruits (peach, plum, blackcurrant), spices (pepper, ginger, cardamom, clove), flowers (tuberose, carnation, narcissus, jasmine, ylang ylang) and grasses (patchouli, vetiver), sandalwood, musk and incense, almost over-ridden with rosewood and cedar. Dark, mysterious, smouldering, seductive and tenacious, **Montana** is unrivalled for dramatic entrances (Pisces) and flashing victories (Aries).

Fracas — *because it triumphs*

This intoxicating perfume was created in 1945 and developed a fanatical fan club over the years. Imagine the horror these women felt when it was announced recently that first of all **Fracas** was being discontinued for ever! There was an infuriated outcry. Things then got worse when it was announced **Fracas** would stay, but with a new 'younger' formula

— there was almost blood again on the *boulevardes* of Paris! 'We Want **Fracas** — the *real* **Fracas**!' they screamed. Finally, commonsense prevailed and **Fracas** is back with us in all its tuberose-laden glory, although its distribution is very limited, so the hunt is on! So is it worth all the fuss? You bet! **Fracas** is a fabulous disturbance of peach and orange blossom over masses of tuberose supported by gardenia, rose, carnation and jasmine — an all-white fountain of flowers underpinned with musk, oakmoss and sandalwood. Romantic Pisces will worship it and innocent Aries will wonder what's hit them. This is one *fracas* worth fighting for, believe me!

BLUE GRASS
— because it's a thoroughbred

It's also a sentimental favourite, winning devoted fans since the '30s — and yes, it *is* still available in good department stores, especially around Christmas when grannies and great aunts still expect to smell its sweetly romantic and impossibly nostalgic magic created from lavender, neroli, jasmine, rose, carnation, sandalwood, tonka bean and musk. **Blue Grass** was Miss Arden's loving interpretation of the smell of the fields she could see from her home in Virginia where more than one champion thoroughbred was foaled. And if you think it's only for the aged, think again — *they* were young and romantic once too, and I'll bet

Blue Grass will pull many an Aries up in her tracks and slow her down to a feminine canter. As for Pisceans — well, they're pushovers for nostalgia and will probably lead the push for a complete return of **Blue Grass** to the winner's circle. I certainly hope so! Life's too short without it.

SONIA RYKIEL
— because it has panache

This is exactly the sort of warm, rich and endearing perfume you'd expect from a truly innovative designer with a very unique sense of feminine chic. Like her wonderfully wearable clothes, **Sonia Rykiel** has tremendous assurance and sophistication but with a wicked sparkle — it refuses to take itself too seriously. Like fashion, perfume can be fun! Its cute sweater-shaped bottle emblazoned with her signature in silver glitter has just the right sort of irreverent non-chalance, and almost belies the potent suprise inside. **Sonia Rykiel** begins with a rush of luscious fruit — passionfruit, pineapple, blackcurrant and grapefruit, warmed with a sweet heart of violet and cyclamen, softened with cypress, sandalwood and a sensuous whiff of patchouli. It's a scent that's like the woman herself — outspoken, urbane, charming, sparkling and witty — refreshingly original without being eccentric. Pisceans will love it because it's a true one-off, and Ariens will like its challenge. It's certainly not a wimp, but the kind of complex and vivacious perfume you'll find so warmly enveloping that, like one of her great knits, you won't want to stop wearing it!

The Pisces male: gifts to gild the lily

The gift of fragrance to a Pisces male is like adding yet another treasure to the lyre bird's nest, or trying to put another glittering feather in the glorious peacock tail. It's a bit superfluous, but of course he won't see it that way. As far as he's concerned there's no such thing as 'too much of a good thing' and he'll happily add it to his incredibly eclectic collection. All Pisces like variety. They spend their entire lives ferreting out and trying new things — especially building up an arsenal of fragrances that would stun most other signs. It isn't just because they can't make up their minds — they simply don't want to! They live for change, and see no reason whatever to stick to the same old routines, but follow their many and varied moods as an infallible guide to feeling, looking and smelling fantastic. This metamorphosis could take place at least three times a day and not faze them in the least. To a Pisces, boredom is the pits, so it follows you're on safe ground giving him a gift of superior male fragrance. But it's not that easy — nothing ever is where a Pisces is involved. It has to be the *right* fragrance, or the mouth will turn down at the corners, and the eyes glaze as you get a vague 'Gee, thanks a million', which translates as 'Thanks for nothing!'. You know you've bombed. The clue is to ask beforehand, as subtly as possible, what he likes, or would like to have. You may not need to do this, however, because as the time for gift-giving looms large on the Pisces horizon, he will give out his own none-too-subtle hints as to precisely what he wants and expects to be given. Just follow the hint to the letter and all will be solved. Since Pisces have very lofty tastes, it will not be an inexpensive exercise. He will never use anything but the best on his precious face (Pisces have a morbid fear of age but usually never look half of it). So, give in and spend a motza!

- **Dune pour Homme** by Christian Dior
  Pronunciation: duh-YOON poor OM/
  KRIST-ee-an-dee-OR
  Type: green/oceanic
- **Chrome** by Azzaro
  Pronunciation: KROME/azz-AR-o
  Type: fruity/spicy
- **Versace The Dreamer** by Gianni Versace
  Type: floral/herbal
- **Bvlgari pour Homme** by Bvlgari
  Pronunciation: boull-GAR-ee, (or, as in Italy,
  BOULL-gar-ee
  Type: citrus/spicy

Dune pour Homme

At long last! A men's fragrance that doesn't smell either like an orchard, a pine forest, a soap factory, or a bordello! **Dune** paves the way (just as its female counterpart did) for a new slant on the rather limited range of thinking on the subject. It doesn't break the rules. It ignores them. **Dune** is so original it makes just about all the other men's options boringly unadventurous. It has a freshness and zing that almost hurts! Based on leaves, oceanic scents and woods, it includes basil, blackcurrant leaves (full of chlorophyll), green mandarin, hedione (a jasmine extract), wild sage, figwood, cedar, sandalwood and tonka bean. Its authentic evocation of sun, sand and surf will send your Pisces reeling into a nostalgic Nirvana!

Chrome

This sleek and cool creation was created to take the New Age male into the millennium, not kicking and screaming, but with a headlong leap. The Pisces male is not usually remotely athletic or even very fearless, but take his trembling hand and tell him **Chrome** will smooth the way and make the leap a piece of cake with its wonderful orange notes of bergamot, neroli and bigarade spiked with ginger, bolstered with cardamom, nutmeggy mace, rosewood and sandalwood. But the clincher will be the aquatic (he'll like that word) notes of ivy and lichen to cool his fevered brow. In any case,

Chrome's square glass bottle fits so comfortingly into his sensitive hand, he'll be glad to leave the tired old twentieth century behind and steel himself for the wonders of the new one.

Versace The Dreamer

Interpret it as prophetic if you like, but this was supposedly the last fragrance Versace created before his death. But that's not why I've chosen it, although its name might seem to suit the clichéd idea of Pisces lost in some Never-Never Land. I've chosen it because it's such a distinctive departure from the normal run-of-male stuff with its intriguing and intoxicating herbs, and its brilliantly original central accord of what are described as 'linen flowers.' But first the herbal bit. There's juniper (used in good gin) and artemisia (once used in the now-banned absinthe as wormwood, sometimes called 'lad's love and maid's ruin') and aniseed-pungent tarragon. Then comes the linen bit — amber lily, iris roots (smelling of woody violet) and 'linen essence'. I don't know precisely how this essence is achieved but the middle notes smell distinctly of fresh creamy linen and stay that way throughout. Finally tobacco flowers and amber waft in to finish off the cocktail with a camouflaged punch. Unusual? Certainly, but with typical Versace vaudevillian virtuosity as well. Pisces men with a bent for theatrics are such impressionable suckers they'll take **Versace The Dreamer** to their super-emotional hearts. I can just hear them crying into the shaving mirror as they splash this on — *in memoriam* to their dear departed Gianni!

Bvlgari pour Homme

This is a fabulous fragrance any romantically-inclined Pisces will fall in a heap for. On the surface in its austere but classy bottle, **Bvlgari** seems to be full of the citrus freshness of bergamot and orange flowers with a dash of blackcurrant. But at its heart are aromatic Turkish cardamom, pepper, iris and rosewood, plus the exotic guaiac wood (Paraguayan *palo santo* from which is extracted a tea-scented essence). Amber and musk fix things, but not before that signature **Bvlgari** drop or two of tea — this time Darjeeling with its orangey aroma. They went to a lot of trouble with this one! But it works so smoothly it never intrudes or invades — in fact it was designed to blend with the skin so as not to blow its own brilliant trumpet too much. But you can bet any Pisces wearing **Bvlgari** will be blowing his!

Who suits what, and when: getting the best out of your perfumes

Because perfumes become not only extensions of your personality but also give emphasis to the way you look and the mood you're in, naturally, to bring out their best, they must be treated with due understanding in regard to their characteristics and qualities. They too have limitations and strengths, just as we all have. So, the following table outlines when best to wear them (Day, Night), the age-group most suited to them (Young, Mature), the general complexion of the wearer (Fair, Dark), and the seasons they bloom best in (Spring/Summer – S/S, or Autumn/Winter – A/W). This table is meant only to be used as an approximate guide or reference point — it is not a hard and fast set of rules by any means.

Perfume	Day	Night	Young	Mature	Fair	Dark	S/S	A
Samsara	•	•	•	•	•	•	•	
1000		•		•		•	•	
Vent Vert	•	•	•	•	•	•	•	
L'Heure Bleue		•		•		•	•	
Paloma Picasso	•	•		•		•	•	
Dune	•	•	•	•			•	

Perfume	Day	Night	Young	Mature	Fair	Dark	S/S	A
Asja		•		•		•		
Passion Flower	•		•		•	•		
Acqua di Gio	•		•	•	•	•	•	
Ô de Lancôme	•		•	•	•	•	•	
Gianfranco Ferre	•	•	•	•		•		
Jean-Louis Scherrer		•	•	•	•	•		

Perfume	Day	Night	Young	Mature	Fair	Dark	S/S	A
Montana Parfum de Peau		•		•		•		
Fracas	•	•		•		•		
Blue Grass	•	•	•	•	•	•	•	
Sonia Rykiel	•	•	•	•	•			

Perfume	Day	Night	Young	Mature	Fair	Dark	S/S	A
Les Belles de Ricci	•	•	•		•	•	•	
Folie douce	•	•	•		•	•	•	
Eau de Camille	•		•		•	•	•	
Parfum de Jour	•		•	•	•	•		

Perfume	Day	Night	Young	Mature	Fair	Dark	S/S	A
Dune pour Homme	•		•		•		•	
Chrome	•		•	•	•	•		
Versace The Dreamer	•	•	•	•	•	•		
Bvlgari pour Homme	•	•	•	•	•	•		

The Perfume Zodiac

464

The perfume index

Index
467